Palgrave Studies in Race, Ethnicity, Indigeneity and Criminal Justice

Series Editors
Chris Cunneen, University of Technology Sydney, Sydney, NSW, Australia
Katheryn Russell-Brown, University of Florida, Gainesville, FL, USA
Shaun L. Gabbidon, Penn State Harrisburg, Middletown, PA, USA

This pioneering series brings much-needed attention to minority, excluded, and marginalised perspectives in criminology, centred on the topic of 'race' and the racialization of crime and criminal justice systems. It draws on a range of theoretical approaches including critical race theory, critical criminology, postcolonial theory, intersectional approaches and Indigenous theory. The series seeks to challenge and broaden the current discourse, debates and discussions within contemporary criminology as a whole, including drawing on the voices of Indigenous people and those from the Global South which are often silenced in favour of dominant white discourses in Criminology.

More information about this series at
https://link.springer.com/bookseries/15777

Tryon P. Woods

Pandemic Police Power, Public Health and the Abolition Question

Tryon P. Woods
University of Massachusetts
Dartmouth, MA, USA

Providence College
Providence, RI, USA

Palgrave Studies in Race, Ethnicity, Indigeneity and Criminal Justice
ISBN 978-3-030-93030-1   ISBN 978-3-030-93031-8 (eBook)
https://doi.org/10.1007/978-3-030-93031-8

© The Editor(s) (if applicable) and The Author(s), under exclusive license to Springer Nature Switzerland AG 2022
This work is subject to copyright. All rights are solely and exclusively licensed by the Publisher, whether the whole or part of the material is concerned, specifically the rights of translation, reprinting, reuse of illustrations, recitation, broadcasting, reproduction on microfilms or in any other physical way, and transmission or information storage and retrieval, electronic adaptation, computer software, or by similar or dissimilar methodology now known or hereafter developed.
The use of general descriptive names, registered names, trademarks, service marks, etc. in this publication does not imply, even in the absence of a specific statement, that such names are exempt from the relevant protective laws and regulations and therefore free for general use.
The publisher, the authors and the editors are safe to assume that the advice and information in this book are believed to be true and accurate at the date of publication. Neither the publisher nor the authors or the editors give a warranty, expressed or implied, with respect to the material contained herein or for any errors or omissions that may have been made. The publisher remains neutral with regard to jurisdictional claims in published maps and institutional affiliations.

Cover illustration: GettyImages-471115570

This Palgrave Macmillan imprint is published by the registered company Springer Nature Switzerland AG
The registered company address is: Gewerbestrasse 11, 6330 Cham, Switzerland

Epigraph

Alter the speed
Or the direction of Change.
Vary the scope of Change.
Recombine the seeds of Change.
Transmute the impact of Change.
Seize Change.
Use it.
Adapt and grow.

—Octavia Butler, *Parable of the Talents* (New York: Seven Stories, 2017), 33

I dedicate Pandemic Police Power *to my daughters, Naomi Marie and Assana Simone. May the wisdom of your ancestors in the black freedom struggle, as well as the courage of all independent thinkers across the ages, guide your personal journeys to spiritual, physical, and emotional whole living.*

Acknowledgments

My gratitude to Josie Taylor, Punitha Balasubramaniam, and the entire editorial and production team at Palgrave Macmillan for supporting this work. It has been an honor and a pleasure working with all of you. A small portion of *Pandemic Police Power* was previously published as "Public Health Policing and the Case Against Vaccine Mandates," *St. Thomas Law Review* 33(2) 2021: 220–282. I thank the editors of *St. Thomas Law Review* for their invitation to publish in their journal, and for their gracious permission to republish my article in a different form here.

Thank you, as always, to my dear friends Dr. Donald F. Tibbs and Dr. Khalil Saucier.

A special thank you to Logan Hill, J. D. for generously sharing his legal research and insights with me.

This book would not have been possible without the partnership of my wife Deborah Bowen. Her research, analysis, outrage, and inquisitiveness regarding the COVID-19 pandemic inform every page. Thank you for walking with me on this path of self-determination and transformation.

Contents

1 Introduction: Racial Sacrifice and Abolition
  in the Pandemic Year   1
2 Reconceptualizing How Policing Works   27
3 Reform, Violence, Capital, and Prison Abolition   43
4 The Police Power of Finance, Technology, Housing,
  and Education   87
5 Evaluating COVID-19 Testing, Infection, Mortality,
  Treatment, and Vaccines   109
6 Efficacy, Eugenics, and Law in the Modern Vaccine
  Regime   163
7 Black Life-Matters, Medical Racism, and Health
  Self-Determination   217

8	Conclusion: The Abolition Question for Medical Science	253
Index		267

About the Author

Tryon P. Woods is Associate Professor of Crime and Justice Studies at the University of Massachusetts, Dartmouth and Special Lecturer in Black Studies at Providence College. He is the author of *Blackhood Against the Police Power: Punishment and Disavowal in the "Post-Racial" Era* (Michigan State, 2019), and co-editor of *Conceptual Aphasia in Black: Displacing Racial Formation* (Lexington, 2016) and *On Marronage: Ethical Confrontations with Antiblackness* (Africa World Press, 2015). His research articles and commentary can be found at www.tryonpwoods.com.

1

Introduction: Racial Sacrifice and Abolition in the Pandemic Year

In the twentieth year of the twenty-first century, the Pandemic Year, not even the virus could displace policing from its usual share of the news headlines. The current global economic and public health crises are unprecedented in modern human history. The antiblack violence of state and civil society is not; it is typical, banal, and contiguous with times gone before and times yet to come. These two facts—what is alarmingly new and grotesquely familiar—are of the utmost analytical and political importance. We need to think them together in order to understand policing. The unprecedented and the precedential, which is also the precedent for all else—two data sets, if you will, from which we can scientifically discern a larger pattern, a historical process in which we remain mired. There can be no simple reading of a text, however, be it literary or legal, scientific or historical, nor of the social or political text in the most general sense. Rather, we must turn the question of policing upon itself, no less than its putative object, as a matter of *interpretation* confronting *representation* and, more importantly, as a matter of the *forces* at work in the interpretative activity under way. In this regard, for the task at hand, we appear to swim upstream; but in fact, we

© The Author(s), under exclusive license to Springer Nature
Switzerland AG 2022
T. P. Woods, *Pandemic Police Power, Public Health and the Abolition Question*, Palgrave Studies in Race, Ethnicity, Indigeneity and Criminal Justice, https://doi.org/10.1007/978-3-030-93031-8_1

are pulled along by a deep and powerful current. Interpreting policing within the historical forces of the Pandemic Year, or any earlier or later moment besides, ascribes voice to what is otherwise muted, attributes a face, or reveals the placement of a mask—and ultimately attests to a veiled reality that is oftentimes indistinguishable from self-delusion on a systemic scale.[1]

In order to interpret policing through the forces that have produced the Pandemic Year, we need to retrain our reading practices. In this essay I return to the long history of black social movement and the archives of black thought for guidance. While the analysis I put forth here may cut against the grain of much of the leading discourse on both policing and public health today, it strives for fidelity with the black liberation struggle. Indeed, it is my contention that were we more faithful to this record, not simply when confronting the state's narrative of law and order, but again, for interpreting *all* facets of the social text generally, we might have more clarity and unity of purpose. Or, at least things might be different than what we find today—which is, the acute expansion of inequality, suffering, and relations of dominance, *and at the same time*, an almost rabid suppression of dissent and independent thought.

There has been ample critique of how the modern world is structured to sacrifice black life to white interests, and it is necessary to remember that this assessment has been lodged from no less of an institutionalized position than the highest levels of the legal academy. The late Derrick Bell, patriarch of sorts within the Critical Race Theory movement in the law, was one source of such an interpretation of U.S. history. Bell's famous Space Traders parable told of how aliens from outer space offered to cure all of the social and structural ills of American society—environmental degradation and pollution, poverty and debt, inequality and violence—in exchange for the country's black people.[2] In Bell's story, American leaders agree to the deal, and black Americans are, once again, trotted onto ships and transported to an unknown fate. Bell makes it clear that American society views blacks *as* its most caustic social ill and as a lesser class of beings useful for addressing its myriad of other problems, and would leap at the chance to clear black people off the country's historical ledger of accounts.

Bell's Space Traders parable simply takes his earlier legal theory of "interest convergence" and renders it as an evocative pedagogical narrative. In his 1980 *Harvard Law Review* article, "*Brown v. Board of Education* and the Interest-Convergence Dilemma," Bell argues that the landmark civil rights decision in *Brown* does not mark progress toward racial justice, but merely the momentary convergence of white and black interests.[3] According to his interest convergence theory, racially progressive policies only occur when they advance, or at least do not impede, the interests of whites. Furthermore, such policies are systematically undone when those measures no longer serve the interests of whites. For this reason, Bell argues that education reform should not seek racial balance, but rather hold out real educational effectiveness as its goal. This may entail improving desegregated schools, but it may also require preserving or creating black schools. Bell's argument is informed not only by the failures of legal and institutional reform in the post-civil rights period, but also by his experience as an attorney working with Charles Hamilton Houston and Thurgood Marshall at the NAACP Legal Defense Fund constructing the school desegregation cases that would result in the *Brown* decision. Bell explains that many of the black families the LDF represented did not want their children integrated into white schools, they simply wanted better funding for black schools.[4] These black families recognized that integration was a false promise for the very reasons Bell would later come to articulate as the pitfalls of interest convergence. Contrary to the analysis of black families, however, the elite civil rights organizations pursued integration through legal reform.

We can use black "fungibility" as shorthand for the historical reality that Bell describes in terms of a society structured to sacrifice black needs to white interests. To be fungible is to be available for all manner of usage. Fungibility implies an objectified status as well as a relation between subjects and objects. The fungible object has no input in, nor any capacity to intervene on, the uses to which it is put; hence, fungibility connotes how a human subject acts upon an objectified non-human being. The only people construed as non-human beings are slaves, and indeed, fungibility is the central characteristic of enslaved status. While slaves frequently worked to produce surplus value for the slaveholder and wealth for the slavocracy as a whole, there were many who did not labor—and yet all enslaved people were fungible for establishing the concept of humanity that Europeans created in their image.[5] No less than five centuries of racial slavery secured humanity as white and its negation as black. The purpose of the enslaved person, in short, was to serve as a surrogate human being: the slave existed so that the master could become "human."[6] The resulting social system has come to be grounded in *antiblackness*, wherein blackness serves as that which orients not only the standing of human beings (no matter how immiserated or dispossessed under white supremacy or capital or patriarchy or empire or settler colonialism), but also the institutions that arose through, or coincident with, the antiblack violence of the slave trade: the nation-state form and its international system, democratic governance, rule of law, capitalist political economy, science and modern medicine, and so forth. Racial slavery created the "antiblack world" as an epistemic system wherein blackness is only present as an absence—of value, of identity, of meaning, of bodily integrity.[7] The very lexicon of the modern world is thus structured in a systemic form of bad faith: because modern principles of fairness, equality, and democracy rest on the disavowal of the violence which inaugurated the modern era (the slave trade) and which continues to structure modern institutions and social life (antiblackness), the modern world and its everyday discourses are structured in a profoundly obtuse misrepresentation of reality.

The Pandemic Year has inspired many related observations about black sacrifice. A recent piece from *Essence* magazine, for instance, claims that so-called essential workers—disproportionately black and female—are inadequately protected from virus transmission and sacrificed to the public health crisis so that the economic crisis can be averted.[8] The *Essence* article cites the history of J. Marion Sims, recognized by Western medicine as the Father of Gynecology, who conducted experiments on enslaved women without anesthesia, claiming that black people do not experience pain the way whites do. These enslaved women were tortured to enable advances in modern medicine.[9] Evoking this history to call for better protection from transmission of the COVID-19 virus today, however, is a treacherous formulation of the problem at hand because it trades on a historical truth (antiblack violence) to obscure a contemporary set of half-truths and untruths related to the pandemic. The history of slavery does indeed continue to structure our present: black people continue to experience medical discrimination and malpractice, as well as disproportionate illness, chronic disease, and premature death related to a range of social factors.[10] Citing this reality, however, only contributes to the mystification that the pandemic relies upon for its coherence. To put it differently, the police power makes good use of black history when it serves its policing aims. This is part of the price we continue to pay in the post-civil rights era for the suppression of black self-determination.[11]

The main argument in *Pandemic Police Power* is that in order to understand what policing is we need to learn how to read it where it is least legible, because policing is most effective precisely where and when it goes unnoticed *as* policing. I use the Pandemic Year to demonstrate this claim because it concentrates the many diffuse forms of social policing unlike ever before *and* stands as the latest case study in fungible blackness. Examining the Pandemic Year in terms of the police power reveals the centrality of medical science and public health to the complex structure of social control, capital accumulation, and antiblack racism. The COVID-19 pandemic is *not* what we think it is any more than policing is as it appears. The efficacy of any legal case is no different from a medical one in that it rests on an accurate establishment of the facts from which the case issues. I begin, therefore, with law, first establishing how policing by law enforcement is subordinate to the police power of state and civil society. I then review, in Chapter 3, the relatively recent trends in criminal justice reform, including the push to abolish prisons and police, the role of private capital in shaping past and future changes, and the problem of violence. In Chapter 4, I briefly consider antiblack policing by means other than criminal justice, namely finance, housing, education, and technology. Chapters 2–4 will establish four things. First, they will enable us to reconceptualize how we understand policing, and in so doing, prepare the analytical ground to discern public health policing for what it is in the present pandemic. Second, the idea of police and prison abolition has gained momentum in recent years as the criminal justice system has consistently come under attack from all quarters, leaving the state with an unprecedented legitimacy problem in this arena. Third, this threat of illegitimacy faced by the criminal justice system, however, has not yet translated to other areas of society, which all told, are far more injurious and consequential to freedom than criminal justice. Fourth, the historical evidence requires the same independent abolitionist research and critical evaluation of medical and public health practices and policies that was applied to law and order to produce the current widespread objection to the system of mass incarceration.

With this evidence in hand, I turn in the fifth chapter to the COVID-19 situation, applying the historical praxis of black struggle to a critical evaluation of the Pandemic Year. I examine the scientific evidence on testing, infection, treatment, and vaccination. In addition to the fraudulent reliance on inaccurate diagnostic tests, the avoidance of reliable, safe, and affordable treatment and prevention, and the xenotropic problem with vaccine production, this chapter scrutinizes the kind of public health model that heavily relies upon vaccination. Chapter 6 deepens this analysis of the COVID-19 situation by looking at vaccination in historical context. Of particular interest here is the historical record of vaccine efficacy, its connections to the racist science of eugenics, and the legal discourse of the vaccine regime. Vaccine law, *in the context of suspect vaccine efficacy*, provides the backdrop and the object of analysis for examining the pandemic police power in this chapter. While there are serious legal implications to the Pandemic Year—including civil liberties, tort damages, fraud, white-collar and state crime, international treaty conventions, and class action lawsuits—law remains constitutive and subordinate to all policing, not external or supraordinate to it. Law's relation to policing in all its myriad forms, in other words, is structural, not instrumental. Chapter 7 interrogates the assertion that black people and other historically marginalized groups need better "access" to medical and public health institutions. Such an approach flaunts the historical struggle and political insights of abolitionism. What will emerge in due course is a portrait of policing by medical science and public health institutions in the service of an expanded social control apparatus at the expense of the public's further diminished capacity for dissent and self-determination. That is, the Pandemic Year represents a severe cost to public health in almost every way *besides* viral infection.

Abolition

This study is heavily dependent upon, and seeks to leverage, the political, historical, and analytical insights of abolition. There are many different iterations, practices, and discourses operating under the title of abolitionism, and a comprehensive overview of them all is beyond the scope of this work. Today abolition is most commonly associated with the call to abolish prisons and police, but it also has its applications where ever structures of social control are perceived as oppressive and impervious to change. Within a complex of Western European and North American academic discourses on punishment, custody, and incapacitation, and identifying itself variously as prison abolition, penal abolition, or carceral abolition, abolitionism has been characterized as "a manifestation of the general human urge to do away with and to struggle against those phenomena or institutions of a social, political, or religious nature that at a given time are considered to be unjust, wrong, or unfair."[12] Most people working with abolitionist thought in these veins acknowledge debts to larger historical, ethical, and spiritual traditions, and they commonly situate contemporary forms of punishment with respect to historical structures such as slavery, empire, settler colonialism, racial capitalism, hetero-patriarchy, and genocide. At the same time, there is a tendency to privilege academic discourse that arcs back philosophically to Michel Foucault and institutionally to the Western academic discipline of criminology, a decidedly limited and compromised framework of knowledge for understanding abolitionism.[13] In the late 1990s, North American academics and activists from various fields came together to develop an abolitionism focused on confronting the specifics of U.S. criminal justice system expansion in the post-civil rights era, analyzing mass incarceration in terms of a "prison industrial complex," specifying the global and transnational sinews of this carceral network, and advancing abolition as a practical change agenda. This work has had a major impact both on abolitionism writ large and on how people across a variety of institutional contexts grapple with the unprecedented problems of U.S.-led carceral practices.

Many abolitionists prefer the term "prison industrial complex" to "criminal justice system" for a number of reasons. First, it highlights how the system fuses profit and punishment such that criminal justice policy decisions are driven less by crime control or public safety needs, and more by the variety of economic interests invested in criminal justice system operation and expansion. In this way, "prison industrial complex" builds on the insights of the "military industrial complex" where observers from peace activists to former five-star general and U.S. President Dwight Eisenhower noted how foreign policy after World War II had become captured by military contractors such that war-making was driven by the profit motive rather than by threats to national security. While the military industrial complex has produced permanent warfare, the prison industrial complex demands constant escalation in policing, imprisonment, and the reach of criminal law throughout society. Second, while capital has always been enmeshed in war and punishment, as the reliance on mercenaries in medieval Europe and the persistence of debtor's prisons across the modern era illustrate, the current period of the PIC stands out for how it signifies radical changes to state formation. With the rise of neoliberal economic globalism, the state's raison d'être in the social policy arena has shifted away from social welfare to law and order. Third, from MIC to PIC, the state's retreat from social investments in areas like education, housing, transportation, healthcare, and so forth, combined with permanent war against enemies foreign and domestic, requires constructing paranoias that justify this extraordinarily lopsided state presence. When they buy into the notion that their lives are threatened by "crime," people more easily tolerate their government's increased spending on law and order while it defunds mostly everything else their communities need. Fourth, through their analysis of the prison industrial complex, abolitionists recognize that the criminal law is less about crime control, or safety and accountability, and more geared toward advancing the social control needs of the state-corporate nexus. In its most historically grounded iterations, then, this abolitionism understands the PIC as a historically specific manifestation of social control structures based on racial, gender-sex, settler colonial, and imperial violence. Finally, the PIC significantly expands the scope of abolition well beyond the traditional criminological concerns of the Eurocentric tradition of penal abolition. By focusing on the "complex" of interests and forces that converge on the site of the prison, the PIC analysis reveals how punishment, policing, incapacitation, and surveillance occur through modalities and institutional contexts irreducible to the criminal justice apparatus. Abolitionists, therefore, pay close attention to how schools, clinics, hospitals, mediascapes, food production, labor, reproduction, sexualities, and more, are sites of domination and violence and thus warrant a fundamental dismantling similar to, and connected with, the abolition of prisons and police.

Abolitionists conclude from this analysis that the only viable solution to the prison industrial complex is to abolish prisons and all systems of control, punishment, and surveillance altogether. They generally reach this conclusion for two reasons. First, according to the insights identified above, the system itself is designed to harm, not to remedy harms, and therefore reforms to the criminal law end up strengthening rather than ameliorating these harmful systems of control, and extending the basic structures of power they represent. Secondly, solving the harms of the prison industrial complex, not to mention the oppressive structures that gain expression through it, means finding alternatives to state power and corporate control. Abolitionists urge community control over resources and problem-solving to foster the local self-determination on which radical social transformation can develop. There is great debate, of course, among abolitionists as to how these principles should translate into practice. While there is a utopian element to abolitionism, there is nothing more pragmatic than asking what do people need and how can individuals and collectives build their capacities to realize these needs for themselves. Moreover, the suggestion that abolition is impractical implicitly dismisses the prerogative of oppressed people to determine their own liberation. Black people's needs, in particular, are closely tied to abolitionist aims and methods, not simply because they bear a grossly disproportionate burden under the present social arrangement, but also because black freedom hinges on the thorough eradication of structures of power that manifest as the prison industrial complex.

Criminal justice is merely symptomatic of more fundamental problems with how society is set up, but as I have written in my recent study *Blackhood Against the Police Power: Punishment and Disavowal in the "Post-Racial" Era,* and elsewhere, the abolitionist focus on the criminal justice system risks turning the symptoms of problems into hypervisible stand-ins for these problems. While any serious abolitionist will agree that the way society is organized must undergo a fundamental overhaul in order to positively impact the problems that manifest as, and *in*, the criminal justice apparatus, in practice there is a decided lack of analytical breadth and ethical consistency in applying these insights to aspects of society beyond institutions customarily associated with punishment, surveillance, and policing. This deficiency is the reason why I have written this book: to draw attention to the role of medical science and public health in carrying out precisely those punishment, surveillance, and policing functions most commonly identified with criminal justice, and therefore, to underscore the necessity of applying the same rigorous abolitionist thought to these institutions as well. The problem that I explore in *Pandemic Police Power*, therefore, impugns abolitionism as much as it relies upon its insights. As it turns out, the contradictions that inhere in contemporary abolitionism stem from a historical context in which abolition has been the source of society's ills as much as it has sought antidotes to them.

Abolition is usually presumed to have arisen as a response to slavery and other forms of oppression across the eras. *Pandemic Police Power's* critical take on abolitionism, however, is grounded in the fact that abolition has served as the *precondition* for enslavement in each successive historical period. Emerging Europe's relationship to human bondage, which eventually would bring virtually the entire planet within the ambit of its yoke, began with a paradox between slavery and freedom peculiar to Western culture and unique in human history. Slavery of some kind has been part of most human societies throughout time. Indeed, such was the case throughout the premodern European subcontinent. In early medieval England, for instance, just over 10 percent of the population was classified as slaves in 1086.[14] The presence of European slaves on the subcontinent would fairly quickly disappear from this point forward, however, such that despite the persistence of various forms of limited compulsion, by the end of the fifteenth century, labor relations were qualitatively distinct from slavery and largely conformed to modern conceptions of free labor.[15] The abolition of slavery for western Europeans, therefore, made the emergent modern civilization of the subcontinent distinctive in human history. Where avoiding or rejecting slave status has been necessary for people in societies everywhere, and non-Western cultures have extensive records debating which persons are eligible for slavery under which conditions, the notion that society should be free of slavery altogether was a uniquely Western phenomenon.[16]

With the abolition of enslavement for Europeans came the uniquely Western conceptions of individual rights and possessive individualism. The increasing freedoms for the individual were symptomatic of two consequential developments underwriting the emergent Western civilization: a shift away from property-in-common to individual property rights, and the capacity to express self-possession as a right to hold property in other people. Europeans might exercise their possessive individualism as freedom from social bonds, or increasingly, by avoiding hiring out these rights to others in return for wages; they might enter the labor market and temporarily trade their rights in persons for wages; or they might purchase property rights in others outright. Indeed, northwestern Europeans in particular developed the most sophisticated conceptions of personal freedom *as* they increasingly concentrated the right to other people as property in the hands of an elite few.

The key to unraveling the slave-free paradox of Western civilization, therefore, lies within European culture itself. Given the high costs of transit from Africa to the Americas, it would have been more profitable to enslave Europeans and transport them to the New World.[17] Indeed, the precedents for European enslavement were ample and coincident: beyond the long history of bondage and servitude on the subcontinent, Europeans in the early modern period were already developing institutions for controlling the dispossessed among them, including exporting bonded or convict labor to the overseas colonies.[18] But the steady abolition of bondage and the concomitant appearance of the possessive individual throughout the medieval period conjoined with an insular civilization structured in racial persecution to make it culturally untenable for Europeans to enslave their own in the emergent modern world.[19]

> European overseas expansion could not have occurred without such a scope, which implied the freedom to enslave others. If neither Africa nor the Americas expanded overseas, it was, perhaps, because of their *social structures* rather than any limited wealth and technology. A corollary is that the impact of European values and social relationships on the non-European world may have been more important than the impact of European wealth and technology. [emphasis added][20]

The European as *racialized* possessive individual thus sits at the heart of the slave-free paradox—and vitally, directs us to the African, but in ways previously misunderstood.

If the racialized autonomous individual is the product of European civilization's abolitionism, then it is also the result of a prior, much more longstanding trade by non-Europeans in African slaves going back at least to the eighth century that shaped the manner of the subcontinent's emergence into the modern era.[21] Western Europe's persecutorial racialism permitted the increasing freedoms of the individual—but only as it congealed its construction of the slave as African. The emergence of the possessive individual, therefore, was only the removal of group bonds *internal* to European civilization. In point of fact, and in historical reality, abolition meant the formation of a group-based power relation at a much grander scale, wherein an emergent slaveholding and slave-trading civilization established its individual liberties in relation to racialized groups external to its borders. Abolition and bondage, free and chattel, and the possessive individual European's rights to hold property in Africans not only developed in tandem with each other, but the former in each of these binaries was parasitic on each of the latter. This means that abolition produces enslavement, not the other way around, and propagates it in order to sustain a free society constituted in bondage. This goes some way toward explaining why emancipation has not meant the end of slavery as culture, but rather has been the site of its expansion and transmutation such that it could exist without any individual being legally enslaved, and moreover, that it could reproduce itself through the very mechanisms ostensibly geared toward its eradication.[22] In short, in the Western tradition, abolitionism has meant the retrenchment of power, not its contestation, eradication, or redistribution.

Abolitionism as the retrenchment of power is amply evident as Western societies moved to abolish slavery in the nineteenth century. This era reveals how the stories about slavery and abolition in the Western tradition are always twofold, bifurcated, and continually enfolding upon themselves: they first set about creating the servile body—unfit, incapable, and alternately vulnerable and threatening; and then, this first kind of story enables a second kind, about those who would bring salvation, the martyrs and saviors, whether through Christianity or the various modes of civility on which the modern democratic polity relies.[23] Extended to the convict and to prison abolition, this dual narrative has been remarkably consistent throughout the twentieth century and into the twenty-first. Implicit in the role of the emancipator is the claim of political authority grounded in the master/slave relation that takes the form, at once, of the Euro-American possessor of both the power to hold others captive and to grant freedom, and of barbaric masters and helpless slaves. Likewise, wholesale emancipation relieves slavery of its function as a social category without eliminating it as an institution and a set of cultural assumptions that structure power relations.[24] To argue that blacks did not deserve slavery was to reinforce the flattering assumption that freedom was both evidence and reward for moral worth, rather than the fact that freedom itself has always been a function of racial violence tied to the historical production of free whites and unfree blacks. When abolitionists criticized slavery thusly, in terms geared to persuade the majority of society which supported enslavement, they advanced a rejection of slavery couched in a contempt for enslaved persons—a sentiment not uncommon within contemporary police and prison abolition discourse.

Whereas the premodern abolition of bondage in Europe was the cultural prerequisite for the African slave trade in the first place, the abolition of racial slavery, in turn, provided the necessary condition for the elaboration of slavery's antiblackness as custom. Abolitionist discourse reveals how status is applied asymmetrically in slaveholding society: masters could be deprived of their slave property after emancipation with no loss of status because ownership of slaves conferred no special status upon them. Deprived of claims over individual chattel human beings, slaveholders could remain proprietors over blacks as a singular class of beings-for-others—"indeed implicit in the conception of slavery as property is the assumption that mastery is an accidental property of the owner, a property she can alienate without altering her own identity."[25] By the time of nineteenth century abolition, therefore, slavery as an institution was sociologically inessential to the structure of antiblack society. Antiblackness since the formal end of slavery, then, can be summarized as constituted in a related version of abolition's twin perversity: alleviating the harm that you have caused, in order that benevolence may cover the ongoing brutality; giving freedom in order to take it away again through an endless series of qualifications, contradictions, and transpositions.

The ongoing vitality of this nuanced historical context means that any invocation of abolition today must pay close attention to the matter of self-determination, to the conformity between civil society and state power, and to customs that present themselves as neutral or life-affirming—such as going to see the doctor. I draw upon abolition in this study, therefore, to build on the many insights of the prison industrial complex noted above, while also elevating the rigors of self-determination pursued by the black freedom movement against *both* slaveholding culture *and* its abolitionism across the eras. In the chapters that follow, I further excavate the police power of slaveholding culture in order to better assess public health's relationship to modes of social control inimical to black freedom and self-determination, and thus to human liberation writ large. Tracking the contradictions of contemporary abolition will help unravel the duplicity of the Pandemic Year.

Contemporary abolitionism's contradictory dimensions are evident in the burgeoning scholarly output on policing and prisons in the past decade. In Chapter 3, I investigate some illustrative examples of recent abolitionist scholarship on prisons, but since policing is in fact the first moment of punishment by the criminal justice system, I briefly assess at this point some of the shortcomings in recent scholarly takes on police to further delineate how *Pandemic Police Power* pursues a different path. Most of the scholarship critical of policing is an elaboration on the basic theme that the purpose of policing is not crime control, but rather social control of the "dangerous classes" as determined by race and class hierarchies. The "dangerous classes" are those groups deemed a threat to the social order by virtue of their potential for rebellion or resistance against race or class oppression, or those groups whose very existence or behaviors offend society's morality, despite fulfilling key cultural and economic functions (such as racialized groups, immigrants, lower-class sex workers, and drug dealers). The analysis of policing in terms of controlling the "dangerous classes" is fine as far as it goes—but it only takes us so far. Alex Vitale's 2017 book, *The End of Policing*, illustrates the problem at hand.[26] *The End of Policing* is an update on what numerous other analysts have already documented, from Kristian Williams' 2004 *Our Enemies in Blue: Police and Power in America* to Radley Balko's 2014 *Rise of the Warrior Cop: The Militarization of America's Police Forces*, to only cite work since 2000. Whereas some of the other studies that Vitale retreads, such as Christian Parenti's 2000 *Lockdown America: Police and Prisons in an Age of Crisis* and the classic 1978 study *Policing the Crisis: Mugging, the State, and Law and Order* by Stuart Hall and his colleagues, actually analyze how shifts in capitalist accumulation at particular historical junctures translate into certain developments in criminal justice and its representations of "crime," Vitale's contribution teaches us nothing about how today's policing is connected to the early twenty-first century political economy. If policing is indeed, as Vitale and everyone else before him has noted, an expression of the inequalities of a racist capitalist system, then in order to abolish it, or fundamentally reconceive it, would we not need to spend more time understanding these connections and less time on the litany of details about how policing happens? Vitale gives us lots of "how" but very little "why."

The End of Policing illustrates the limitations of recent research on policing in the abolitionist vein because the primary responsibility for social control does *not* lie with policing in the ways that Vitale and others suggest. The defensive work of countering the narrative of policing as crime control, again, only takes us so far. As I argue elsewhere, this focus on what the criminal justice apparatus actually does is itself a feature of the social control function of criminal justice.[27] We are policing ourselves by keeping the focus on the police and how to change the criminal justice system. Vitale reproduces the common error of neglecting the culture of slaveholding—that is, the fungible blackness at the center of white-over-black dominance no matter the institutional arrangements of any given political economy—that is foundational to the development of society's police power. He only acknowledges slavery to note some parallels between the early constabulary in England and uniformed officers in antebellum New Orleans and Savannah. Without an actual analysis of slavery, Vitale thus leaves a vast chasm of unarticulated inference in which readers are invited to connect racial inequities in criminal justice practice today to an unspecified legacy of slavery, as mere residue of a long-ago past. Vitale fails to grasp, as do most contemporary abolitionist analysts, how slavery's most important function was the creation of custom, as noted above. The police power of slavery was the reproduction of custom, and that was not primarily the job of a select group of deputized whites (slave patrols, police officers, constables), it was the duty of everyday white people. When we lose track of the fact that white society as a whole was the seat of the original police power, we forget that the primary policing function in society has always been carried out by non-state actors, across half a millennium of slavery and a century of segregation. It was not until the latter stages of the civil rights period in the mid-twentieth century that this duty nominally transitioned to the state—in other words, it has only been seen as the purview of state authority for a mere five decades.

With this historical context in mind, we can recognize that this transition was not a hand-off, but rather part of what legal scholar Anthony Farley calls "slavery perfecting itself."[28] Farley notes that "the story of progress up from slavery is a lie, the longest lie…told juridically in the form of the rule of law."[29] For example, Farley notes the continuities between *Plessy v. Ferguson*, the 1895 "separate but equal" case in which the U.S. Supreme Court held that segregation does not violate the 13th and 14th Amendments to the U.S. Constitution, and *Brown v. Board of Education*, the 1954 desegregation decision that overturned *Plessy*. The dissenting opinion in *Plessy* found common ground with the majority regarding the perpetuity of white supremacy. This dissenting opinion, in turn, was cited favorably by the *Brown* majority who found that segregation created a harmful sense of inferiority in black children, but not an equally destructive false notion of superiority in white kids, and that this damage in blacks "was to be repaired by the healing presence of white children."[30] From slavery to segregation to neo-segregation, explains Farley, the law perfects white-over-black dominance.

Vitale has no sense of this process and can only throw racial discourse *du jour* ("antiblackness") at his basic palette of "excessive" policing of the "dangerous classes." *The End of Policing* rehearses an ahistorical theme in contemporary abolitionism that policing is *newly* militarized and that attendant institutions of control (such as education) are *newly* carceral.[31] Slaveholding culture has always been heavily militarized and acutely carceral toward black people. *The End of Policing* ends up amplifying amorphous solutions that are already well trod across the mainstream: better training for officers, better services for communities in need, better funding for schools and other institutions at the community level. Instead of approaching "the end of policing," then, such proposals tender a more effective police power by offering greater inclusion in state and civil society, rather than an end to the antiblack structure of civil society that demands state authority over all aspects of black life. Even restorative justice methods remain unthought in Vitale's study. Restorative justice, once again, is fine and well as far as it goes, but what is worth restoring in a society constituted in slaveholding? In his study of the Haitian Revolution, C. L. R. James wrote that when the slaves rose up they necessarily burned everything because everything was against them:

> They burned San Domingo flat so that at the end of the war it was a charred desert. Why do you burn everything, asked a French officer of a prisoner. We have a right to burn what we cultivate because a man has a right to dispose of his own labour, was the reply of this unknown anarchist.[32]

Restorative justice models advance individual-level remedies for problems that are structural in nature. When restorative justice programs are posed as alternatives to police, they function as social control insofar as they distract from the slaves' prerogative to destroy tirelessly, as James put it.[33]

The fetish-like focus on the criminal justice system, at the expense of the multi-faceted process by which the police power reproduces historical structures of dominance, means it is unsurprising that so few critics of policing have had anything substantive to say on public health in general, and on the present pandemic specifically. Brendan McQuade and Mark Neocleous' recent article "Beware: Medical Police" thus stands out. McQuade and Neocleous correctly point out that medical policing was a feature of the first modern police entities formed in the late eighteenth century to manage the social upheaval of early industrial capitalist society.

> It was police as *social policy* and hence *social policy as police*. It was, in other words, an art of government and an exercise in technologies of power through a network of institutions and animated by ways of knowing that produced modern social order. While policing was oppressive, its real power is manifest in the management of life and ways of living. Hence, medical police focused on the promotion of the collective health of the population which in turn involved the policing of the health of individuals. This health of individual bodies and the collective body politic was expected to underpin the economic productivity of the labour force.[34]

Schematically, this apprehension of how the police power works is generative. In practice, however, McQuade and Neocleous only direct this analysis to capitalist production and the policing of its "dangerous classes," once more. Policing, it seems, is only what the police do, and hence, there is no analysis of the police power of slaveholding culture, of the reproduction of white-over-black custom throughout society. Most problematically, moreover, McQuade and Neocleous take the medical science and public health aspects of the present pandemic at face value. They are only concerned with how the pandemic gives further license to excessive, discretionary, and biased law enforcement.

In fact, the pandemic reiterates how social analysis on abolition and the police power remains mired within scholars' various institutional disciplines, despite the academy's oft-expressed fondness for "interdisciplinarity." Those who think in terms of police are disciplined by socio-criminological frameworks to privilege the criminal justice system.

Those who think in terms of spatial politics are similarly disciplined by criminological discourse to only see the geography of policing in terms of criminal justice encroachment in areas presumed to be beyond the scope of the police, such as architecture, housing policy, and homeless shelters, as if these features of modern society were not already intrinsic expressions of the police power.[35] Abolitionist geographers present robust critiques of "carceral spatiality," including the toxicities of certain spatial arrangements, built environments, and constructed landscapes, but seem unable to pose abolitionist critiques of medical science's fundamental colonization of space at all levels: biome, species, body, family, collective, nation, planet. Political philosophers, for their part, have found Agamben, Benjamin, Foucault, and other European thinkers useful to inveigh against the "medicalization of politics" and the pandemic's invocation of the "state of exception," but in today's philosophers' hands at least, the Western philosophes are not up to the task of reading medical science against the state-corporate grain as they too fail to call into question any aspect of the public health model.[36] This disciplinary approach to examining the pandemic is equally evident in Patrice Douglass' "Unnatural Causes: Racial Taxonomies, Pandemic, and Social Contagion." A scholar of black feminist theory, Douglass compares the deaths of black patients from COVID-19 to police killings of black people, arguing that the production of blackness as social contagion leads to both kinds of deadly outcomes.[37] Although she is at pains to emphasize that disproportionate black death during the pandemic is not simply a function of inequities in healthcare, but rather an expression of black excision from all social spaces, not just hospitals, Douglass, as well, takes the medical science and public health narrative about the pandemic for granted. As a result, she finds herself in the customary abolitionist conundrum of reproducing the state-corporate narrative on the disease, while calling for greater attention to those lives summarily extinguished by state-corporate management of health.

Along the same lines, the COVID-19 Policing Project is seeking to track the expansion of law enforcement powers during the pandemic.[38] Despite its explicitly abolitionist rhetoric, this project also accepts the state's narrative on medical science and public health, missing a golden opportunity to use its media savvy and community connections (not to mention extensive philanthropic support network) to promote non-statist, independent analysis of medical science, and to foment a public health model that circumvents state-corporate control over medicine and wellness. Instead, the Project seems to prefer advocating for equitable public investment in healthy communities rather than in policing; the Project even inverts these two things by calling for police officers to stop harassing people and instead give out useful health information during the pandemic. It is ironic enough that abolitionists are requesting that law enforcement cease its social control function; but the supreme irony lies with the fact that by advocating vaccination, mask-wearing, and social distancing as the basis for healthy publics, the abolitionists are carrying out the state's own social control agenda. Another case of abolitionist bad faith—asking the state to do better is like trying to make stone soup while submitting to a clientele relationship that never delivers. Similarly, a recent edited volume, *Sick of the System: Why the COVID-19 Recovery Must Be Revolutionary*, charts many of the political fault lines in modern society exposed by the pandemic.[39] Again, while there are gestures to non-statist public health solutions here, all of this work takes the medical science of the present pandemic at face value, leaving the collective proposition for recovery far short of "revolutionary."

The severe worldwide consequences of how this pandemic has been constructed demand analysis of medical science and public health from a historical perspective on abolition that can illuminate why things are happening now and in the manner that they are occurring. It is imperative that we cross into previously unfamiliar terrain, carrying with us what we do know from the historical struggle for human liberation, and refuse to allow "experts" in any field to singularly determine what we know about these fields without conducting our own independent evaluations. It is no more tenable for people who have been working in the criminal law to tolerate the suppression of dissent in medical science simply because the contours of the field are unfamiliar, than it would be for medical professionals to accept the marginalization of dissenting perspectives on law and order just because they are only aware of the mainstream narrative. This critique of the medical industrial complex must work toward understanding how finance, education, housing, and technology, for instance, reproduce the police power and thus structure the response to this pandemic. Medical policing does not simply appear out of thin air in 2020, as McQuade and Neocleous rightfully remind us. Its sudden appearance in fully operational form in the Pandemic Year indicates that it has always been here but we have not seen it as such because either we chose not to see it or it was operating under other names. We are collectively, albeit unevenly, paying the cost now for failing to adequately read the medical science and critique public health policing in abolitionist terms prior to 2020.

All told, the analysis of policing and abolition driving *Pandemic Police Power* aims to extricate our thinking from the either/or structures of popular dichotomies typical of the sectarianism characterizing public life today in the U.S. especially, but also in many other nations too: Trump is bad, Fauci is good; politicians are bad, doctors and scientists are good; capitalists are bad, philanthropists are good; anti-vaxxers and re-openers are bad, mask-wearing and social distancing is good; kids are bad, technology is good; science is truth, science is political; and so on. These binaries are in fact state narratives which function as dead-ends for thought: state power promotes anti-intellectualism, the sequestration of critical thought, and the quarantine of independent research and analysis. Legal scholars and practitioners are no different from scientists and medical professionals, who are no different from the rest of us: we are all impacted by the socio-political context of our lives, which tends to shape the kinds of questions we ask and do not ask about the world. At the same time, we all have at our disposal an almost endless trove of evidence with which to make independent determinations about what is going on with the Pandemic Year. This study aims to supplement independent thought against policing everywhere.

Notes

1. This paragraph borrows from Jared Sexton, "Ça: Were It Posed as a Question," *qui parle*, 26(2) December 2017: 298: "There can be no simple reading of a text, be it literary, scientific, or historical, nor of the social text in the most general sense. Rather, the question must turn upon itself, no less than its putative object, as a matter of *interpretation* and, more important, as a matter of the *forces* at work in the interpretative activity under way. There is always the ascription of voice to what is otherwise silent, the attribution of a face or the placement of a mask."
2. "The Space Traders" first appeared in Derrick A. Bell, Jr., *Faces at the Bottom of the Well: The Permanence of Racism* (New York: Basic, [1992] 2018), 197–242. It was adapted for television by HBO in 1994 (Reginald Hudlin, dir.).
3. Bell, "*Brown v. Board of Education* and the Interest-Convergence Dilemma" *Harvard Law Review* 93(3) 1980: 518–533.
4. Bell, "Serving Two Masters: Integration Ideals and Client Interests in School Desegregation Litigation" *Yale Law Review* 85(4) 1976: 476, n. 12, 477–479.
5. See Frank B. Wilderson, III, "Gramsci's Black Marx: Whither the Slave in Civil Society?" *Social Identities* 9(2) 2003: 225–240.
6. See Orlando Patterson, *Slavery and Social Death: A Comparative Study* (Cambridge: Harvard University Press, 1982).
7. See Lewis Gordon, *Bad Faith and Antiblack Racism* (Atlantic Highlands, NJ: Humanities Press, 1995).
8. See https://www.essence.com/health-and-wellness/black-women-sacrifice-economy-covid-19/.
9. See Deirdre Cooper Owens, *Medical Bondage: Race, Gender, and the Origins of American Gynecology* (Athens: Georgia, 2017).
10. Risa Lavizzo-Mourey and David Williams, "Being Black Is Bad for Your Health," *U.S. News and World Report*, April 14, 2016, https://www.usnews.com/opinion/blogs/policy-dose/articles/2016-04-14/theres-a-huge-health-equity-gap-between-whites-and-minorities.

11. On the ways in which black historical struggle is manipulated in the post-civil rights era to abet the further suffering of black communities, see Toni Cade Bambara, *Those Bones Are Not My Child* (New York: Vintage, 2000); and Tryon P. Woods, "Still *Missing and Murdered*: Atlanta's Lost Children Address Today's Plague of Police Violence," *Black Agenda Report*, September 23, 2020, https://blackagendareport.com/still-missing-and-murdered-atlantas-lost-children-address-todays-plague-police-violence.
12. H. Bianchi, "Abolitionism in the Past, Present, and Future," in Z. Lasocik et al., eds., *Abolitionism in History: On Another Way of Thinking* (Warsaw: Institute of Social Prevention and Resocialisation, 1991), 9. See as well the useful overview provided by Nicolas Carrier and Justin Piché, "The State of Abolitionism," *Champ Pénal/Penal Field*, vol. 12, 2015, https://journals.openedition.org/champpenal/9164.
13. For a detailed elaboration of this kind of abolitionism within the Western academy, see Vincenzo Ruggiero, "The Legacy of Abolitionism," *Champ Pénal/Penal Field*, vol. 12, 2015, https://journals.openedition.org/champpenal/9080.
14. John McDonald and Graeme D. Snooks, *Domesday Economy: A New Approach to Anglo-Norman History* (Oxford: Oxford University Press, 1986), 16–17, as cited in David Eltis, *The Rise of African Slavery in the Americas* (New York: Cambridge University Press, 2000), 5.
15. Eltis, 5–6, 8.
16. Eltis, 4, 7.
17. Eltis, 14.
18. Scott Christianson, *With Liberty for Some: 500 Years of Imprisonment in America* (Chicago: Northeastern, 1998); Peter Linebaugh, *The London Hanged: Crime and Civil Society in the Eighteenth Century* (London: Verso, 2006).
19. R. I. Moore, *The Formation of a Persecuting Society: Authority and Deviance in Western Europe, 950–1250*, 2nd ed. (Oxford: Blackwell, 2007).
20. Eltis, 23.

21. See for example, R. W. Beachey, *The Slave Trade of Eastern Africa* (New York: Barnes & Noble, 1976); Cheikh Anta Diop, *Precolonial Black Africa: A Comparative Study of the Political and Social Systems of Europe and Black Africa, from Antiquity to the Formation of Modern States* (Chicago: Lawrence Hill, 1987); Ronald Segal, *Islam's Black Slaves: The Other Black Diaspora* (New York: Farrar, Straus, and Giroux, 2001).
22. Guyora Binder, "The Slavery of Emancipation," *Cardozo Law Review* 16(2063) 1996: 2064.
23. Joan Dayan, *Haiti, History, and the Gods* (Berkeley, CA: University of California Press, 1998), 205.
24. Guyora Binder, "The Slavery of Emancipation," *Cardozo Law Review* 16 (1996): 2075.
25. Dayan, 203; Binder, 2097.
26. Alex S. Vitale, *The End of Policing* (London: Verso, 2017). Again, *End of Policing* is representative of some of the issues within contemporary scholarship on policing, but it does not exhaust the variety of approaches scholars are taking on the topic. A brief and uncomprehensive list of other titles in the recent critical scholarly output on policing include, Simon Balto, *Occupied Territory: Policing Black Chicago from Red Summer to Black Power* (Chapel Hill: North Carolina, 2020); Geo Maher, *A World Without Police: How Strong Communities Make Police Obsolete* (London: Verso, 2021); Derecka Purnell, *Becoming Abolitionists: Police, Protests, and the Pursuit of Freedom* (New York: Astra House, 2021); Stuart Schrader, *Badges Without Borders: How Global Counterinsurgency Transformed American Policing* (Berkeley, CA: University of California Press, 2019).
27. Tryon P. Woods, *Blackhood Against the Police Power: Punishment and Disavowal in the "Post-Racial" Era* (East Lansing: Michigan State, 2019).
28. Anthony Farley, "Perfecting Slavery," *Loyola University Chicago Law Journal* 36 (2005): 222.
29. Farley, 222.
30. Farley, 241.
31. The militarism intrinsic to U.S. society has been duly noted throughout the long tradition of independent black thought, from

David Walker's 1829 *Appeal to the Colored Citizens of the World*, to Robert F. Williams' 1962 *Negroes with Guns*, to George Jackson's 1971 *Blood In My Eye*. There is no more authoritative text on slaveholding culture's construction of a carceral education for black children than Carter G. Woodson's 1933 *The Mis-Education of the Negro*.

32. C. L. R. James, *The Black Jacobins: Toussaint L'Ouverture and the San Domingo Revolution* (New York: Vintage, 1989), 361.
33. James, 88.
34. Brendan McQuade and Mark Neocleous, "Beware: Medical Police," *Radical Philosophy* 2.08 (Autumn 2020): 4.
35. See for example, Madeline Hamlin, "The Abolition Geographies of COVID-19," *Society + Space*, May 6, 2020, https://www.societyandspace.org/articles/the-abolition-geographies-of-covid-19.
36. See for example Carlo Salzani, "COVID-19 and the State of Exception: Medicine, Politics, and the Epidemic State," *Depictions: The Paris Institute Newsletter*, March 12, 2021, https://parisinstitute.org/depictions-article-covid-19-and-state-of-exception-medicine-politics-and-the-epidemic-state/.
37. Patrice Douglass, "Unnatural Causes: Racial Taxonomies, Pandemic, and Social Contagion," *Prism: Theory and Modern Chinese Literature* 18(1) March 2021: 256–270.
38. https://communityresourcehub.org/covid19-policing/.
39. Between the Lines, *Sick of the System: Why the COVID-19 Recovery Must Be Revolutionary* (Toronto: Between the Lines, 2021), https://btlbooks.com/book/sick-of-the-system.

2

Reconceptualizing How Policing Works

We continually misread policing because we begin with law and the criminal justice system in the abstract, rather than understanding them in the historically grounded reality which produces them. It is insufficient to observe that current policies and practices in the criminal law do not correspond to the principles of fairness, equity, and due process codified in law. The state's job is to preserve the status quo, and one way that it does this is by establishing the parameters of acceptable debate and dissent. If we limit our analysis about law to a critique of its inequitable outcomes, then we are strengthening the state's control over our understanding of what the law is and how it works. That is, we are doing the state's job of preserving the status quo. We must also develop an accurate and rigorous assessment of how power works by examining the violence that produces law. This focus means attending to the world as it is, not the one we wish it were nor the one that the law purports it is. Only in this manner can we begin to understand what policing really is. My recent book *Blackhood Against the Police Power: Punishment and Disavowal in the "Post-Racial" Era* employs this approach to redefine

© The Author(s), under exclusive license to Springer Nature
Switzerland AG 2022
T. P. Woods, *Pandemic Police Power, Public Health and the Abolition Question*, Palgrave Studies in Race, Ethnicity, Indigeneity and Criminal Justice, https://doi.org/10.1007/978-3-030-93031-8_2

policing as a sociohistorical process of implementing and reproducing the modern world's onto-epistemic structure of antiblackness.[1] In so doing, I demonstrate how racism is policing's other name, and as such, is foremost an act of sexual violence that produces the punishment of "race." Antiblack policing, therefore, saturates the society in ways large and small, and reveals an anxiety about the threatening specter of black liberation that is both foundational and persistent to social organization at all levels. In this first chapter, I briefly summarize this redefinition of policing.

Beginning where we are now, and walking it back conceptually and historically: most of the harm caused to our society today—in terms of financial loss, bodily injury, communal disarray, and premature death—comes from the realm of white-collar crime and state crime, not from so-called street crime, and yet we focus the overwhelming brunt of our attention, resources, and fear on the latter realm of criminal behaviors.[2] I call this the "justice contradiction": society focuses mostly on those behaviors that cause the least amount of harm, socially speaking, while devoting the least amount of attention to those behaviors that wreak the most destruction on society.[3] The justice contradiction turns our attention away from crime and onto the police themselves: we have a *policing* problem, not a crime problem per se. Members of all races and classes participate in law-breaking, and yet whites and the wealthy go relatively unpoliced and decriminalized. This means that what gets counted as "crime," and who shows up as "criminal," is not a reflection of what is actually happening in terms of law-breaking behavior but is merely a catalog of police behavior, not to mention an index of the law's disposition itself. Third, given this policing problem, we face the reality that we are not policed for what we do, but for who we are or what we represent in the historical structure. This is why the determining factor in who gets punished with imprisonment is whether a person is black, not whether that person is a law breaker.[4] Policing is thus a cultural and structural phenomenon. It is not principally about enforcing law, making us safe, or keeping a lid on chaos.[5]

As a cultural and structural problem, the cultural content of policing is antiblackness. This cultural content derives from the historical structure that police exist to maintain, racial slavery. Contemporary policing does not descend from the colonial night watch or from the London constabulary; it is a distant cousin to these institutions. Those who point to the slave patrols as the progenitors of today's police hit much closer to the mark.[6] But this too is a kind of misdirection because the original police power was not a discrete cadre of deputized individuals, riders in the night hunting down fugitive slaves—rather, it was white society itself, writ large. For four hundred years of slavery, in the least, followed by one hundred years of lynching, it was everyday white people who policed all black people. At the compulsion of the black freedom movement during the civil rights era, this duty transferred from the average white citizen to the state in the form of the criminal justice system by the 1970s—which means it has only been in the hands of the cops for less than five decades (compared with five centuries).[7] The recent killings of Ahmaud Arbery, Trayvon Martin, Renisha McBride, Jordan Davis, and many others at the hands of non-police officers remind us that the police power rests first with civil society, not with law enforcement.[8] The cultural implications of this historical structure are threefold: modern policing formed through the policing of blackness; it has always been militaristic with respect to black people; and it thus serves as a key mechanism for racialization.[9] Put differently, policing is racism's other name.

Slavery as the condition of possibility for modern society means that policing precedes law. We can trace law's subordinate position relative to policing through every historical period, beginning with the manner in which the United States itself was conceived in a counter-insurgent warfare against both rebellious slaves and the British abolitionism they compelled. The frequency and intensity of African rebellion in the Caribbean, let alone its periodic success and the omnipresent threat of marronage amid the plantations, had portended the collapse of Britain's slave holdings in the region.[10] The decades leading up to the American Revolution in 1776 were marked by notable slave rebellions across North America as well, most significantly in Manhattan in 1712 and 1741 and South Carolina in 1739.[11] The British were eventually persuaded to adopt abolition in the face of mounting losses at the hands of African rebels, with the 1772 judgment of the English Court of King's Bench in *Somerset v. Stewart* signifying the abolitionist direction of British policy.[12] In *Somerset*, Charles Stewart, a colonial customs officer for the British Crown, purchased the enslaved person James Somerset in Boston and brought him back to England. After Somerset escaped and was recaptured, Stewart directed him sent to the slave market in Jamaica to be sold to a plantation. British abolitionists filed writ of habeas corpus and Somerset was brought before the Court, which eventually declared slavery unknown to English common law, ordering Somerset released from his unlawful imprisonment.[13]

The North American colonists, by contrast, dug deeper into the morass of greater investment with the slave trade and paranoia regarding black freedom. Ben Franklin fairly represented colonist sentiment, almost two decades before the Revolution, when he asserted, "Every slave might be reckoned a domestic enemy."[14] The landed elite of the North American British colonies were deeply indebted to London creditors, with their slave property among their only liquid assets.[15] The *Somerset* decision was therefore read by the colonists as an existential threat as serious as that posed by African rebels. As the American slave trade increased, and revolts of the enslaved rose accordingly, abolitionism began to spread and the division between the colonists and London sharpened on the slavery question.[16] Whereas the colonists famously presented their cause as revolutionary because it sought to throw off the shackles of British despotism, their resistance was in fact *counter-revolutionary* in that it endeavored to keep the shackles *on* the Africans, even at pains of war with their European motherland. Indeed, the American Revolution's declaration of the rights and liberties of man is more accurately understood as the assertion of an imperative freedom to buy and sell Africans as they pleased, than it is a principled objection to tyranny.

Given that the preservation of slavery was a central impetus for the Revolution, the primary legal institution that it created, the U.S. Constitution, unsurprisingly enshrines the interests of the slaveholding class. As former Supreme Court Justice Thurgood Marshall put it on the occasion of the Bicentennial celebration of the 1787 Constitution,

> Nor do I find the wisdom, foresight, and sense of justice exhibited by the Framers particularly profound. To the contrary, the government they devised was defective from the start, requiring several amendments, a

civil war, and momentous social transformation to attain the system of constitutional government, and its respect for the individual freedoms and human rights, we hold as fundamental today.[17]

Marshall's point that the Constitution enshrined slaveholding is clear. By suggesting that the country has righted its historical wrongs, by dint of civil war, the civil rights movement, judicial decree, and legislative reform, the first black Supreme Court Justice invoked the "false start" narrative about democratic governance. Not only does contemporary jurisprudence fail to bear out Marshall's suggestion that the country has overcome its false start, but moreover, the high court's interpretation of law has consistently followed the police powers of slaveholding class interests.

The 1801 *Fletcher v. Peck* case before the Supreme Court of the United States stemmed from a thirty-five-million-acre land grant authorized in 1795 by the Georgia legislature to private speculators. When it was later revealed that most of the legislators who voted for the grant had been bribed to do so, the legislature voided the grant. A subsequent dispute over said land parcel between two speculators, John Peck and Robert Fletcher, eventually landed the case before the Supreme Court. Chief Justice John Marshall ruled that the Georgia legislature's voiding of the land grant was unconstitutional, reasoning that the contracts clause of the U.S. Constitution prevents states from rescinding an agreement even if that agreement was reached illegally.[18] The Marshall Court is generally remembered by legal historians for establishing the "foundations of power" for the Court and the federal government.[19] Put differently, the Marshall Court enshrined the power of slave traders and slaveholders to have laws created and interpreted to meet their propertied interests in black people. The *Fletcher* decision established the principles that a contract is inviolable and that property is absolute; these principles are now the accepted conclusion of the contract clause of the U.S. federal constitution.[20] Again, put differently, the Court's decision ignored the illegality of the original contract in order to pave the way for the sale of millions of acres for slavery's expanding footprint in the U.S. South.

> Marshall's ruling also gave every future defender of slavery and its expansion an incredible tool. Consider this: If the people of Georgia couldn't overturn a contract born from obvious corruption, how could a legislature or any other government entity take slaves away from owners? Enslaved African Americans were property acquired by contract, according to the law of slave states. Nor, the decision implied, could legislatures constrain enslavers' right to treat said property as being an absolute, as mobile, and as alienable as they liked.[21]

In this way, slavery stands as the synecdoche for all of subsequent contract law: grounded in barbaric theft and human social death, it is the illicit contract that establishes the legal supremacy of contracts, but renders any contracts that conflict with slavery's extralegal compacts secondary or null and void.

Chief Justice Marshall, who actively bought and sold slaves during his lifetime, used black social death to build the supremacy of property law.[22] In *Hezekiah Wood v. John Davis and Others*, Wood purchased Davis and his siblings from a slave trader despite the fact that Davis' mother, Susan Davis, had been born free and was never enslaved during her life.[23] Since their mother was not a slave, John Davis and his siblings argued that they had been born free as well and had never been slaves. Ever since the 1662 act of the Virginia General Assembly which decreed "Negro womens children to serve according to the condition of the mother, [sic]" it has been the law of *all* slaveholding jurisdictions in the United States that children born to a free mother are also free, no matter how they ended up in the hands of others who illegally held them as slaves.[24] Chief Justice Marshall ignored the universal acceptance of this rule and decided that the Davis children were not free. Marshall claimed that the judgment of the lower court recognizing Susan Davis' freedom "was not conclusive evidence in the present case" because there was "no privity" between Wood and the man who had claimed to own her.[25] The case had nothing to do with Susan Davis' owner and yet Marshall justified rejecting the settled slave law of *every* state by evoking an irrelevant contract theory in order to configure the exchange between erstwhile slaveholders as contractual and legal. Again, the extralegal or illicit contractual relations between free whites are allowed to bypass the actual law that ostensibly bound relations between white society and its black inhabitants, free or enslaved. In other words, actual law is subordinate to the police power of slaveholding.

The 1837 decision in *New York v. Miln* is largely remembered for the Court's early enunciation of the police power in law. Writing for the Court majority, Justice Philip Barbour decreed the "indefinite supremacy" of the police power and that it possesses an "undeniable and unlimited jurisdiction over all persons and things."[26] The matter in *Miln* involved an 1824 New York State statute requiring ship masters to register immigrants that they import from abroad, to detain immigrants who might become wards of the state due to their poverty, and to deport noncitizen immigrants whom the mayor determined to be potential wards. The New York law was challenged on the grounds that it interfered with Congress' exclusive power to regulate commerce. The Court found that the law in question was a police action, not a regulation of commerce. Legal scholars have long failed to notice the bald contradiction in this decision.[27] When compared with the Court's earlier decision in *The Antelope*, we see how slavery at once stands in excess of law, constitutes the basis for the nation's legal regime, and *is* the limitless police power.[28] Law is integrated into the structure of slavery, not the other way around.

The Antelope was a slaver registered in Spain, perhaps owned by Spanish and Portuguese shipowners, but perhaps owned by an American. The ship was seized by American privateers off the coast of Africa, with scores of captives on board. These slave-trading pirates then acquired additional Africans before being intercepted by a coast guard cutter off the coast of Florida. The pirates seized some of the additional African captives from a Portuguese vessel, while others probably came from an American ship operated on behalf of a prominent Rhode Islander who, by the time the case reached the courts, was a U.S. senator.[29] This international web of shadow ownership, piracy, and complicity itself indicates the manner in which the formal institutions of civil society and its governance systems are beholden to an illicit economy organized by the desire for black flesh.[30] Representatives of Spain and Portugal sued for the return of the African captives to the supposedly Iberian shipowners rather than to their own homelands in Africa.

At the time of *The Antelope* decision in 1825, U.S. federal law recognized property in slaves, but at the same time prohibited the importation of slaves. The 1807 statute outlawing international slave trading also provided for captive Africans illegally imported into the United States. to be returned to Africa. This suggested that the Supreme Court in *The Antelope* would not recognize foreign title to slaves being imported into the country. Moreover, in international law, British precedent asserted that the slave trade violated the law of nations and could no longer give rise to good title anywhere.[31] Justice Marshall, however, writing for the Court, held in favor of the foreign shipowners who claimed ownership over the slaves. He reasoned that the confiscatory sanctions entailed in the statute prohibiting international trade in slaves could not be applied to foreign slave traders who had never themselves attempted to import slaves into the United States.[32] Where was the police power in *The Antelope*? Only two years after *The Antelope*, the Court would cite "the police power" of the federal government to invalidate a Maryland law taxing foreign imports in *Brown v. Maryland*.[33] And in *Miln*, shortly thereafter, the Court interpreted facts very similar to *The Antelope* as cause for police action. Indeed, while the facts in *Miln* and *The Antelope* may be essentially the same, the fact of slavery proves again to be the essence on which law turns. Millions of Europeans immigrated to the United States in the first half of the nineteenth century. The transport of these immigrants was not charity; it was business, much like the transport of enslaved Africans. The New York law was an early effort by the state to both regulate this business and shape the contour of immigration. The Court chose to read *Miln* as a police action, but when slavery was involved in *The Antelope*, it overlooked the police action provided in the prohibition against the importation of slaves in favor of promoting the larger global institution of slavery, which included the ongoing illicit international commerce in enslaved Africans long after the 1807 law proscribing it.

These cases remind us that slavery was never a matter of law; but the law has always been a matter of slavery. The extensive statutory and jurisprudential apparatus of slave law is a testament to the complex justificatory needs of modern civil society; this legal regime *follows* the exigencies of particular cases, and as such, does not adjudicate *to* them. Slavery is the antiblack violence that forms the modern world, and as such, it precedes and paves the way for law. In these cases, we see the formation of contract law, property rights, the state's police power, and international law through the propertied interests of slaveholders and slave traders. The disaggregation of laws and judicial decisions that do not have obvious direct correspondence to slavery from the larger structure of a society based on slaveholding is a grievous analytical error plaguing legal scholarship that continues to incapacitate our understanding of policing. This becomes especially evident in the post-Emancipation era, where the advantageous interpretation of the 14th Amendment to establish corporate personhood is viewed as merely coincidental to the degraded legal persona of ex-slaves.

One of the three so-called Reconstruction Amendments passed after the Civil War, the 14th Amendment was first interpreted by the Court in the 1873 *Slaughterhouse Cases*. When Louisiana granted one company a monopoly to operate a slaughterhouse in New Orleans, local butchers alleged that the monopoly had deprived them of one of the "privileges and immunities" of citizenship by denying them the right to earn a living.[34] While the Court majority found that the privileges and immunities clause applies to national citizenship, not state citizenship, the split decision allowed that the 14th Amendment could not be construed as only protecting former slaves. The 1886 case *Santa Clara County v. Southern Pacific Rail Road* then solidifies the precedent for using the 14th Amendment to establish corporate personhood.[35] Between 1868 when the Amendment was ratified and 1912, the Court would rule on 312 cases involving the rights of corporations and only 28 cases on the rights of African Americans.[36] There is a direct line from *Santa Clara County* to the more recent decisions of corporate personhood in *Citizen's United v. Federal Election Commission* and *Burwell v. Hobby Lobby Stores*.[37] The burgeoning rights of the corporation are not simply parasitic on the ex-slave, they are the constitutive inversion producing the ongoing degradation of black personhood before the law.

Thurgood Marshall's suggestion that the United States has overcome its "false start" is further waylaid by post-civil rights 4th Amendment jurisprudence. I refer to this body of law, from *Terry v. Ohio* in 1968 through at least the 2013 District Court decision in *Floyd, et al. v. City of New York, et al.*, as the "jurisprudence of racial profiling." In *Floyd*, Judge

Shira Scheindlin found the New York Police Department's implementation of its stop-and-frisk policy to be in violation of the 4th and 14th Amendments and ordered its immediate remediation. Although advocates hailed a victory against racial profiling, *Floyd* occurred in the first place because the NYPD failed to comply with the consent decree stemming from an earlier case, *Daniels, et al. v. City of New York, et al.* . In the decade between the city's settlement of *Daniels* in 2003 and the *Floyd* decision in 2013, the NYPD actually *increased* its stop-and-frisks dramatically, from 314,000 stops in 2004 to a high of 686,000 in 2011, joining a tradition of court decrees, commission reports, and police scandal exposés that produced no lasting reforms but simply more of the same police practices.[38] *Floyd* is very clear that the constitutionality of stop-and-frisk is not at issue, only that the NYPD systematically carried it out in a racially prejudicial manner. In other words, the Supreme Court's reasoning in *Terry* did not come under examination in *Floyd*; indeed, Judge Scheindlin paid tribute to *Terry*, claiming that the NYPD was in violation of the Constitution because it had strayed from the principles of "reasonable suspicion" set forth in the 1968 decision. What, then, did the *Terry* Court mean by "reasonable" police action?

When the Court created the legal fiction of "reasonable suspicion" in *Terry*, it essentially amended the law to better conform with what the police were already doing. When asked during cross-examination at the trial court on what basis did he suspect John Terry and his companions, all of whom were black, of criminal activity, the white police officer who made the arrest, Detective Martin McFadden, explained simply: "I didn't like them…I was attracted to them."[39] What the Court found "reasonable" in this response, then, is nothing more than classic Negrophobia, the sexual neurosis of white supremacy, a disavowed desire for and fear of immoral shameful things—black bodies.[40] Although ostensibly applied to individual-level behaviors, the practice of suspicion itself is conceptually and empirically wedded to the social and political construction of blackness—in other words, suspicion functions at the level of populations, not the individual.[41] "Danger," "threat," and "security" are racialized constructs that define black people as intrinsically suspicious as a group, irrespective of individual behaviors. Justice Marshall's questioning of the attorney for the State of Ohio during oral argument reveals the farcical racial profiling intrinsic to the case, but he nonetheless joined the majority opinion—and in so doing, provides us with additional historical evidence that policing precedes law, not the other way around. Moreover, since none of the 4th Amendment decisions since *Terry* have called into question "reasonable suspicion" or even "probable cause," we are faced with the reality that the state and its legal apparatus as the arena for petitioning and adjudicating claims to justice, on the one hand, and the police as the agents of lethal violence with impunity, on the other hand, are in fact two sides of the same coin.[42] Things are working as intended: if the police relate to those whom they profile as "suspect" as a law unto themselves, endorsed by the judicial process, then the law itself is moot, null and void—for what is the meaning of law in the face of routinized impunity before it?[43]

The brief review here of how law conforms to slavery begets the analysis of how policing precedes law. Although "reasonable suspicion" does not appear in 4th Amendment jurisprudence until 1968, *Terry* merely codified what has been this society's default orientation toward black people at least since Benjamin Franklin named all slaves "domestic enemies" almost exactly two hundred years prior. Slavery was itself, at base, the profound and fundamental expression of search and seizure powers over black people's bodies, over black spaces, and over black lands. Colonial settlers conjured the principles of individualized justice that would become the 4th Amendment to the Constitution only in relation to this capacity to seize blackness with impunity. The 4th Amendment is a feature of the counter-revolutionary warfare against African rebels, and as such, the principle of individualized justice and the prohibition against the general warrant are products of the American struggle for sovereignty *as* a struggle *for* slavery. It is not ironic or contradictory, therefore, that the colonists' objection to the generalized and arbitrary suspicion of the British Crown is the precise same objection today against racial profiling and stop-and-frisk. It is simply the persistent tyranny of antiblackness that continues to underwrite democratic governance.

Notes

1. See Tryon P. Woods, *Blackhood Against the Police Power: Punishment and Disavowal in the "Post-Racial" Era* (East Lansing: Michigan State, 2019).
2. See Steven Box, *Power, Crime, and Mystification* (London: Tavistock, 1983), 5–6.
3. Woods, *Blackhood*, 8.
4. Angela Y. Davis, "Race and Criminalization: Black Americans and the Punishment Industry," in Joy James, ed., *The Angela Y. Davis Reader* (Malden, MA: Blackwell, 1998), 61–73.
5. Woods, *Blackhood*, 8.
6. See Kristian Williams, *Our Enemies in Blue: Police and Power in America* (Boston: South End, 2007).
7. On the "professionalization" of the police, see *The Iron Fist and the Velvet Glove: An Analysis of the U.S. Police* (Berkeley: Center for Research on Criminal Justice, 1975).
8. Woods, *Blackhood*, 10.
9. Woods, *Blackhood*, 9.
10. Gerald Horne, *The Counter-Revolution of 1776: Slave Resistance and the Origins of the United States of America* (New York: NYU, 2006), 9.
11. See Thomas J. Davis, *Rumor of Revolt: The "Great Negro" Plot in Colonial New York* (New York: Free Press, 1985); Thelma Wills Foote, *Black and White Manhattan: The History of Racial Formation in Colonial New York City* (New York: Oxford, 2004); and John Hope Franklin and Loren Schweninger, *Runaway Slaves: Rebels on the Plantation* (New York: Oxford, 1999).
12. *Somerset v. Stewart* (1772) 98 ER 499.
13. See https://www.nationalarchives.gov.uk/pathways/blackhistory/rights/docs/state_trials.htm.
14. Cited in Horne, 19.
15. Horne, 19.
16. Horne, 27, 149, 152, 156, 159.
17. http://thurgoodmarshall.com/the-bicentennial-speech/.

18. *Fletcher v. Peck. Oyez,* www.oyez.org/cases/1789-1850/10us87. Accessed 10 November 2020.
19. See George Lee Haskins and Herbert A. Johnson, *History of the Supreme Court of the United States: Foundations of Power: John Marshall, 1801–1815* (New York: Macmillan, 1981).
20. See Contracts Clause, Article 1, Section 10, Clause 1, U.S. Constitution; Legal Information Institute, Cornell University Law School, https://www.law.cornell.edu/constitution-conan/article-1/section-10/clause-1. Accessed 11 November 2020.
21. Edward E. Baptist, *The Half Has Never Been Told: Slavery and the Making of American Capitalism* (New York: Basic Books, 2014), 33.
22. Paul Finkelman, *Supreme Injustice: Slavery in the Nation's Highest Court* (Cambridge: Harvard, 2018).
23. *Hezekiah Wood v. John Davis and Others,* 11 U.S. 271 (1812).
24. *Encyclopedia Virginia,* https://www.encyclopediavirginia.org/_Negro_womens_children_to_serve_according_to_the_condition_of_the_mother_1662. Accessed 11 November 2020.
25. Finkelman, "John Marshall's Proslavery Jurisprudence: Racism, Property, and the 'Great' Chief Justice," *The University of Chicago Law Review Online,* August 31, 2020, https://lawreviewblog.uchicago.edu/2020/08/31/marshall-slavery-pt2/, accessed 11 November 2020.
26. *State of New York v. Miln* 36 U.S. 102 (1837).
27. See Walter Wheeler Cook, "What is the Police Power?" *Columbia Law Review* 7(5) May 1907: 322–336 at 326–327, https://www.jstor.org/stable/pdf/1109666.pdf.
28. *The Antelope* 23 U.S. (10 Wheat.) 66 (1825).
29. John T. Noonan, Jr., *The Antelope: The Ordeal of the Recaptured Africans in the Administrations of James Monroe and John Quincy Adams* (Berkeley: California, 1977), 27–31.
30. For more on how *The Antelope,* piracy, and slave trading connect to the contemporary migration of African migrants across the Mediterranean basin, see P. Khalil Saucier and Tryon P. Woods, *Ex Aqua in the Mediterranean: Excavating Black Power in the Migrant Question* (Manchester: Manchester UP, forthcoming).
31. Noonan, 56.

32. Binder, 2079.
33. *Brown v. Maryland* 25 U.S. (12 Wheat.) 419 (1827).
34. *Slaughterhouse Cases* 83 U.S. 36 (1873).
35. *Santa Clara County v. Southern Pacific Rail Road* 118 U.S. 394 (1886).
36. Adam Winkler, "'Corporations are People' is Built on an Incredible 19th-Century Lie," *The Atlantic*, March 5, 2018, https://www.theatlantic.com/business/archive/2018/03/corporations-people-adam-winkler/554852/. Also see Winkler, *We the Corporations: How American Businesses Won Their Civil Rights* (New York: Liveright, 2019).
37. *Citizen's United v. Federal Election Commission* 573 U.S. 682 (2014); *Burwell v. Hobby Lobby Stores* 558 U.S._(2010).
38. Woods, *Blackhood*, 153. For more on the *Floyd* and *Daniels* cases, see the Center for Constitutional Rights, the organization that led the legal team, https://ccrjustice.org/home/what-we-do/our-cases/floyd-et-al-v-city-new-york-et-al. The long line of police reform studies include, the Kerner, Mollen, and Christopher Commissions, the Rampart Corruption Task Force, the Riders Scandal in the Oakland Police Department, and the Justice Department's 2015 and 2017 findings of civil rights violations by the Ferguson and Chicago Police Departments, respectively (see https://www.justice.gov/opa/pr/justice-department-announces-findings-two-civil-rights-investigations-ferguson-missouri and https://www.justice.gov/opa/pr/justice-department-announces-findings-investigation-chicago-police-department).
39. Transcript of oral argument, *Terry v. Ohio* 392 U.S. 1 (1968), http://users.soc.umn.edu/~samaha/cases/terry_v_ohio_oral_arguments.htm.
40. See Greg Thomas, *The Sexual Demon of Colonial Power: Pan-African Embodiment and Erotic Schemes of Empire* (Bloomington: Indiana, 2007), 83–89.
41. Woods, *Blackhood*, 152.
42. Steve Martinot and Jared Sexton, "The Avant-Garde of White Supremacy," *Social Identities* 9(2) 2003: 170.

43. Woods, *Blackhood*, 154–155. For a more robust argument for overturning "reasonable suspicion" and ending the legal cover for stop-and-frisk altogether, see Donald F. Tibbs and Tryon P. Woods, "Requiem for Laquan: Policing as Punishment and Prosecuting 'Reasonable Suspicion,'" *Temple Law Review* 89(4) Spring 2017: 101–117.

3

Reform, Violence, Capital, and Prison Abolition

The foregoing chapter elaborates some of the ways in which the police are merely an appendage of power, not the seat of power itself. Their operations are symptomatic of society's governing structure and call for a capacious redefinition of policing that can address how power actually operates. While today's criminal justice system has its roots in slavery, each historical period since the end of the Civil War has contributed to the build-up, to the point that the U.S. now has 2.27 million people behind bars, with an additional 5 million people under community supervision of some kind (mostly probation or parole).[1] Most of this expansion has come since 1980, reaching a high point in 2009, and has declined 7.3 percent since then.[2] But despite being at its lowest in twenty years, the U.S. rate of incarceration remains by far the highest in the world. The degree to which the U.S. is out of pace with the rest of the world's humanity is that a full quarter of all prisoners worldwide are held in U.S. jails and prisons, and the U.S. incarceration rate of 639 per 100,000 people is 5–10 times higher than other industrialized democracies.[3]

These dramatic increases in the numbers of people brought into the criminal justice system, and how long they remain under its control, are the result of aggressive policymaking over the past forty years to enhance punitiveness at every stage in the criminal justice process: arresting, charging, sentencing, confining, releasing, and supervising. A point that will become important later in this article is that this process begins and ends with surveillance—which is to say that it never ends; in between is punishment, with each of the six stages simply naming the varied institutional mandates to punish. These effects are not accidental byproducts of well-intended policy solutions to social problems. As Ruth Wilson Gilmore showed over two decades ago, despite dominant explanations that the crack-down responded to increases in crime, drug use, and poverty-related property offences, in fact the opposite is the case.[4] The overall crime rate declined in the 1970s and early 1980s, *prior to* the expansion of the criminal justice apparatus, and it was precipitous declines in both drug use and property crimes in particular that pushed down the overall rate.[5] The dawn of the prison industrial complex in the 1980s, however, opened a period of attenuated lethality in black communities that was made to appear to be the result of self-destructive forces internal to these communities—drug addiction, gang violence, worklessness—when in fact it was an expression of state power. Regarding the construction of a drug problem, journalist Gary Webb's seminal investigation revealed that the CIA was operating a gun-running and drug-smuggling operation that brought guns to the Nicaraguan contras that the U.S. was using to destabilize the popular government in that country, while bringing cocaine into the U.S. and funneling it to street-level dealers with access to black inner-city neighborhoods.[6]

Black street gangs present a complex history that can be succinctly summarized in terms of the afterlife of COINTELPRO, the FBI's counter-intelligence program that actively sabotaged black social movement throughout the long civil rights era.[7] Bobby Lavender, one of the founders of the Bloods in Los Angeles, explained that the COINTELPRO assassinations of black leaders, and the terrorizing of rank-and-file activists, left a leadership vacuum in many communities that youth like him filled with their "own brand of leadership."[8] The Crips and the Bloods sought to end their conflicts as early as 1972–1974, only to have their truce sabotaged by police interference. This pattern of black self-determination thwarted by the state would repeat itself in the undermining of Los Angeles gang truces in 1992 after the rebellion following the verdicts in the Rodney King case, and in 1994, 1998, 2002, and 2004.[9] The backdrop to drug and gang warfare was the dramatic restructuring of the post-industrial welfare state. The shift from an industrial manufacturing political economy to one in which the financial and service sectors drive profits and economic growth has meant the loss of stable working-class jobs, the rise of part-time, low-wage work, and the inflated importance of unaffordable higher education.[10] Deindustrialization has been coupled with changes in welfare policy that have contributed to soaring precarity for vast numbers of people as the cost of housing, food, transportation, child care, and health care simply exceed people's ability to pay for these essentials.[11]

Given the analysis in the preceding chapter, that law and criminal justice are symptomatic of how slaveholding culture organizes power, the prison industrial complex is foremost a cultural problem, not simply a policy issue. It is expressive of a culture of politics ready and willing to sacrifice black interests, that generally views black people fearfully and as problems to be controlled, and is in fee to the antiblack violence in which the society remains grounded. There is no overselling this point: the dramatic transformations in U.S. society since the 1980s were all made possible by racist mythologies about black familial pathology: fear of black crime, black sex, black mothers, black kids, black music, and black spaces.[12] Carol Anderson explains it in terms of white rage. Writing in the *Washington Post* after the uprisings in Ferguson, MO following Officer Darren Wilson's killing of black teenager Michael Brown, Anderson says,

> When we look back on what happened in Ferguson, MO during the summer of 2014, it will be easy to think of it as yet one more episode of black rage ignited by yet another police killing of an unarmed African American male. But that has it precisely backward. What we've actually seen is the latest outbreak of white rage. Sure, it is cloaked in the niceties of law and order, but it is rage nonetheless. Protests and looting naturally capture attention. But the real rage smolders in meetings where

officials redraw precincts to dilute African American voting strength or seek to slash the government payrolls that have long served as sources of black employment. It goes virtually unnoticed, however, because white rage doesn't have to take to the streets and face rubber bullets to be heard. Instead, white rage carries an aura of respectability and has access to the courts, police, legislatures and governors, who cast its efforts as noble, though they are actually driven by the most ignoble motivations.[13]

White rage, explains Anderson, lashes out in each historical juncture. Jim Crow and lynching were backlashes to Emancipation; the Great Migration of blacks out of the South was met with white riots throughout the North.[14] When the Supreme Court ordered desegregation of public schools in *Brown v. Board of Education*, public school districts throughout the South closed down and paid for white families to send their children to private school, while whites rioted in northern cities like Boston to prevent the implementation of desegregation plans.[15] The wars on crime, drugs, and gangs were backlashes against the gains of the civil rights era, as were notions of "colorblindness" and "reverse discrimination." The election of Barack Obama has been followed by an ongoing effort to suppress the vote through electoral redistricting, voter ID laws, and limits on early and absentee voting.[16]

Concerted efforts to expose the antiblack violence of policing go back at least to the anti-lynching campaigns led by journalist Ida B. Wells in the late nineteenth and early twentieth centuries.[17] Challenges to the post-1980s incarceration juggernaut, too, are longstanding, especially at the community level as black families, churches, and organizations work ceaselessly against the comprehensive impact of carceral policies. In recent years, a burgeoning bi-partisan consensus in favor of criminal justice reform has emerged to give momentum and hope to families and organizations that have been pushing for change for decades.[18] This development has recently amplified calls for prison abolition and the defunding of police.[19] A comprehensive deconstruction of both police-prison abolitionism and the emergent bi-partisan consensus on the need for criminal justice reform is beyond the scope of this book. As I have argued elsewhere, however, the focus on reforming criminal justice practices, although desperately needed, is not the same as addressing the structure of antiblackness that continues to give rise to the kinds of punishment we have today.[20] While prison abolitionists have long maintained that abolishing prisons entails a fundamental reorganization of society, especially key institutions impacting family, work, housing, safety, and healthcare, there is also a tendency to reify the problem of the prison when it should be treated like the symptom that it is by focusing on the structure that gives rise to it. Moreover, the longer historical context for abolitionism in Western society, going back to the end of bondage for Europeans by the fifteenth century that paved the way for the systematic enslavement of Africans for the next seven centuries, followed in due course by the movement to abolish racial slavery in the eighteenth and early nineteenth centuries, and proceeding through contemporary abolitionist movements against human trafficking and so-called modern-day slavery, reveals a contradictory culture of politics that is parasitic on blackness.[21]

If we apply Anderson's analysis of white rage, and adhere to Bell's theory of interest convergence noted in the Introduction—which is to say, fidelity to the tradition of critical black thought—then not only were the ensemble of carceral policies that have directly and indirectly wrought despair and destruction on the majority of black Americans intentionally created to sacrifice black needs, advance white interests, and ameliorate white rage, but moreover, it would be irrational to expect the potential policy reversals underway now to do anything but advance this essential parasitic structure, albeit in refined ways. This chapter, then, investigates the relations of force behind the tension of our historic moment: how the legitimacy for law-and-order discourse has been diminished to the extent that police-prison abolitionism has entered mainstream consciousness; and how, in turn, the mainstreaming of abolitionism signals its accommodation to the very social structures it ostensibly aims to eradicate. I consider three of the generative factors behind the current moment: how the edifice of criminal justice was built through liberal reform; how the current displacement of law-and-order ideology has been achieved without uncoupling the race-crime nexus and its key articulating figure, the construct of black pathos; and how private capital has quietly shaped the direction of change. The purpose here, again, is to deepen our understanding of what policing actually is by exploring how police–prison abolition may itself serve a policing role. This argument will be a critical step toward the latter chapters in which I demonstrate the police power in medicine and health science.

Liberal Reform

The construction of a criminal justice system characterized by mass incarceration, the harassment and terrorizing of people of color, and the relative decriminalization of white and wealthy law breakers is not the result of a fringe racist bent in American governance. It has been the handiwork of bi-partisan consensus and compromise from the start, as has been oft-noted regarding the Clinton Administration's oversight of the 1994 Violent Crime Control and Law Enforcement Act. During her failed run for president in 2016, candidate Hillary Clinton rightfully took a lot of heat for championing this legislation during the 1990s. President Joe Biden, however, did not receive the same scrutiny during his campaign in 2020 when, in fact, he was the one who authored the Senate's version of the bill in cooperation with the National Association of Police Organizations.[22] That bi-partisanship has been a continuous fact throughout the rise of the prison industrial complex from the 1980s through its current reckoning in the 2020s should be unsurprising; fears of black violence and the interests of capital have been *the* unifying features of slaveholding culture since the Revolutionary era. What has received less attention is how at each historical juncture it has been liberalizing reforms touted as remedies for the excesses of earlier periods that have built, step by step, the massive criminal law apparatus. This history, reviewed in cursory fashion here, underscores the well-established observation that reforms constitute the system, rather than stand opposed to it in any way, and as such, strengthen instead of weaken its social control capacity.[23] They work *within* structural logics, not outside of them.

As noted in the section above, the U.S. Constitution institutionalized the counter-revolutionary struggle to extend slaveholding during the eighteenth and early nineteenth centuries. Likewise, the Thirteenth, Fourteenth, and Fifteenth Amendments, the so-called Civil War or Reconstruction Amendments, mark a renovation without rupture in slaveholding culture. As Frederick Douglass explained, the Civil War was begun "in the interests of slavery on both sides. The South was fighting to take slavery out of the Union, and the North was fighting to keep it in the Union; the South fighting to get it beyond the limits of the United States Constitution, and the North fighting for the old guarantees—both despising the Negro, both insulting the Negro."[24] Preserving the Union meant preserving slavery, but as W. E. B. DuBois showed in *Black Reconstruction*, the collective response of the enslaved forced the war to become a war to end slavery.[25] Slave emancipation, then, was an expression of black self-determination, opportunistically forced upon the whole of the country during the exigencies of war. From the point of view of the enslaved, the conflict within the slaveholding class (North vs. South) produced a brief cease fire in the centuries-old war against their white oppressors that they strategically wielded to end the formal institution of slavery. It was the ultimate heist: while your adversaries are fighting each other, you pull the rug out from beneath both of them.

The ex-slaves were powerless, however, to withstand slavery's transmutation in the war's aftermath. As many people are now aware, close reading of the Thirteenth Amendment reveals that it does not actually abolish slavery, but instead relocates it into the domain of the criminal justice system.[26] Debates about mass incarceration today point to this feature of the Thirteenth Amendment and misconstrue the clause stating that criminal convicts can be enslaved as a "loophole" that has been exploited to produce the gross injustice of industrialized punishment today.[27] This interpretation is incorrect. The clause in question is a design feature, not a design flaw, historically consistent with the original agenda of the war to extend, not end, black unfreedom. Since criminalization is first and foremost a political-symbolic tool, it refers not to individual behavior but rather to the social itself, to an onto-epistemic framework structuring social relations. The Amendment's authors knew exactly who they had in mind with the penal servitude clause because this framework of black dangerousness and lawlessness had long informed the culture of slaveholding. For instance, consider the 1855 Missouri Supreme Court case, *Missouri v. Celia*.[28] Celia, an enslaved young woman, had been raped regularly by her owner from the time he purchased her until the night she killed him four years later.

Enslaved people did not have the right to their own bodies by law, and therefore could neither give nor withhold their consent to sex. Celia had no legal claim to self-defense; she was prosecuted for murder, but was prevented from speaking at trial in order to preempt her self-defense claims. Although at first it appears that the law is contradictory in putting a slave on trial for murder, because this requires the law to recognize that which it otherwise disavows, slave humanity. But the Celia case demonstrates that there is no contradiction because the law recognizes black humanity precisely in order to ascribe criminal liability. In short, slavery had long asserted that black people are only one kind of human being: the criminal kind. As such, the Thirteenth Amendment oversees the reiteration of democracy's basis in social captivity—no plantations, no auction blocks, no laws, no prisons necessary.[29] If blackness is criminalized a priori, irrespective of whether blacks break the law or not, then the stain of enslavement rests on all black people, imprisoned or not. Far from the end of slavery, therefore, the Thirteenth Amendment marks the continuation of slaveholding culture despite the fact that no one is legally held in bondage as a slave: slavery without slaves.[30]

With the demise of Reconstruction, the post-Emancipation era saw the swift institutionalization of black criminality through the Black Codes, the convict lease system, sharecropping, and lynching. Despite the facile transfer of ex-slaves into the grip of penal servitude, turning Southern penitentiaries from all-white prior to the War to swollen institutions with almost entirely black inmate populations after Emancipation, black leaders at the time offered very little by way of opposition to the atrocities of convict leasing. Frederick Douglass, W. E. B. DuBois, Mary Church Terrell, Booker T. Washington, and Ida B. Wells were at least as critical of black criminality as they were of the injustice blacks faced before the criminal law. Historian Milfred Fierce contends that

> black leaders fell victim to the notion the "criminals" were getting what they deserved and, despite the cruelty of convict leasing, a crusade on behalf of prisoners was not seen as more important than fighting the lynching bee, opposing voting restrictions, or protesting the acts of racial bigotry that abounded. Those who accepted this analysis failed to

fully appreciate how many of the convicts were kidnapped, held beyond their sentences, or actually innocent of the crimes for which they were incarcerated, the total number of which will never be known.[31]

Douglass was *the* preeminent abolitionist and black public intellectual of his era, but as Angela Davis suggests, his faith "in the law blinded him to ways in which black people were constructed, precisely through law, as only fit for slavery."[32] The reticence on the part of Douglass and other black leaders of the early twentieth century to question convict leasing is testament to a misplaced faith in the law's supremacy over policing. This failure to recognize how policing actually precedes law would similarly keep black leadership in the late twentieth century relatively silent regarding penal servitude.[33] Indeed, at both ends of the century, black leadership turned away from the discomfiting reality that the past was not yet over in favor of more comforting evidence unseen regarding the democratic rule of law.[34]

Northern blacks also discovered that the tyranny of law was in fact as much a source of terror as the mob itself. The emergence of crime statistics in the early twentieth century enabled the discourse on black crime to appear rational and obscured race liberals' fear of black aggression.[35] Mob rule was not simply a Southern phenomenon but was also a feature of Northern cities as whites responded to the Great Migration of blacks out of the South with deadly violence and punitive segregationist policies. Liberal reformers in the 1940s responded by establishing a federal law-and-order mandate strong enough to curb racial violence in the streets and to control racial bias in criminal justice administration. Rule of law and the rights-based state were seen as the antidote to race war: "lawmakers constructed the *civil rights* carceral state, in which liberal notions of racial violence and agendas for race-neutral machinery actually propelled development of a punitive carceral state" (emphasis added).[36] In practical terms, this meant the professionalization of police forces nationally, and the integration of local departments with regional and federal agencies. By the time federal law enforcement had shifted from containing racial violence in the 1940s and 1950s to wielding its newly expanded repressive apparatus against civil rights organizations in the 1960s, successive federal agencies were providing enhanced funding and technical assistance to law enforcement departments across the country.[37] In other words, the state was already in the process of preparing itself to undermine, co-opt, negate, and overcome the very changes that social movements would soon succeed in winning.

The 1960s war on poverty programs were bound up with the war on crime, and also played a key role in the liberal reforms that built the state infrastructure for the prison industrial complex to come. Social service programs were required to partner with police, courts, and corrections in order to receive funding, thereby fusing criminal justice with community service, jobs training, after-school programming, public housing, and so forth.[38] But the only meaningful job creation was the war on crime itself. The insinuation of law enforcement directly into neighborhood-level social services in this way effectively installed a surveillance network that brought greater numbers of people under criminal justice control, but more importantly, later served as the foundation for using criminalization as the leverage through which to withhold services, one of the draconian features of the prison industrial complex era.[39] The conception of poverty popularized during the 1960s as a learned behavior of the resource-poor translated into a predictive model for preventing crime. The infrastructure for the prison industrial complex to come was now largely in place thanks to liberal civil rights reform. As one liberal congressman put it in 1965 during hearings for the Law Enforcement Assistance Act, "we must fight this battle on two fronts. We must fight crime today and, at the same time, we must prevent the growth of tomorrow's criminal and thereby protect the future safety of our own children and grandchildren."[40]

Since the 1960s, the courts have, accordingly, endorsed the larger clamp down of the mass incarceration era, while at the same time configured liberal reforms that appear to ameliorate the excess and injury of prior moments, but actually serve to re-entrench the larger system of punishment. As noted in the preceding chapter, the *Terry* Court, following the police in due course, sanctioned racial profiling with the new imprimatur of "reasonable suspicion"—and legal scholars ever since have generally viewed it as part of the liberal expansion of the rights of the accused.[41] The courts show no inclination to revisit the precedent *Terry* established, as *Floyd* makes clear. Indeed, Judge Scheindlin explicitly aligned her decision in *Floyd* with *Terry*, explaining that the NYPD's stop-and-frisk program was unconstitutional because it violated the principles of reasonable suspicion as set forth by the *Terry* court. And for her conformity to Fourth Amendment precedent, the Court of Appeals for the Second District removed Scheindlin from the case and presumably was on its way to overturning her decision when the de Blasio administration came into the mayor's office and withdrew the city's appeal.

Not surprisingly, the punitive career of the prison industrial complex has occasioned numerous legal challenges on behalf of the incarcerated. Beginning in the 1980s with a series of cases contesting inadequacies in medical care for prisoners, visitation rights, prisoners' access to reading materials and law libraries, use of force, and conditions of confinement, most of the decisions have resulted in the steady evisceration of the substance of the Eighth Amendment's protections against "cruel and unusual" punishment.[42] These decisions have winnowed the legal persona of prisoners to the point that they are merely caged bodies, not human beings. In so doing, the courts demonstrate the continuities between the slavocracy and our present period of slaveholding. Slave codes uniformly provided for the slave's basic needs of food, shelter, and security. The law of slavery also featured prohibitions against excessive punishments and willfully or maliciously killing a slave, except when the slave died resisting a master or when "dying under moderate correction."[43] As Colin Dayan explains, to style the "correction" of a slave that causes death "moderate" is to guarantee tyranny, while the attempt to curb torture hides law's brutality behind vague standards of "humane" care.[44] Each of the Supreme Court's seven Eighth Amendment decisions between 1976 and 1994 were cited by the Bush Administration's torture memos as laying the legal framework for the U.S.'s treatment of prisoners at Abu Ghraib, Guantanamo, and other as-yet-unnamed detention sites around the world.[45]

In the context of this legal revanchism, a court decision against gladiator fights and burning a prisoner's skin off of his body have been taken as modest victories against the prison industrial complex. In *Madrid v. Gomez*, a class action suit against California's Pelican Bay state prison in 1993 heard by the federal District Court in California, prisoners challenged the constitutionality of a broad range of conditions and practices to which they were subjected.[46] Finding in the plaintiff's favor, Chief Judge Thelton Henderson wrote that "defendants have unmistakably crossed the constitutional line," citing the habit of caging inmates naked outdoors in freezing temperatures "like animals in a zoo," the unnecessary and sometimes lethal force used in cell extractions, and the scalding of a mentally disabled inmate, burned so badly that "from just below the buttocks down, his skin peeled off."[47] Regarding Pelican Bay's Special Housing Unit, the separate self-contained super-maximum security housing unit, Henderson noted that while indefinite solitary confinement in the SHU "may well hover on the edge of what is humanly tolerable for those with normal resilience," such conditions remain within the limits of permissible pain. According to Henderson, these conditions of "extreme social isolation and reduced environmental stimulation" do not violate "exacting Eighth Amendment standards" in regards to all inmates, but only when imposed on those inmates "at risk of developing an injury to mental health of *sufficiently serious magnitude*."[48] Whereas the prisoners had filed suit against the conditions of the prison in toto, including against the basic inhumanity of solitary confinement, the court found unconstitutional only discrete institutional practices, relying on technical legalism and extreme verbal qualifications to permit cruelty to pass for the necessary incidents of prison life.[49] *Madrid* thus stands as a liberal rapprochement with the carceral regime to curtail its more heinous practices, and in so doing, endorse its intrinsic inhumanity.[50] This brief review of how liberal reforms to the endemic racial violence of slaveholding society across the eras have built a massive criminal justice juggernaut will be instructive for my subsequent interrogation of COVID-19 and the pandemic police power. Much like the prison industrial complex, the medical industrial complex has emerged from liberal reforms geared towards expanding access to healthcare, promoting medical scientific discovery, and eradicating disease. The nature of this complex system, therefore, is not reducible to political ideology; and the problems we face today in public health are intrinsic to the development of medical science itself.

Leaving Violence Alone

The inextricable relationship between race and crime in the American popular imagination has been central to the foundation of slaveholding society and to its steady evolution into today's carceral society. It has never been sufficient to dismiss this discourse by simply exposing the notion of the black criminal for the stereotype that it is. For this reason, today's police–prison abolition movement has critiqued the racialization of crime by exposing the institutional contexts through which this stereotype is reproduced—from racial profiling to sentencing disparities by race to felon disenfranchisement laws. Nonetheless, this strategy, too, falls short when it is uncoupled from what is *inside* the racialization of crime: violence. Since the human race is normatively white, racialized human beings exist as a non-white subspecies of humanity, with the negation of white being its supposed opposite, black. For this reason, in the antiblack world there is but one race—black—and to be racialized is to be pushed down toward blackness, while to be deracialized is to move up toward whiteness.[51] This means that race is itself a product of racism, not the other way around; it is a function of the dominance that white society claims for itself and expresses through the prerogative to explain the hierarchy created by such dominance in terms of racialization and to name the society it creates as "natural." The very category of the "human" in the antiblack world, then, is constituted in violence against black people.

Since racism is first and foremost violence, white society displaces onto black people the antiblack violence by which it establishes itself as "free," "civilized," "democratic," and "just." This is why stereotypes are self-referential: they tell us more about those conjuring the stereotype than about its targets. Constructing black people as inherently violent is how white society misrecognizes its own predatory ways and its disavowed rationalization for this violence. The fear of crime, therefore, is more fundamentally about the fear of black violence, which is at root the disavowal of antiblack violence. For this reason, attempts to redress the police power of antiblackness without confronting the issue of violence will come up short. The common factor in the chain of reforms explored above is that the blackness of crime goes unthought, enabling antiblack violence to replenish itself anew. Today we see this problem in the unwillingness of abolitionists and reformers alike to be addressed by the matter of violence. The most popular renunciation of mass incarceration is the assertion that non-violent drug offenders have been the main grist for the prison mill.[52] The efficacy of this as an argument against prevailing policies is that drug offenders need to be in treatment, not behind bars.[53] Furthermore, since everyone uses substances of whatever kind (be it heroin, nicotine, codeine, or caffeine) for the same reason—to change their emotional state—then drug offenders are no different from other people. The argument for reform based on the wrongness of locking up the non-violent drug offender, therefore, is essentially an argument of identification. The problem with a non-violent identity, however, is that it is constituted in what it is identified *against*: violence. In other words, the argument for releasing non-violent offenders works because it is simultaneously an argument for keeping violent offenders locked up. The bi-partisan consensus for criminal justice reform, such as it is, is more properly conceived of as based on keeping violent offenders locked up. In short, the consensus is still the blackness of crime and the danger of blackness.

Abolitionists take safety seriously, which is why they aim to reduce violence of all kinds, at least theoretically or rhetorically, including the act of putting human beings in cages. Confronting violence in the question of police–prison abolition is inescapable and it becomes a strategic organizing decision as to *how* to deal with it in the course of advancing the abolitionist goal of undoing a carceral society. Most abolitionists seem to follow the lead of people like Ruth Wilson Gilmore who takes the approach that weighing non-violent offenders against violent offenders, or inmates at a low risk versus a high risk for re-offending or for negatively impacting public safety, is unproductive. Instead, Gilmore says that if we take seriously the fact that most people leave prison anyway, and if we simply cut their lengthy sentences by a matter of days, months, or years, then we can reduce the amount of harm we are causing by locking them up, and we can get on to the important work of addressing the "organized abandonment" that contributes to incarceration in the first place and that most people face when leaving prison.[54]

3 Reform, Violence, Capital, and Prison Abolition   57

This approach is imminently rational and practical, and it corresponds to the harm and risk reduction methodologies applied across a range of different policy arenas. The problem with this approach to addressing the police power is that blackness is anathema to reason: as Frantz Fanon once put it, blackness inspires all manner of madness in others. Fanon writes,

> there is nothing more neurotic than contact with unreason. I felt knife blades open within me. I resolved to defend myself. As a good tactician, I intended to rationalize the world and to show the white man that he was mistaken…Reason was confident of victory on every level. I put all the parts back together. But I had to change my tune. That victory played cat and mouse; it made a fool of me. As the other put it, when I was present, it was not; when it was there, I was no longer.[55]

Reason is accounted for only when blackness is absent; when black people are present, reason flees the scene. Today's bi-partisan consensus for criminal justice reform, for instance, pursues policy solutions to the methamphetamine and opioid addiction crises that are imminently more rational than those of the previous war on drugs approach not because it has learned the lessons of the failed drug policies of the 1980s–2000s, but rather because those "failures" were suitable to black people whereas this latest drug problem is construed as disproportionately white.[56] The irrationality of the police power acts like "the a posteriori proof of the inferiority of inferior people," which "is that one is able to degrade them."[57] In this case, the proof that blacks are a dangerous and violent race is the fact that they are "stop-eligible" anytime anywhere for police interdiction and for warehousing in cages—even as society moves on to an ostensibly less punitive approach to substance use by non-blacks.[58]

Recent polls affirm this problem, showing that people support ending mass incarceration only if it means releasing non-violent drug offenders.[59] They want violent offenders to remain locked up. This is a racial dichotomy that will not be undone through a non-racial approach that avoids the singular paranoia about black violence. This is not to say, to be clear, that non-violent offenders are non-black and violent offenders are black; indeed, many black people will directly benefit from decarceration of non-violent offenders. Nor is to say that violent offenders are disproportionately black, which is also not the case. The point is simply that the continued intransigence regarding inmates who committed violent offences is a racialized phenomenon. The fact of the matter is that violent offenders make the most reliably safe ex-convicts of all. They are far less likely to return to prison for another violent offense than non-violent offenders are to re-offend.[60] Research findings on violent offender recidivism bear this out today and it has been true for more than a half century, at least. John Monahan reports the problem with psychiatric predictions of violence:

> The conclusion to emerge most strikingly from these studies [predicting violence] is the great degree to which violence is overpredicted…Of those predicted to be dangerous, between 65 and 95 percent are false positives—that is, people who will not, in fact, commit a dangerous act. Indeed, the literature has been consistent on this point ever since Pinel took the chains off the supposedly dangerous mental patients at La Bicetre in 1792, and the resulting lack of violence gave lie to the psychiatric predictions that had justified their restraint.[61]

The ability of psychiatry to accurately predict dangerousness has been shown to persistently hover around fifty percent, rightfully garnering comparisons to "flipping coins in the courtroom."[62] Antiblack racism is a leading source of "false positives," from racial profiling's ineptitude at predicting the presence of contraband in traffic stops and stop-and-frisks, to psychology's and psychiatry's slip-shod record of predicting violence by inmates, the formerly incarcerated, or any other racialized population.[63] Indeed, science's notion of the "false positive" effectively covers for the systemic failures of institutions that are constituted, at least in part, in antiblack violence. The "false positive" is meant to be read as a situational error in diagnosis, but when read through the historical lens of black struggle the "false positive" itself is diagnostic of an institutional disposition toward tyranny. This historical awareness translates into a political readiness to call into question such truth claims, as we will encounter in subsequent chapters regarding COVID-19. The tyranny of law and order is by now well understood; we will see that this disposition in criminal justice is, in fact, an expression of a more fundamental despotism in other institutional settings more central to the social body.

The matter of violence that some abolitionists prefer to elide also includes the reality that sometimes violence is absolutely necessary for survival, while at the same time, the experience of violence permanently alters people's lives. People tend to bear considerable rage about these facts, usually directed toward the person directly responsible for harming them, but sometimes also finding expression in a variety of additional directions. While enduring violence is traumatizing enough, the debilitating effect is compounded by the silence, abandonment, and disrespect that survivors frequently go through, whether or not their case is handled by the criminal justice system.[64] Conversely, when trauma is repaired, survivors are often able to carry on with their lives with less negative consequences than if there is no constructive response to the violence.[65] This reality underscores the well-known but under-attended fact that *all* violence is socially produced. Since violence is *social*, not individual, it is more properly understood as a collective trauma and/or abandonment temporally entangled and expressing itself through individuals and their communal intercourse at a moment in time. Most inmates serving time for violent crimes were themselves victimized by violence of some kind earlier in life.[66] It takes a collectivity under erasure—a broken community—to generate these acts of violence by failing to support, protect, intercede, hold accountable, repair, or alleviate the socially produced burdens, harms, and fears that find expression in violence. The criminal justice system, moreover, does not get involved in most incidents of interpersonal violence—which means the system does not contribute additional harm, but usually this also means that there is no formal recognition of the injury, let alone remedy or resolution, for the survivors.[67] Abolitionists argue that winnowing the carceral apparatus will begin reducing the overall harm in society, and better equip us to deal more productively with interpersonal violence in the community, but the merits of this position remain abstract and theoretical without simultaneously addressing the multi-scalar realities of violence. More to the point, however, violence, like the various institutions of law and order, is itself symptomatic of a more fundamental social disposition. Dealing with symptoms is important; but we need to also seek a deeper cut. In other words, violence is always a symptom of power: it is either an expression of the powerful and their corruption, or of the powerless and their injury, desperation, or resistance. Addressing the police power, in other words, requires confronting the structural and interpersonal ways in which power produces violence of all kinds, something that abolitionism has often failed to do.

Private Capital Shapes Change

Although rumors of its demise are greatly exaggerated, as the saying goes, the currently diminished status of law and order raises the need for us to evaluate how we got here and how can we study this process to better understand what policing is actually all about. The present investigation is not exhaustive, of course, and much of the work has been done elsewhere to tell the story of the recent emergence of abolitionism into mainstream debates on what to do with police and prisons.[68] I am interested in presenting the muted components of this portrait, those dynamics that have been slighted in both the leading explanations and the dissenting narratives. I am highlighting those components of the present situation that deepen our comprehension of the police power; as will become evident, it is these factors that are also central to the pandemic police power. In addition to the role of liberal reform in building the law-and-order problem, and the way in which violence has been neglected in its dissent, the third issue to incorporate into our analysis of the police power is the role of private capital in shaping change in its image.

Among the leading backers of the bi-partisan coalition for criminal justice reform is Charles Koch of Koch Industries. Koch campaigns for sentencing reform for non-violent offenders, "smart decarceration," and "policing alternatives" for communities through his company's philanthropic entities, the Charles Koch Foundation and the Charles Koch Institute. Koch philanthropies make grants principally to academic researchers "to help all learners realize their potential," which is part of their strategy for building an intellectual infrastructure that utilizes universities and K-12 curricula to foster the Koch version of socially conservative, big capital, libertarianism.[69] Although some liberals dismiss the Koch philanthropies' involvement in criminal justice reform as nothing more than savvy public relations aimed at rebranding the Koch name, this overlooks the convergence of libertarian and progressive interests in this policy area.[70] For the Koch philanthropies, shrinking the criminal justice apparatus will have short-term benefits for non-violent drug offenders *and* for white-collar and corporate criminals.[71] These short-term effects fit into the larger goal of the "Koch network" that coordinates big money funders, idea producers, issue advocates, and innovative constituency-building efforts to pull U.S. politics further to the right.[72] In the long run, then, the right-wing vision for criminal justice reform will make life harder for the working poor, especially without commensurate structural changes in labor and housing markets, in the least. This is the complex terrain on which private capital shapes the direction of social change.

The most recent example of successful corporate philanthropy shaping criminal justice policy is the case of New York City's Rikers Island jail. The NYC Council voted in October 2019 to shut down the Rikers facility and replace it with four smaller jails situated in four of the city's boroughs. Under the new plan, the Rikers jail will close by 2026.[73] The city council appointed the Independent Commission on New York City Criminal Justice and Incarceration Reform to create a plan of action for reforming the city's jail system.[74] The Commission featured a number of foundation officers, including the president of the Ford Foundation, Darren Walker.[75] Walker writes that the Commission produced a compromise that rescued the reform effort from what he views as the politically extremist position of abolitionists who had been demanding the closure of Rikers for years. He states that these longtime activists are incapable of the political "nuance" necessary for a "constructive" social "path forward," arguing that "we cannot let the perfect be the enemy of progress. If we skip steps, we risk creating a new kind of gap—a gap of missed opportunities and lost alliances. Indeed, these examples help inform the path forward—a journey away from the extremes."[76] As Keeanga-Yamahtta Taylor explains, this is "subterfuge for his actual intervention," which is to manage the capitalist system's excesses.[77] As Walker puts it:

> We can see how our capitalist systems have broken down, *while also* appreciating that markets have helped reduce the number of people around the globe who live in poverty…We can be critical of ill-gotten fortunes, *while also* appreciating the current need for private capital to fund certain valuable public goods, and encouraging wealthy individuals to understand their own privilege and support institutional reforms.[78]

The logic of philanthropy, then, is that these multi-billion-dollar organizations work to preempt the coalescence of the diverse interest blocs that could produce the kind of social change that would be intolerable to the corporations to which they are systemically tethered. The influence of foundations is thus to extend the life of the system by moderate amendments to the status quo.

Foundation impact on racial justice matters today is the result of a well-honed practice going back at least a century. In the 1920s and 1930s, foundations wielded their financial influence to redirect the NAACP away from its focus on lynching and white terrorism to education instead, a far less-threatening agenda.[79] During this time, the Carnegie Foundation was a substantial supporter of the Hampton Institute and the Tuskegee Institute, and in 1938 it commissioned Swedish economist Gunnar Myrdal to do a study of race relations in the U.S. The Carnegie report, which would later be published in 1942 as *An American Dilemma: The Negro Problem and Modern Democracy*, provided the ideological scaffolding for the 1954 Supreme Court decision in *Brown v. Board of Education* which relied on Myrdal's sociological claims about black pathos.[80] In 1961, Attorney General Robert F. Kennedy asked four major foundations to fund the Voter Education Project.[81] The aim was to divert civil rights efforts from the sit-ins, boycotts, and mass demonstrations that garnered spectacles of white supremacist violence which were bad publicity for the Kennedy Administration. The foundations formed a coalition with the leading national civil rights organizations, but anointed the Southern Regional Council (SRC) as the sole grantee.[82] The SRC, a mainly white organization formed to avoid interracial violence through the moderate improvement of social, economic, and political conditions, would not take a stand against legal segregation but was empowered with financial oversight of the civil rights organizations whose explicit missions included the eradication of such forms of structural oppression.[83]

The fact that philanthropy's aims are frequently at odds with the goals of their grantees betrays the structural antagonism between black liberation and the existing system of multicultural capitalist democracy. The Ford Foundation's impact on black struggle has been particularly insidious in this regard. During the 1960s and 1970s, explains Karen Ferguson, Ford sought to disarm the Black Power movement by fostering a new black leadership elite who could manage the poor black masses from within the American establishment, "a kind of elite pluralism that would at once demonstrate the nation was living up to its egalitarian ideals and dampen black insurgency."[84] Ford correctly understood that Black Power represented a "true social revolution at home," and interpreted this development as a crisis that required a response at the "level of effort…we now make as a nation in Vietnam."[85] The resulting model of elite affirmative action institutionalized black arts and black studies programs within the nation's cultural and educational establishment, promoted private–public partnerships through community development corporations that incubated black public entrepreneurs, and expanded the black professional class through a college scholarship program.[86] In Ferguson's words, Ford generally "paved a path of least resistance against the claims of Black Power…that spawned a new regime of race management that has served the nation's elites, not black freedom. It helped lay the seed for the 'progressive neoliberalism' which celebrates elite multiculturalism and promotes 'diversity' while ignoring or masking structural inequalities"—an ongoing blueprint for the post-civil rights era that defuses radical social change before it gains programmatic traction, giving the system a new lease on life, even as it shudders to itself at narrowly escaping Black Power's true potentiality.[87]

The real lesson of philanthropy's intervention in the long civil rights era is the necessity of subverting black self-determination through moderate institutional change. For this reason, the foundations are circling around the organizations and networks comprising the Movement for Black Lives today. In 2016, the Ford Foundation announced a major new funding initiative targeting the M4BL, pledging $40 million in "capacity"-building support over six years.[88] Ford is also partnering with Borealis Philanthropy which in 2015 established the Black-led Movement Fund to attract, consolidate, and oversee major gifts from other liberal funders, such as George Soros' Open Society Foundation.[89] Indeed, the philanthropic field's attention to racial justice movements today is both sophisticated and focused.[90] Today's foundation interest in black movement is geared toward pacifying black liberation in the manner practiced during the civil rights era. For instance, Ford situated its funding commitment to M4BL not in terms of the litany of black deaths at the hands of law enforcement, but rather with reference to two rare moments of violent blowback against this state violence, namely the killing of five Dallas police officers and three Baton Rouge police officers in separate incidents in July 2016 in the midst of nation-wide outrage at the police murders of Philando Castile and Alton Sterling.[91] Claiming that these officers died for the "larger democratic principles at play," including "protecting the right to freedom of expression and peaceful protest," Ford warned that the killing of police officers had "the potential to either deepen empathy and understanding among Americans or divide us even more sharply along lines of race, ethnicity, and gender."[92]

Philanthropy's interest in corralling black self-determination is also connected to the surge in academic research critical of the post-civil rights law and order regime.[93] What does it mean that research critical of state violence translates into institutional advancement for its authors in corporate spaces such as foundations and elite universities? Are elite scholars pushing the envelope for social change, or are they being used to consolidate against it? Elite universities are deeply invested in preserving the status quo, and it is almost axiomatic that you do not go to the university in search of the cutting edge; in fact, once the university gets hold of that edge, it is usually a sign that the edge is no longer cutting, but instead has become a fence. It must mean that these critiques are good for business—but in what way? Many of the most prominent scholars now advancing abolitionist or abolition-leaning critiques of criminal justice, or at least scholars using abolitionist rhetoric, receive support from major philanthropies, corporate universities, or the state in the form of elite public research universities or grants from federal agencies. While their scholarly contributions usefully enhance knowledge about the prison industrial complex, the context for this research raises three observations about how the police power works in this area.

First, thought is not individual; like violence, it is *social.* The thought that researchers produce is institutionally situated, socially produced, and an expression of power. The institutional life of research findings may work at cross-purposes with the critique intended by the scholars who produce the research. Academic research scholars are no different from police officers in the sense that an officer may conduct her day-to-day business of policing with respect for the rule of law and constitutional liberties, but her individual behavior does not counteract the institution's purpose to affirm the basic dispossession of the policed. Likewise, scholars and scientists operate within an institutional setting that is not undone or reoriented by virtue of their individual actions. Put differently, the academy is part of the state-capital nexus, even if many of those operating within it would like to see that structure dismantled. Secondly, the institutional setting for research brings up the historical context of thought. Abolitionists in the academy today present ideas that function in relation to power very differently from the institutional life of the same ideas produced decades ago by black thinkers in the midst of autonomous social movement. What is happening outside of the academy, in other words, is crucial in determining the efficacy of what is produced from within it. Third, the popularity of "critical resistance" in the academy, then, is foremost a reflection of the historical reality in which the police power regards black liberation as effectively quarantined in the present period.[94] Funders and universities richly reward such critiques and research now that the social movements of the long civil rights era that originally generated them have been rendered ineffectual. This is not a prognosis or a judgment of currently existing social movements; it is simply a historical diagnosis of how power works: as a rule, it does not promote ideas that would lead to its dissolution. If the idea is popular in the academy, then it is no longer a threat to the structure of power against which the idea itself is ostensibly wielded.

We can further consider these three observations by examining two prominent scholars popular today for their research on the prison industrial complex and our carceral society. Although any examples would suffice, my choices here are not arbitrary. Dorothy Roberts has been producing trenchant analyses of law, race, science, policy, and social justice for over two decades, while Elizabeth Hinton is a rising star in the historical treatment of the prison industrial complex. Since my objective here is to call into question the institutional life of police–prison abolitionism in academia as a way of reading the status of the police power in the early twenty-first century, it is most useful to draw attention to scholarship that deals critically with carceral society and that has been supported and honored at the highest institutional levels. To be clear, I have the utmost respect for both of these scholars, and have found their research imminently useful for my purposes as an educator. My interest in highlighting their work is to demonstrate the political and historical situatedness of knowledge production—which is always simultaneously the unmaking of other ways of knowing, since power is inextricably relational. Roberts, currently a professor of law at the University of Pennsylvania, has been a grantee of the Robert Wood Johnson Foundation, National Science Foundation, and the National Institutes of Health. Her oeuvre is too extensive to succinctly summarize here, but in many ways she has encapsulated it for us in her recent *Harvard Law Review* article "Abolition Constitutionalism," where she argues for interpreting the U.S. Constitution in an expansive abolitionist fashion and putting it to work to advance the cause of dismantling the prison industrial complex.[95] Roberts notes the Supreme Court's decidedly anti-abolitionist jurisprudence, and acknowledges that an abolitionist constitutionalism would be instrumental in its deployment of law to chip away at the carceral structure, pointing out that this approach is consistent with how black people have historically pursued constitutionalism "because it offers 'practical advantages' to their struggle for equal citizenship."[96] Despite the historical evidence that precisely such approaches to the Constitution have heretofore yielded only a deeper quagmire, Roberts remains hopeful.

Roberts' argument for working through the Constitution sets up a false dichotomy between futility and utility on constitutionalism that forecloses on other alternatives.[97] Given that law did not create slavery and will not make it go away, because it was slavery that created law and it is slaveholding culture that continues to manifest itself throughout the social structure, of which law is but one feature, Roberts' emphasis on renovating law relies on either presumption or on faith, but not on

3 Reform, Violence, Capital, and Prison Abolition

evidence. She has to *imagine* what the Thirteenth Amendment "could" do, not what it is or does. Granted, this exercise of imagination is crucial for creating the world that does not yet exist, and has been characteristic of how black families have nurtured freedom across the generations for centuries. But put differently, law remains unthought in Roberts' analysis. Why work *through* the constitution? Since law stands apart from relationality, it institutionalizes relations of power, not human relations, and if abolitionists are serious about "changing everything," then why do they take for granted that law will govern an abolitionist future differently?[98] More to the point for Roberts, it seems, as a legal scholar the law is the *sine qua non* for thought, it is the taken-for-granted starting point for her scholarship—but how potent would it be if a prominent legal scholar started thinking about law from outside of it? A law professor fugitive from legal thinking—it would reveal how the law and legal consciousness, no matter how imaginative or abolitionist, are themselves central to the police power, and as such, fortify the very institutions of control that abolitionist legal scholars like Roberts ostensibly seek to dismantle.[99] Roberts' many richly institutional rewards reflect her exemplary leadership in legal scholarship *and* her service in buttressing the very structures crucial for managing structural antiblackness—the law, the legal academy, and the corporate-state nexus.

Hinton is a historian at Yale University, with a joint appointment in the Yale Law School. She was formerly on the faculty at Harvard University, and has also been a Ford Foundation and a Carnegie Corporation Fellow. She embodies the Ford Foundation's effort to defuse Black Power by cultivating a black leadership class through higher education. Hinton states that the Yale Law appointment was a "major factor" in her decision to leave Harvard. "The opportunity to be a part of the faculty at Yale Law School, I think is really important in terms of the moment that we're in right now in confronting issues of racism in the criminal justice system, and considering new pathways for reform," Hinton said. "Yale provides me a new kind of platform and I think an important one for my scholarship moving forward."[100] At Yale, Hinton joins the law school's Justice Collaboratory, an interdisciplinary project that brings together Yale faculty to find new ways "to improve the criminal justice system."[101] As both her own words and those of the Justice Collaboratory's mission state clearly, the work of Hinton and her new colleagues at Yale is geared toward reforming the carceral state by improving its capacity to deliver policing and punishment services without the race and class-based inequities that have been, in fact, intrinsic to both the state and its carceral apparatus all along. This kind of reform-minded research is well situated to offer voluminous rhetoric about justice and change, but precious little substance in these areas.[102] Witness the Collaboratory's Policy Director, Jorge Camacho, formerly an Assistant District Attorney for Manhattan and counsel in various capacities for the Mayor's Office. In response to the latest outraged protests about antiblack state violence, Camacho turns to the state itself for guidance: "We need our politicians and policymakers to finally lay the groundwork necessary to readily define what policing is, its failures and successes, and the public's safety needs. Only then can we even attempt to chart where we go from here."[103] In other words, as communities rise up to clarify exactly what kind of public safety they do *not* need, the Policy Director of Yale Law's Justice Collaboratory says that, no, the state needs to determine what safety means for people and how policing fits into that framework. This is the police power of the academy.

Hinton's presentation of reformism is more complex than some of her new colleagues at Yale Law because she uses abolitionist rhetoric, is active within academia's prison abolition networks, and is involved with prison-based education endeavors. As a panelist at a recent academic conference on mass incarceration, Hinton fielded a question from an audience member about how to get universities to financially divest from corporations that profit from the prison industrial complex. Her response was to argue for *more* investment by the university:

> How does this university have a responsibility to the Boston community and communities in Massachusetts and prisons, and how can we invest in educational opportunities for people who are incarcerated; and use Harvard resources to do so while also using Harvard resources to support various community groups in their campaigns and to help them reach their needs to help work with them to address, to think about dynamic research, questions, and programs. So, I think it just leads to disclosure

in divesting. We can also push these universities to invest in new ways because, again, it's going to take these universities to help decarcerate, to help end mass incarceration.[104]

This kind of reformism-as-abolition mystifies how the corporate university wields its influence. How the university's endowment portfolio managers grow its assets is not qualitatively distinct nor politically at odds with how its administrators and faculty invest its institutional resources through community programming. Camacho's call for the state to define policing (as if its definition was not already crystal clear) is no different from Hinton's assertion that ending mass incarceration will require university support. Both appeal to the corporate-state nexus to do the right thing—a decidedly *un*-abolitionist approach, by any measure.

Hinton's scholarship reflects this reliance on the state at the expense of crowding out what the black movement has been doing and saying about the police power. Her books focus on policymaking in the 1960s and 1970s that laid the foundation for mass incarceration in the post-1980 period. What appears as a useful fill-in-the-gap function, shoring up the historical chronology of the prison industrial complex where the account of its antecedent periods was thin, ends up playing a role in the state's counter-insurgent project itself. If we understand policing as war, which is precisely the terms in which black activists have always put it, then it is a profoundly asymmetrical genocidal war.[105] By focusing on the policy decisions through which this war-making is implemented, historians like Hinton are more properly understood as narrating diplomatic history, the machinations within and between elite structures of power. Even worse, this diplomatic history is itself grotesquely asymmetrical as she does not give commensurate air time to the insurgent politics from below, but instead focuses mainly on the counter-insurgency. Absent from her historical account is the extensive archive of black thought analyzing state power. Her claims that social programs are central to the state's social control apparatus, and that urban riots are in fact social rebellions sparked by police violence and fueled by poverty and inequality are *not* the "untold" story that she claims them to be.[106] On the contrary, the literature assessing the welfare state in these terms is longstanding and extensive, as is the library on black social rebellions.[107]

Numerous studies foreground black women's confrontation with the punitive and policing functions of social policy across the generations.[108] In his 1995 study of the Watts uprising, *The Fire This Time*, Gerald Horne analyzed the state-civil society structure, including the black disunity wrought by the intra-race class divide, against which the black rebellion took its stand.[109] Likewise, Thomas Sugrue's 1996 account of Detroit's turbulence in the postwar period details the police power of industry, labor, and homeownership against insurgent blackness.[110] Sugrue reminds us of the lesson that nineteenth century black intellectuals like Ida B. Wells taught us, that race riots have historically been the domain of civil society, not of the black community, making available the analysis that white riots transmute into police actions in the post-civil rights era.[111]

As we move back in time, closer to the zenith of the black revolutionary period, the black studies library reveals that black activists and thinkers analyzed the police power through principles of black self-determination that have gone missing in today's literature on police–prison abolition. George Jackson and Lerone Bennett, Jr., each in their own ways, underscore the reality that when social change is not authored by the slave's revolt, it bears a false promise. Jackson writes:

> In every sense of the term, in every sense that's real, I'm a slave to, and of, property. Revolution within a modern industrial capitalist society can only mean the overthrow of all existing property relations and the destruction of all institutions that directly or indirectly support existing property relations. It must include the total suppression of all classes and individuals who endorse the present state of property relations or who stand to gain from it. Anything less than this is reform.[112]

Bennett likewise excoriates the black movement's faith in legal reform: "Even more disastrous was the miring of the Negro's basic constitutional rights in legalism…Bound and gagged by legalism and bad faith, the Negro walked down a road called freedom. As he walked, his enemies and his disabilities multiplied."[113] Kwame Ture amplifies this theme: "All of these experiences and lessons have taught us that we must look only to *each other* in finding the solution of our problems."[114] Bennett, again, in response and repose:

> And an ideology of revolution needs to deal with *our* options and *our* obstacles. One possible policy would be a strategy of permanent confrontation linked to a black cooperative-economy movement and a long-range, phase-by-phase program for taking over the major *institutions* (police department, fire department, school system, teachers and transit unions) in the major American cities in which black people constitute the largest single ethnic bloc.[115]

Clark Squire, one of the defendants in the New York Panther 21 conspiracy case of 1969–1971, reflects on the colonizing effects of institutional inclusion, concluding that he never found "much respect for the black bourgeoisie, teachers, preachers, intelligentsia, and so-called leaders."[116] Squire is pointing to the problem of culture internal to black social movement, which brings us to *The Wretched of the Earth* where Frantz Fanon asked, "ought one to say that the battle for freedom however fertile a posteriori with regard to culture is in itself a negation of culture? In short, is the struggle for liberation a cultural phenomenon or not?"[117] In the least, two decades of sustained black rebellion, then, posed the matter of what kind of evolutionary process is necessary before revolution can become possible, as James and Grace Lee Boggs put it in 1963.[118]

Hinton's scholarship, in short, is in good company, but the reason why private capital and the corporate university are fond of her version and loath that earlier iterations might authorize contemporary consciousness is because she displaces black self-determination by excising black radical voices and narrating the era of black rebellion through the lens of state power. In other words, her investment in institutional reform is mirrored in her scholarship by the manner in which she writes *through*, rather than against, the history profession's disciplinary formation, eschewing the radical voices of earlier generations in favor of the decorum of policy history. This changes the narrative of black power and leaves police–prison abolition adrift in today's counter-revolutionary times without a compass. Boggs and Boggs once observed that a "revolutionary period is one in which the only exit is a revolution."[119] The fact that police–prison abolition has become captured by the foundations and the elite universities is testament to the prior capture of black revolutionary praxis. In these counter-revolutionary times, reformism looks radical, institutions constituted in antiblack violence embrace abolitionist discourse, and the only exit looks to be an extension of state power masquerading as social justice. As we will see, private capital's capacity to shape the direction of social change is particularly insidious in the public health and medical science arenas. The history presented in this chapter reminds us that the pandemic police power expresses itself through a variety of channels that may appear to be progressive and change-minded, but in fact are aimed at displacing structural critiques in favor of preserving the system's longevity.

Notes

1. https://www.sentencingproject.org/news/new-prison-jail-population-figures-released-u-s-department-justice/; Michael Gelb, "Racial Disparities Still Mar Probation, Parole Despite 14% Decline," *The Crime Report*, August 13, 2020, https://thecrimereport.org/2020/08/13/racial-disparities-still-mar-probation-parole-despite-14-decline-report/.
2. https://www.sentencingproject.org/news/new-prison-jail-population-figures-released-u-s-department-justice/.
3. https://worldpopulationreview.com/country-rankings/incarceration-rates-by-country.
4. Ruth Wilson Gilmore, "Globalisation and U.S. Prison Growth: From Military Keynesianism to Post-Keynesian Militarism," *Race & Class* 40(2/3) 1998/1999: 171–188.
5. Gilmore, 172–173.
6. Gary Webb's investigation was first published in summer 1996 in the *San Jose Mercury News*. It was later published in book form as Gary Webb, *Dark Alliance: The CIA, the Contras, and the Crack Cocaine Explosion* (New York: Seven Stories, 1998). On the U.S. effort to destabilize Nicaragua, with effects still reverberating

throughout the Hemisphere to this day, see Noam Chomsky, "The Contra War in Nicaragua," https://libcom.org/history/articles/nicaragua-contras.
7. On COINTELPRO, see Dhoruba bin Wahad et al., *Still Black, Still Strong: Survivors of the War Against Black Revolutionaries* (Brookly: Semiotext(e), 1993); Ward Churchill and Jim Vander Wall, *The COINTELPRO Papers: Documents from the FBI's Secret Wars Against Dissent in the United States* (Boston: South End, 2001); William Pepper, *An Act of State: The Execution of Martin Luther King* (London: Verso, 2018).
8. See Bobby Lavender's interview in Randy Holland (dir.), *The Fire This Time* (1994). On the Black Panther Party, including its relationship to black street gang formations, see Kathleen Cleaver and George Katsiaficas, eds., *Liberation, Imagination, and the Black Panther Party: A New Look at the Panthers and Their Legacy* (New York: Routledge, 2001); Mike Davis, *City of Quartz: Excavating the Future in Los Angeles* (New York: Vintage, 1990); Charles E. Jones, ed., *The Black Panther Party Reconsidered* (Baltimore: Black Classic Press, 1998); Cle Sloan (dir.), *Bastards of the Party* (2005).
9. William Covington, "Prelude to a Truce, 1972–1974," *Our Weekly Los Angeles*, August 4, 2016, http://ourweekly.com/news/2016/aug/04/prelude-truce-1972-1974/; Frank Stoltze, "Forget the LA Riots—Historic 1992 Watts Gang Truce Was the Big News," *Southern California Public Radio*, April 28, 2012, https://www.scpr.org/news/2012/04/28/32221/forget-la-riots-1992-gang-truce-was-big-news/. Similar processes have been underway in other black communities outside of Los Angeles: see Kate Briquelet, "Bloods and Crips Team Up Together to Protest Baltimore's Cops," *The Daily Beast*, July 12, 2017, https://www.thedailybeast.com/bloods-and-crips-team-up-to-protest-baltimores-cops.
10. Manufacturing jobs have declined 37 percent since 1979, with the average earnings of a high school graduate in decline by 28 percent in the same period. See Bureau of Labor Statistics https://www.bls.gov/webapps/legacy/cesbtab1.htm.

11. See Simon Black, *Social Reproduction and the City: Welfare Reform, Child Care, and Resistance in Neoliberal New York* (Athens: Georgia, 2020); Kaaryn Gustafson, "The Criminalization of Poverty," *The Journal of Criminal Law & Criminology* 99(643) 2009; Joel F. Handler, *The Moral Construction of Poverty: Welfare Reform in America* (Newbury Park, CA: Sage, 1991).
12. See Laura Briggs, *How All Politics Became Reproductive Politics: From Welfare Reform to Foreclosure to Trump* (Berkeley: California, 2017); Ange-Marie Hancock, *The Politics of Disgust: The Public Identity of the Welfare Queen* (New York: NYU, 2004); Dorothy Roberts, *Killing the Black Body: Race, Reproduction and the Meaning of Liberty* (New York: Vintage, 1997); Katheryn Russell-Brown, *Color of Crime: Racial Hoaxes, White Fear, Black Protectionism, Police Harassments, and other Macroaggressions* (New York: NYU, 2008).
13. Carol Anderson, "Ferguson Isn't About Black Rage Against Cops. It's White Rage Against Progress," *Washington Post*, August 29, 2014, https://www.washingtonpost.com/opinions/ferguson-wasnt-black-rage-against-copsit-was-white-rage-against-progress/2014/08/29/3055e3f4-2d75-11e4-bb9b-997ae96fad33_story.html. See as well, Anderson, *White Rage: The Unspoken Truth of Our Racial Divide* (New York: Bloomsbury, 2017).
14. See *United States v. Cruikshank* 92 U.S. 542 (1876); Thomas J. Sugrue, *The Origins of the Urban Crisis: Race and Inequality in Postwar Detroit* (Princeton: Princeton, 2014).
15. See Matthew D. Lassiter and Andrew B. Lewis, *The Moderates' Dilemma: Massive Resistance to School Desegregation in Virginia* (Charlottesville: Virginia, 1998); Robert Formisano, *Boston Against Busing: Race, Class, and Ethnicity in the 1960s and 1970s* (Chapel Hill: North Carolina, 2004); *Milliken v. Bradley* 418 U.S. 717 (1974).
16. See *Regents of the University of California v. Bakke* 438 U.S. 265 (1978); *Gratz v. Bollinger* 539 U.S. 244 (2003); *Grutter v. Bollinger* 539 U.S. 306 (2003); *Fisher v. University of Texas* 570 U.S.

297 (2013); https://www.brennancenter.org/our-work/research-reports/state-redistricting-litigation.
17. See Ida B. Wells, *The Light of Truth: Writings of an Anti-Lynching Crusader* (New York: Penguin, 2014).
18. https://www.nationalreview.com/2015/09/mass-incarceration-prison-reform/; https://eji.org/news/bipartisan-support-criminal-justice-reform-still-strong/; https://www.sentencingproject.org/wp-content/uploads/2015/12/Ending-Mass-Incarceration-Charting-a-New-Justice-Reinvestment.pdf.
19. https://www.cnn.com/2020/06/06/us/what-is-defund-police-trnd/index.html. Abolitionism is not simply taken to mean that carceral practices cease altogether overnight. Prison abolitionism predates the emergence of the prison industrial complex, affirming that punishment was a problem long before the 1980s. In 1976 the Prison Research Education Action Project published the landmark pamphlet *Instead of Prisons: A Handbook for Abolitionists* that outlines the "attrition model" of moratorium, decarceration, and excarceration, a practical strategy for achieving a prison-less society. See PREAP, *Instead of Prisons: A Handbook for Abolitionists* (Syracuse: PREAP, 1976), https://www.prisonpolicy.org/scans/instead_of_prisons/; Angela Y. Davis, *Are Prisons Obsolete?* (New York: Seven Stories, 2003).
20. Woods, *Blackhood*, 143–194.
21. See Tryon P. Woods, "Surrogate Selves: Notes on Anti-Trafficking and Antiblackness," *Social Identities* 19(1) 2013; P. Khalil Saucier and Tryon P. Woods, "Ex Aqua: The Mediterranean Basin, Africans on the Move, and the Politics of Policing," *Theoria: A Journal of Social and Political Theory* (141) December 2014.
22. Michael Kranish, "Joe Biden Let Police Groups Write His Crime Bill. Now, His Agenda Has Changed," *Washington Post*, June 8, 2020, https://www.washingtonpost.com/politics/joe-biden-let-police-groups-write-his-crime-bill-now-his-agenda-has-changed/2020/06/08/82ab969e-a434-11ea-8681-7d471bf20207_story.html. Arguably more significant was Clinton's signature welfare reform law, the Personal Responsibility and Work Opportunity Reconciliation Act of 1996.

23. Michel Foucault, *Discipline and Punish: The Birth of the Modern Prison* (New York: Vintage, 1995), 234. On reform as fascism see Dylan Rodriguez, *White Reconstruction: Domestic Warfare and the Logics of Genocide* (New York: Fordham, 2021).
24. W. E. B. DuBois, *Black Reconstruction in America, 1860–1880* (New York: Atheneum, 1979), 61.
25. See DuBois, "The General Strike," in *Black Reconstruction*, 55–83.
26. Amendment XIII, Section 1. Neither slavery nor involuntary servitude, except as a punishment for crime whereof the party shall have been duly convicted, shall exist within the United States, or any place subject to their jurisdiction. Section 2. Congress shall have power to enforce this article by appropriate legislation.
27. See Ava DuVernay (dir.), *13th* (Netflix, 2016).
28. See *Missouri v. Celia* (1855) http://kalamu.com/neogriot/2017/10/28/history-missouri-v-celia-a-slave-she-killed-the-white-master-raping-her-then-claimed-self-defense/.
29. Woods, *Blackhood*, 177.
30. See Guyora Binder, "The Slavery of Emancipation," *Cardozo Law Review* 16 (1996): 2063. Thirteenth Amendment jurisprudence includes the decision in the *Civil Rights Cases* where the Court interpreted the Amendment to prohibit all of the "badges and incidents" of slavery. See *Civil Rights Cases* 109 U.S. 3 (1883). A number of legal scholars have argued that the "badges and incidents" interpretation might be productively applied to address a range of issues, from housing segregation to environmental racism. For an example of the "badges and incidents" argument applied to abolishing police, see Brandon Hasbrouck, "Abolishing Racist Policing with the Thirteenth Amendment," *UCLA Law Review Discourse* 68 (2020): 200, https://www.uclalawreview.org/abolishing-racist-policing-with-the-thirteenth-amendment/#_ftn6; P. Khalil Saucier, "Traces of the Slave Patrol: Notes on Breed-Specific Legislation," *Drexel Law Review* 10(2018): 673, 680.
31. Milfred Fierce, *Slavery Revisited: Blacks and the Southern Convict Lease System, 1865–1933* (New York: Brooklyn College, CUNY, Africana Studies Research Center, 1994), 229.

32. Angela Y. Davis, "From the Prison of Slavery to the Slavery of Prison: Frederick Douglass and the Convict Lease System," in Joy James, ed., *The Angela Y. Davis Reader* (Malden, MA: Blackwell, 1998), 85.
33. Davis, "From the Prison of Slavery," 84.
34. See James Forman, Jr., *Locking Up Our Own: Crime and Punishment in Black America* (New York: Farrar, Straus & Giroux, 2018).
35. See Khalil Gibran Muhammad, *The Condemnation of Blackness: Race, Crime, and the Making of Modern Urban America* (Cambridge: Harvard, 2010).
36. Naomi Murakawa, *The First Civil Right: How Liberals Built Prison America* (New York: Oxford, 2014), 3–4.
37. See Tony Platt et al., *The Iron Fist and the Velvet Glove: An Analysis of the U.S. Police* (Berkeley: Center for Research on Criminal Justice, 1975).
38. See Elizabeth Hinton, *From the War on Poverty to the War on Crime: The Making of Mass Incarceration in America* (Cambridge: Harvard, 2016).
39. See Marc Mauer and Meda-Chesney Lind, *Invisible Punishment: The Collateral Consequences of Mass Incarceration* (New York: New Press, 2003). Although somewhat dated, I continue to cite *Invisible Punishment* because it lays out still-relevant information on how criminalization has become central to social service delivery, forever blurring the boundary between criminal justice and other institutions. Contrary to the editors' conception of this extra-criminal justice punishment, these are not "collateral consequences of mass incarceration"—rather, they are intended outcomes, the production of which predate the contemporary imprisonment boom.
40. Hinton, 61.
41. See Eric J. Miller, "The Warren Court's Regulatory Revolution in Criminal Procedure," *Connecticut Law Review* 43(1) 2010: 1–82, https://papers.ssrn.com/sol3/papers.cfm?abstract_id=1575356.
42. See *Estelle v. Gamble* 429 U.S. 97 (1976); *Rhodes v. Chapman* 452 U.S. 337 (1981); *Whitley v. Albers* 475 U.S. 312 (1986); *Wilson v. Seiter* 501 U.S. 294 (1991); *Hudson v. McMillian* 503 U.S.

1 (1992); *Helling v. McKinney* 509 U.S. 25 (1993); *Farmer v. Brennan* 511 U.S. 825 (1994); *Lewis v. Casey* 518 U.S. 343 (1996); *Hope v. Pelzer* 536 U.S. 730 (2002); *Overton v. Bazetta* 539 U.S. 126 (2003); *Beard v. Banks* 548 U.S. 521 (2006).
43. Colin Dayan, "Cruel and Unusual: The End of the Eighth Amendment," *Boston Review*, October 7, 2004, http://bostonreview.net/dayan-cruel-and-unusual, 6.
44. Dayan, "Cruel and Unusual," 6–7.
45. Dayan, *The Law Is a White Dog: How Legal Rituals Make and Unmake Persons* (Princeton: Princeton, 2011), 95–96. These cases, which decided when punishments are judged as cruel and unusual, are *Estelle v. Gamble* 429 U.S. 97 (1976); *Rhodes v. Chapman* 452 U.S. 337 (1981); *Whitley v. Albers* 475 U.S. 312 (1986); *Wilson v. Seiter* 501 U.S. 294 (1991); *Hudson v. McMillian* 503 U.S. 1 (1992); *Farmer v. Brennan* 511 U.S. 825 (1994); *Hope v. Pelzer* 536 U.S. 730 (2002).
46. *Madrid v. Gomez* 889 F. Supp. 1146 (N.D. Cal. 1995).
47. As cited in Dayan, "Cruel and Unusual," 9–10.
48. As cited in Dayan, "Cruel and Unusual," 9–10.
49. Dayan, "Cruel and Unusual," 8.
50. Not only has the international human rights community long condemned the U.S. prison system overall, but solitary confinement in particular has been found to be severely deleterious to basic human mental health. See https://www.hrw.org/legacy/advocacy/prisons/u-s.htm; https://www.aclu.org/blog/national-security/supermax-prisons-cruel-inhuman-and-degrading; https://truthout.org/articles/un-human-rights-committee-finds-us-in-serious-violation/; https://www.americanbar.org/groups/crsj/publications/human_rights_magazine_home/2015--vol--41-/vol--41--no--2---human-rights-at-home/the-united-states-and-human-rights-treaties--can-we-meet-our-com/; https://thecrimereport.org/2020/10/21/solitary-confinement-and-mental-illness-its-time-to-stop-the-harm/; http://jaapl.org/content/38/1/104.
51. Lewis Gordon, *Her Majesty's Other Children: Sketches of Racism from a Neocolonial Age* (Lanham, MD: Rowman & Littlefield, 1997), 76.

52. See Michelle Alexander, *The New Jim Crow: Mass Incarceration in the Age of Colorblindness* (New York: New Press, 2010).
53. See https://www.huffpost.com/entry/nonviolent-drug-offenders_b_6104256.
54. See Ruth Wilson Gilmore and Naomi Murakawa, "COVID-19, Decarceration, and Abolition" (Part 2), 10:00 min mark, April 16, 2020, https://www.youtube.com/watch?v=xk3K3xLWL_o. "Organized abandonment" refers to the complex of state policies that shift resources away from the needs of people and communities to the needs of capital. For instance, people's need for affordable, safe, and non-toxic housing conveniently located near viable places of work, means of transportation, sources of food, and spaces for recreation have been systematically sacrificed to a deregulated private marketplace that distributes housing as a commodity.
55. Frantz Fanon, *Black Skin, White Masks* (New York: Grove, 1967), 118–120.
56. See Anjali Om, "The Opioid Crisis in Black and White: The Role of Race in Our Nation's Recent Drug Epidemic," *Journal of Public Health* 40(4) December 2018: e614–e615, https://academic.oup.com/jpubhealth/article/40/4/e614/5035761.
57. Lewis Gordon, *Fanon and the Crisis of European Man: An Essay on Philosophy and the Human Sciences* (New York: Routledge, 1995), 26.
58. On "stop-eligible," see Margaret Raymond, "Down on the Corner, Out in the Street: Considering the Character of the Neighborhood in Evaluating Reasonable Suspicion," *Ohio State Law Journal* 60 (1999): 99–143; Woods, *Blackhood*, 160.
59. See https://www.vox.com/2016/9/7/12814504/mass-incarceration-poll.
60. See Mike Brodheim, "Paroled Killers Rarely Re-Offend," *Prison Legal News*, July 15, 2011, https://www.prisonlegalnews.org/news/2011/jul/15/paroled-killers-rarely-re-offend/.

61. John Monahan, "The Prediction of Violence," in Duncan Chappell and John Monahan, eds., *Violence and Criminal Justice* (Lexington, MA: D. C. Heather & Co., 1975), 20.
62. See Bruce Ennis and Thomas R. Litwick, "Psychiatry and the Presumption of Expertise: Flipping Coins in the Courtroom," California Law Review 62 (1974): 693; John Monahan, "Clinical and Actuarial Predictions of Violence," in *Modern Scientific Evidence: The Law and Science of Expert Testimony* §§ 7–2.0 to 7–2.4, at 300 (David Faigman et al. eds., 1997).
63. On the failure of racial profiling to accurately predict law-breaking by black and brown motorists, see David Harris, *Profiles in Injustice: Why Racial Profiling Cannot Work* (New York: New Press, 2002).
64. See https://law.lclark.edu/live/news/21696-preventing-revictimization; https://breakthesilencedv.org/re-victimization-by-the-court-system/.
65. Marc Umbreit et al., "Impact of Restorative Justice Conferencing: A Review of 63 Empirical Studies in 5 Countries," *Center for Restorative Justice and Peacemaking* (2002); Lawrence W. Sherman and Heather Strang, "Restorative Justice: The Evidence," *Jerry Lee Institute Randomized Trials in Restorative Justice*, The Smith Institute (2007).
66. See Bruce Western, "Violent Offenders, Often Victims Themselves, Need More Compassion and Less Punishment," *USA Today*, August 9, 2018, https://www.usatoday.com/story/opinion/policing/2018/08/09/violence-crime-punishment-policing-usa/930249002/.
67. See Sarah Ryley, "Most Shooters Go Free in Chicago's Most Violent Neighborhoods—While Police Make Non-Stop Drug Arrests," *The Trace*, November 11, 2019, https://www.thetrace.org/2019/11/most-shooters-go-free-in-chicagos-most-violent-neighborhoods-while-police-make-non-stop-drug-arrests/.
68. See Rose Braz et al., guest editors, "Critical Resistance to the Prison-Industrial Complex," *Social Justice: A Journal of Crime, Conflict & World Order* 27(3) 2000; Angela Y. Davis, *Abolition*

Democracy: Beyond Prison, Torture, and Empire (New York: Seven Stories, 2005).
69. See https://www.charleskochfoundation.org/.
70. See Jane Mayer, *Dark Money: The Hidden History of the Billionaires Behind the Rise of the Radical Right* (New York: Anchor, 2017).
71. On Koch Industries' criminal record, see https://www.justice.gov/archive/opa/pr/2001/April/153enrd.htm; on Koch Industries' history of environmental pollution, see Daniel Schulman, *Sons of Wichita: How the Koch Brothers Became America's Most Powerful and Private Dynasty* (New York: Grand Central, 2014).
72. See Theda Skocpol and Alexander Hertel-Fernandez, "The Koch Network and Republican Party Extremism," *Perspectives on Politics* 14(3) September 2016: 681–699.
73. https://www.cbsnews.com/news/rikers-island-closing-new-york-city-council-votes-to-close-jail-complex-today-2019-10-17/.
74. See http://islg.cuny.edu/sites/our-work/independent-commission-on-nyc-criminal-justice-incarceration-reform/.
75. See https://www.morejustnyc.org/.
76. See https://www.fordfoundation.org/just-matters/equals-change-blog/posts/in-defense-of-nuance/.
77. Keeanga-Yamahtta Taylor, "Five Years Later, Do Black Lives Still Matter?" *Jacobin*, September 30, 2019, https://www.jacobinmag.com/2019/09/black-lives-matter-laquan-mcdonald-mike-brown-eric-garner.
78. https://www.fordfoundation.org/just-matters/equals-change-blog/posts/in-defense-of-nuance/.
79. See Megan Ming Francis, "The Price of Civil Rights: Black Lives, White Funding, and Movement Capture," *Law & Society Review* 53(1) March 2019: 275–309.
80. *Brown v. Board of Education of Topeka* 347 U.S. 483 (1954). See Gunnar Myrdal, *An American Dilemma: The Negro Problem and Modern Democracy*, vol. 1–2 (New York: Routledge, 1995).
81. Sean Dobson, "Freedom Funders: Philanthropy and the Civil Rights Movement, 1955–1965," National Committee for Responsive Philanthropy, June 2014, https://www.ncrp.org/wp-content/

uploads/2016/11/Freedom_Funders_and_the_Civil_Rights_Movement-FINAL.pdf, 12.
82. Dobson, 13.
83. Randall L. Patton, "Southern Regional Council," *New Georgia Encyclopedia*, https://www.georgiaencyclopedia.org/articles/government-politics/southern-regional-council.
84. Karen Ferguson, "The Perils of Liberal Philanthropy," *Jacobin*, November 26, 2018, https://jacobinmag.com/2018/11/black-lives-matter-ford-foundation-black-power-mcgeorge-bundy. Also see Ferguson, *Top Down: The Ford Foundation, Black Power, and the Reinvention of Racial Liberalism* (Philadelphia: Pennsylvania, 2013).
85. Ferguson, "The Perils."
86. See Martha Biondi, *The Black Revolution on Campus* (Berkeley: California, 2014); Noliwe Rooks, *White Money/Black Power: The Surprising History of African American Studies and the Crisis of Race in Higher Education* (Boston: Beacon, 2007).
87. Ferguson, "The Perils." On the historical process by which black activists are induced to work within the system they were confronting, see Cedric Johnson, *Revolutionaries to Race Leaders: Black Power and the Making of African American Politics* (Minneapolis: Minnesota, 2007); on "progressive neoliberalism," see Nancy Fraser, "The End of Progressive Neoliberalism," *Dissent*, January 2, 2017, https://www.dissentmagazine.org/online_articles/progressive-neoliberalism-reactionary-populism-nancy-fraser.
88. See https://www.fordfoundation.org/just-matters/just-matters/posts/why-black-lives-matter-to-philanthropy/.
89. See https://borealisphilanthropy.org/project/black-led-movement-fund/.
90. See Chloe Cockburn, "Philanthropists Must Invest in an Ecology of Change," *Stanford Social Innovation Review*, June 25, 2018, https://ssir.org/articles/entry/philanthropists_must_invest_in_an_ecology_of_change; and https://fundersforjustice.org/resourcing-movement-black-lives/.
91. See https://wjla.com/news/nation-world/pofficers-shot-at-protest-in-dallas-reports; https://www.nbcnews.com/storyline/baton-

rouge-police-ambush/three-baton-rouge-officers-killed-three-injured-ambush-n611101.
92. https://www.fordfoundation.org/just-matters/just-matters/posts/why-black-lives-matter-to-philanthropy/.
93. Research critical of criminal justice related topics abounds across the faculties of law, humanities, and the social sciences at all major research universities…
94. By "critical resistance," I refer to both the prison abolitionist organization of the same name and the general popularity of "resistance" studies in the post-civil rights multicultural academy. See http://criticalresistance.org/.
95. Dorothy Roberts, "Abolition Constitutionalism," *Harvard Law Review* 133(1) November 2019: 1–122.
96. Roberts, 109.
97. Roberts, 9–10.
98. See Ruth Wilson Gilmore, *Change Everything: Racial Capitalism and the Case for Abolition* (Chicago: Haymarket, 2021). A historical problem central to Roberts' argument for an abolition constitutionalism is the fact that abolition in the nineteenth century meant very different things for whites than it did for blacks. For an analysis of the antiblackness of abolitionism in both the nineteenth and twenty-first centuries, see P. Khalil Saucier and Tryon P. Woods, *Ex Aqua in the Mediterranean: Excavating Black Power in the Migrant Question* (Manchester University Press, forthcoming). This historical analysis suggests that "abolition" has earned our skepticism as much as "constitutionalism" has.
99. This issue recalls a debate within the legal academy in the 1980s and 90s between Critical Legal Studies and Critical Race Theory. A particularly sharp point of divergence between CLS and CRT was the CLS critique of rights. CLS generally argued that rights are indeterminate, incoherent, individualistic, and impediments to progressive movements for genuine social justice. See Mark Tushnet, "The Critique of Rights," 47 *SMU Law Review*. CRT's response was essentially, yes, but rights are too important for oppressed groups to give up entirely. CRT argued that rights can be defended and reconstructed, that one's subject position shapes

one's relationship to rights, and that rights can serve an important social psychological function for people of color and women. See Patricia J. Williams, "Alchemical Notes: Reconstructed Ideals from Deconstructed Rights," *Harvard Civil Rights-Civil Liberties Law Review* 22 (1987): 401. It is time to revisit and extend the combined insights of CLS and CRT in light of the further devolution of antidiscrimination law, and of the rights of the accused, the poor, the confined, and the sick in the "post-racial" era. The matter of police–prison abolition suggests that CRT may have been correct that rights are helpful for the upwardly mobile beneficiaries of foundation support for higher education, but they have not done much good for the black masses.
100. James S. Biakales, "High-Profile History Prof. Hinton to Depart for Yale," *The Harvard Crimson*, February 27, 2020, https://www.thecrimson.com/article/2020/2/27/hinton-leaves-harvard-yale/.
101. See https://law.yale.edu/justice-collaboratory.
102. For more analysis of the Yale Justice Collaboratory's Phillip Atiba Goff, for instance, see Tryon P. Woods, "The Implicit Bias of Implicit Bias Theory," *Drexel Law Review* 10(3) Spring 2018: 631–672.
103. Jorge Camacho, "Defining Policing is Essential to Reform It," *The Hill*, January 26, 2021, https://thehill.com/blogs/congress-blog/politics/535813-defining-policing-is-essential-to-reform-it.
104. Elizabeth Hinton, Session 1: Law and Abolition Transcript p. 17, Making and Unmaking Mass Incarceration, University of Mississippi, December 6, 2019, https://mumiconference.com/.
105. See Dhoruba bin Wahad et al., *Still Black, Still Strong: Survivors of the War Against Black Revolutionaries* (New York: Semiotext(e), 1993).
106. See Elizabeth Hinton, *From the War on Poverty to the War on Crime: The Making of Mass Incarceration in America* (Cambridge: Harvard, 2017); *America on Fire: The Untold History of Police Violence and Black Rebellion Since the 1960s* (New York: Liveright, 2021).
107. On the welfare rights movement, see Premilla Nadesen, *Rethinking the Welfare Rights Movement* (New York: Routledge, 2012).

108. See Annelise Orleck, *Storming Caesar's Palace: How Black Mothers Fought Their Own War on Poverty* (Boston: Beacon, 2006); Rhonda Y. Williams, *The Politics of Public Housing: Black Women's Struggles Against Urban Inequality* (New York: Oxford, 2002).
109. Gerald Horne, *The Fire This Time: The Watts Uprising and the 1960s* (New York: Da Capo, 1997).
110. Thomas J. Sugrue, *The Origins of the Urban Crisis: Race and Inequality in Postwar Detroit* (Princeton: Princeton, 1996).
111. See Ida B. Wells-Barnett, *The Crusade for Justice: The Autobiography of Ida B. Wells* (Chicago: Chicago, 2020).
112. George Jackson, *Blood In My Eye* (Baltimore: Black Classic Press, 1972), 7–8….Robert Staples 1977 special issue on the police in The Black Scholar…phylon journal 1974–75 staples piece…Chrisman piece on white law in the early 1970s in the black scholar…which then connects to Bennett and the IBW and the 1970s…
113. Lerone Bennett, Jr., *Confrontation: Black and White* (Chicago: Johnson, 1965), 78.
114. Kwame Ture, *Stokely Speaks: From Black Power to Pan-Africanism* (Chicago: Lawrence Hill, 1971), 177.
115. Lerone Bennett, Jr., *The Challenge of Blackness* (Chicago: Johnson, 1972), 27.
116. Kuwasi Balagoon et al., *Look For Me In The Whirlwind: The Collective Autobiography of the New York 21* (New York: Random House, 1972), 111.
117. Frantz Fanon, *The Wretched of the Earth* (New York: Grove, 1963), 245.
118. James and Grace Lee Boggs, *Revolution and Evolution in the Twentieth Century* (New York: Monthly Review, 1974), 19.
119. Boggs and Boggs, 19.

4

The Police Power of Finance, Technology, Housing, and Education

Philanthropy, the corporate university, and the state seek to focus attention on the spectacles of the prison industrial complex so that we do not see the many diffuse and more central ways in which we are policed. This is partly why police–prison abolition tends toward reformist compromise or gets displaced onto things that do not adequately address the police power, such as the recent calls to defund police. Not only do police and prison managers have ways of recouping the modest cuts in their budgets that advocates are able to occasionally force through state legislatures or city councils but policing and punishment are themselves already sufficiently diversified that should a jurisdiction actually implement a substantive funding decrease, its policing and punishment functions would be readily taken up by other state agencies and by private entities. In other words, policing and punishment, again, are not primarily institutional (criminal justice agencies), nor practice (law enforcement or corrections), nor principle ("justice"). Rather, they relate to blackness as pure power—violence with impunity.[1] Rigorous abolitionism would therefore necessitate defusing the hypervisibility of the police–prison structure in order to reveal the police power in its systemic form. It is these diffuse operations of the police power, especially, that keep black liberation effectively quarantined. Comprehensively analyzing the police power of antiblackness in its fully socialized reality would be impossible within the space of this book, let alone the one chapter that I have allotted to the task. The following analysis, therefore, is cursory and suggestive. It focuses on developments that have unfolded apace with the formation of the pandemic police power in the past year, have anticipated it, or have made it possible, with the understanding that the distinctions between different facets of society are artifices of my deconstructive method—in reality they are all deeply imbricated within and through each other. This chapter is conjoined with the ensuing analysis of the pandemic police power of medical science to elucidate the manifold techniques and technologies by which the culture of politics in slaveholding society *is* the primary police function.

How does the police power operate in ways other than the criminal law? In order to better understand the Pandemic Year in terms of the pandemic police power, rather than as simply a public health crisis, we can connect the financial and technology industries with housing and education. As the state-corporate mediascape tried to focus the nation's attention during the winter of 2020–2021 on the "assault on the capitol" and the second impeachment trial of President Trump, the new Biden administration's economic leadership team took shape. Against the muted backdrop of increased financial insecurity for many Americans due to the pandemic, the spectacle of Trumpism continued to distract from the continuities in economic policy between Republican and Democrat administrations. Former Federal Reserve chairperson Janet Yellen was confirmed in January 2021 by the Senate to become the new Secretary of the Treasury.[2] Yellen chaired President Clinton's Council of Economic Advisors, and was a member of the Federal Reserve Board of Directors under both Presidents Clinton and Obama, and served as Chair of the Federal Reserve for both the Obama and Trump administrations. During Yellen's confirmation hearing before the Senate Finance Committee, a number of senators expressed their concern that the 2008 taxpayer bailout of Wall Street never repeat itself. Yellen concurred, stating,

Our focus should be on Main Street, not Wall Street…During my time at the Fed, I worked very hard to strengthen the banking system, to make sure that these institutions don't operate in ways that would harm Main Street. I am pleased to see that when the pandemic hit and there was a good deal of financial disruption, that especially the largest banks have been able to – due to the reforms that were put in place – continue to lend, to survive with adequate capital, and to support the needs of households and businesses. And, you have my absolute pledge that this will continue to be my focus.[3]

This is the state's customary narrative on the economy: populist rhetoric to mystify the starkly elitist reality of economic policy. In fact, the economic downturn preceded the global pandemic-caused shutdowns, and to the extent that Wall Street banks have any liquidity to speak of today, it is because the Federal Reserve had already begun giving them billions of dollars daily *prior* to the appearance of COVID-19 in the world.

The performance of the ten-year Treasury Note is often taken as a suggestive indicator of economic health. During the epic financial collapse of 2007–2010, the yield on the Treasury Note flopped, foreshadowing the brewing economic catastrophe.[4] In 2019, the yield on the ten-year Treasury Note precipitously fell from 3.22 percent to 1.47 percent—four months *before* a COVID-19 death had been reported anywhere on the planet.[5] At the low point of the T-Note on September 17, 2019, the Fed began repurchasing loan agreements from the leading Wall Street banks in order to avert a repeat of the 2008 crash.[6] The Fed uses repurchase agreements, or "repos," to make collateralized loans to primary dealers. A repo temporarily adds reserves to a bank's balance sheet, offsetting momentary swings in the levels of the bank's reserves.[7] The problem since 2019 has been that this "momentary" shortage in bank liquidity has been so severe that Fed spending has surpassed what it pumped into Wall Street during the 2008 crisis. The Fed's emergency repo payments during the 2007–2010 period reached a high of $126 billion just before the bankruptcy filing of Lehman Brothers on September 15, 2008. By December 18, 2019, the Fed's outstanding repo payments had peaked at $236.6 billion—$100 billion more than during the worst financial crisis since the Great Depression. By the time the United States had recorded its first official COVID-19 death on February 28, 2020, the Fed had already spent a cumulative total of $6.6 *trillion* in super cheap loans to the leading trading houses with no explanation as to whether Wall Street banks are experiencing a funding, liquidity, or insolvency crisis.[8]

For our purposes, we can note two key implications of this economic situation. First, finance capital's steady takeover of the U.S. economy has exceeded the saturation point. Since the late 1960s, industrial manufacturing has been steadily declining in importance to the U.S. economy, giving way to the financial and service sectors. At the macro-economic level, deindustrialization and the rise of finance has proceeded apace with a shrinking of the welfare state, the growth of the security state, including the prison industrial complex, and the withering of worker power across labor markets. At the micro-economic level, deindustrialization has meant a historic disconnect between work and poverty as people are working more for less, an increase in housing and food insecurity, and the massive expansion of debt for both households and industry alike.[9] The financialization of the U.S. economy reached its saturation point with the 2008 collapse; 2019 marks its excess because evidently we are now in a period of economic crisis worse than the 2008 collapse, but the state–corporate nexus has turned yesterday's crisis management into today's daily operating procedure. Crucial to this crisis management is occupying the news media attention through a host of distractions (Trumpism, pandemic), as well as messaging that shrouds the reality of Wall Street's dependency on the state's feeding tube. In May 2020, for example, Treasury Secretary Steve Mnuchin said "there's lots of liquidity" on Wall Street and "this isn't like the financial crisis," and almost all mainstream and left-liberal media have reported it as such, even though $6.6 trillion of Fed spending to prop up the industry says otherwise.[10]

The second implication of the present economic situation is the financialization of everything. The finance sector has expanded to include insurance and real estate to create neo-rentier economies in which wealth derives primarily from the extraction of economic rent through the privatization of goods and services and debt-servicing.[11] One of the consequences of this development is that the entire society is directly yoked to the boom and bust of Wall Street.[12] The pandemic shutdowns caused a sudden spike in unemployment that outpaced that of the Great Depression: in two short months, March and April of 2020, the nation's unemployment rate reached heights that took almost two years to reach after the stock market crash on October 29, 1929.[13] The Trump–Pelosi coronavirus bailout of the banks (the CARES Act of 2020) dwarfed that by Obama in 2008, and in 2020 the small portion that went directly to individual households largely ended up in the hands of banks and landlords anyway in the form of servicing consumer debts, rents, or mortgage payments.[14] Despite a non-binding federal eviction moratorium in effect through March 31, 2021, eviction filings have risen 40 percent since summer 2020 and continue unabated.[15] While some European governments subsidized up to 90 percent of workers' lost wages during the pandemic shutdowns, economic subsidies in the United States correspond to its prior standards by which human needs are subject to the needs of finance.[16] The bailout of the banks in 2008 underwrote the greatest dispossession of property and loss of wealth for black families in U.S. history—that is to say, after that which cannot be measured, the Middle Passage and slavery: between 1998 and 2006, mortgage foreclosures cost black households between $71 and $93 billion.[17]

As we have seen time and again, however, each successive era opens new possibilities for antiblack violence. In the aftermath of the 2008 foreclosure crisis, many of the private equity firms came out of the economic collapse in excellent financial shape and were looking for investment opportunities, which they found in the form of foreclosed homes.[18] Taken in the aggregate, these empty properties offered a large pool of assets at discount prices, which private equity firms like the Blackstone Group turned into "rent-backed securities." Working on the same principles of the mortgage-backed securities that were at the heart of the 2008 mess, rent-backed securities use monthly rental payments instead of mortgage payments to pay bondholders. Profits from the sales of these securitized bonds require Blackstone and other investors to maintain high occupancy rates, raise rents, and enforce a rigid eviction policy to remove all non-paying tenants, and the high annualized returns attract investors from around the world.[19]

Finance capital's interest in black living spaces is not new, but simply reworks the predatory capitalism of Jim Crow segregation, of redlining in the housing and lending industries, and of the subprime mortgage industry.[20] It is in slavery, however, that we can see how the intrinsic antiblackness of the basic methods of finance capital lay the foundation for the present. Enslaved Africans provided slaveholders and their investors with both the means of production and also the collateral needed for acquiring the credit necessary for expanding production. Slaves were thus the ultimate hedge because they would either produce enough for every investor to realize a return, or they could be sold to produce the liquidity to cover the debts incurred in the production process.[21] Slavers purchased new slaves with money they borrowed using their existing slaves as collateral. Slaves were essentially turned into mortgages, which were sold individually or collectively by banks as mortgage-backed securities. Local banks issued stock certificates to stockholders who mortgaged their slaves and land, convinced state legislatures to back the banks' issuance of bonds based on these mortgages, and then sold these banknotes to investment firms in Liverpool, London, Paris, Philadelphia, and New York. The investment firms, in turn, sold the bonds to investors around the world, allowing slaveholders to monetize their slaves by securitizing them and then leveraging them multiple times on the international financial market.[22] The risk represented by the slaves was now shared by all of the citizens of the state, not just the individual slaveholders, and the group of people able to profit from slavery expanded exponentially. For the investors who bought these slave-securitized bonds, they were really buying a "completely commodified slave: not a particular individual, but a tiny percentage of the income flows derived from each one of thousands of slaves."[23] The investor, of course, escaped the risk inherent in owning slaves.

Likewise, slavery explains why the 2008 foreclosure crisis was *not* a crisis for capital, but rather one of the mechanisms by which housing commodities were transformed into profits for the various investors involved in mortgage- or rent-backed securities. During slavery, because of the various insurance contracts, credit-backed securities, and the rate of interest guaranteed by bills of exchange, the interruptions due to the premature death of the enslaved or to their periodic rebellion did not register as losses; they simply meant hastening the transformation of objectified human beings into money for the various parties that had a propertied interest in them.[24] The speculative culture of finance capitalism, in other words, is the practical expression of a particular phenomenology of things. Put differently, as an expression of racial violence, finance capitalism is productive of a prior racial unity. Never merely an economic transaction, the economy of trust that underwrites the finance industry derives from the underlying racial solidarity of being a human being with bodily and spatial integrity that is vouchsafed in the form of the black person chained up in the ship's hold—or as the case may be today, evicted for being late on the rent or for defaulting on the mortgage. As in the slave era when slave-backed securities spawned a trans-Atlantic financial industry, rent-backed securities created from (disproportionately) black foreclosures sustains a hugely profitable investment pool that draws in large institutional investors like public pensions, sovereign wealth funds, and university endowments looking for stable long-term investments with high yield. The financialization of housing is a major driver of gentrification and racial segregation. This is a massive structural investment in black displacement—the police power of finance and real estate.

One of the few things that shape the intimate contours of people's lives as much as housing is technology. We are entirely dependent on corporate infrastructure for the internet. Not only is this infrastructure designed to be ignored and not noticed for what it is, but its efficiency as the police power rests in its ability to recruit users to voluntarily enact its surveillance mechanisms on themselves. Surveillance thus expands by virtue of users' ignorance about the impact of giving away information to other people, to the state, and to corporations. The visible web that we can access with the customary search engines is just the tip of the iceberg; the mass underneath, the unindexed reaches of the internet, is the "deep web" where certain protocols allow you to access hidden service websites where there is no way of knowing who owns the site, and in turn, the server does not know who you are. But you need to understand computer science and how to code in order to subvert internet surveillance in this way, tools that most people do not have.[25] As with the discourse on health disparities, with respect to technology we mostly hear about unequal access to computers and to the internet. The ubiquity of smart cell phone technology, sometimes in lieu of personal computer access, compounds this inequity by enhancing surveillance over precisely the people least likely to be able to escape it. Put differently, the race, class, and national disparities in the science, technology, engineering, and mathematics (STEM) education fields become ever more salient in the context of pandemic lockdowns. As internet technology now mediates almost every human interaction, from school to work to healthcare, simplifying the technical problem to a question of user access (as opposed to computer engineering literacy and the autonomy it offers) is akin to reducing the prison industrial complex to the sheer numbers of people behind bars. As always, the real question is power and how it polices; with technology, then, we need to pay more attention to matters of control and consciousness.

Against a catastrophic backdrop for most people, including the steepest decline of gross domestic product (GDP) on record, the tech companies' fortunes have been stratospheric during the Pandemic Year.[26] As Shoshana Zuboff explains, tech giants like Amazon, Apple, Google, and Microsoft are making money hand over fist in two ways.[27] First, by advancing their core business of surveillance capitalism which is based on extracting user data, feeding it to artificial intelligence programs, and selling the predictive behavioral models generated by AI in their human futures markets; and secondly, through their institutional business. In the first instance, the pandemic lockdowns have been a boondoggle for the tech corporations as people are further driven into online markets. The business model of extracting user data means that *all* online fora, whether for school, work, socializing, entertainment, or consumption, occur within the larger marketplace in which *all* user behaviors are mined, sent to a computational factory, and then sold as human predictions to government and corporations, generating in record time market capitalization in the billions of dollars. In the second instance, the tech corporations host institutional clients on their platforms, inside third-party ecosystems, or stored in their cloud networks where data analytics go to work. These two aspects of the technology industry may appear innately apolitical and unique to the digital age, but in fact they are part of a racist genealogy of pseudo-science that has been central to the police power of slaveholding culture, connecting the slave trade with twenty-first-century social media, as we will see in a moment.

Before the pandemic, Google was the biggest player in the educational technology market. More than half of all public schools were using Google services prior to 2020, including a whole range of colleges and universities.[28] After the pandemic, Google Classroom doubled its reach to 100 million users, with other Google services increasing by as much as 900 percent.[29] The United Nations estimates that pandemic shutdowns affected 94 percent of the world's student population, and upwards of 99 percent in low and lower-middle income countries.[30] Google's ability to capitalize on this sudden and worldwide need for remote learning capacities was the result of many years of the tech giant slowly entrenching itself in schools around the world. This is not coincidental or a stroke of prescient foresight; it is the tech industry's growth strategy: to seek, inhabit, and exploit vulnerabilities in our institutions, economies, and social spaces so that they are ready to provide at an instant's notice what institutions cannot do or cannot afford to do or will not do or dare not do.[31] As the recent lawsuits around the country against Google make clear, states that cannot or will not provide educational resources to its teachers and children are belatedly realizing that the pied piper must be paid: the company's apparent largesse in gifting educational equipment and services to schools is merely a means to an end.[32] New Mexico's attorney general alleges Google violated the federal Children's Online Privacy Protection Act by mining children's personal location and usage data. Recent attempts to bring Google and the other tech giants into compliance with the law have been fruitless and recalls the longstanding pattern of reform futility with police departments. Despite agreeing in 2015 to not collect student data, Google was fined $170 million in New York in 2020 for violating children's privacy on YouTube; it also faces additional privacy suits and a federal anti-trust lawsuit.[33] Microsoft had also previously been the subject of a lawsuit against the U.S. Department of Education for facilitating a massive database on student personal information.[34] We must recognize that these attempts at applying the law to technology companies are akin to seeking obeisance to the rule of law from police departments. As we have seen, policing precedes law in every arena, and since Google and Microsoft are even more central to the police power than law enforcement is, we are once again confronted with the conundrum of appealing to legal oversight in the face of police impunity, which amounts to pretending to a superseding law which impunity has itself already superseded.[35]

During the Pandemic Year, Google has censored viewpoints and information on COVID-19 that dissents from the medical-industrial complex by blocking such videos on YouTube, which it owns. Through its venture capitalist arm, Google Ventures, Google invests heavily in biotechnology, as do most of the other tech companies like Microsoft and Oracle. Google Ventures invests in Vaccitech the biotech firm owned by the lead developers of the Oxford-AstraZeneca vaccine.[36] Google is therefore censoring information that goes against the medical industrial complex in which it has staked a considerable financial interest.

Microsoft, Amazon, and other big tech companies hold between them thousands of contracts with the Department of Defense and federal law enforcement (including ICE, DEA, FBI, and BOP), and thousands more with local law enforcement.[37] Microsoft is also a key part of the infrastructure for police force deployment on streets across the country through its Domain Awareness surveillance system connecting thousands of cameras and radiation detectors with cloud-based data storage capacity. When New York City's implementation of Domain Awareness was revealed in 2012, Mayor Michael Bloomberg dismissed criticism of "Big Brother" omniscience, correctly noting, "What you're seeing is what the private sector has used for a long time. If you walk around with a cell phone, the cell phone company knows where you are."[38] Not appreciating his boss' implication that his officers are merely the backups to a more fundamental policing apparatus that has long been in effect throughout society, Police Commissioner Ray Kelly attempted to reclaim policing for police officers: "The system is a transformative tool because it was created by police officers for police officers…the system allows us to connect the dots by instantly tapping into the details of crime records, 911 calls, license plate readers, videotape footage, and more." On the contrary, police officers are not typically computer engineers, but computer engineers are very much central to the police power.

Microsoft's Domain Awareness illustrates how criminal justice is merely a secondary facet of a vast police power connecting everyday life to surveillance technology. Microsoft's role in modern law enforcement is thus an outgrowth of the policing function of the Gates Foundation in the public schools. For over two decades, Gates has been at the forefront of eviscerating and privatizing public education, promoting non-profits that disparage or attack public schools and teachers, promoting charter schools at the expense of public schools, undermining teacher effectiveness, and replacing books with software.[39] Remote learning may seem unique to life under pandemic lockdowns, but in fact it simply further activates the "personalized learning" model championed by big tech for decades. The leading philanthropic supporters of education are tied to technology corporations: the Dell, Gates, Google, and Hewlett Foundations, and the Zuckerberg Initiative. "Personalized learning" is a euphemism for lessons delivered individually to students on their digital devices. Despite years of struggle by teachers, parents, and students to curtail the standardized testing paradigm in education, "personalized learning" retrenches it by dressing up performance measurement in the neoliberal language of flexibility, individuation, and mastery.[40] As the U.S. Department of Education puts it, sounding like the de facto education technology sales firm that it has become,

> Transitioning away from seat time, in favor of a structure that creates flexibility, allows students to progress as they demonstrate mastery of academic content, regardless of time, place, or pace of learning. Competency-based strategies provide flexibility in the way that credit can be earned or awarded, and provide students with personalized learning opportunities.[41]

As with the introduction of technology into the workplace everywhere, the subtext here is surplus labor. In the case of education technology, the teacher becomes extraneous, de-skilled as an educator, and estranged from the learning relationship.[42] Indeed, since education *is* a relationship, "personalized learning" is arguably not education at all.[43] As Jack Schneider and Jennifer Berkshire explain, "just having more Chromebooks or online learning platforms hasn't allowed for faster or larger batch-processing of students."[44] Or, as Diane Ravitch puts it, so-called personalized learning "is actually *depersonalized* learning because it attempts to replace human teachers with computer instruction" (emphasis added).[45] Unsurprisingly, the measurable negative effects are profound. Education psychologists find that computers interfere with everything from child motor skill development to logic to the ability to discern between fantasy and reality, and over two hundred peer-reviewed studies demonstrate that screen time correlates to increased ADHD, screen addiction, aggression, depression, anxiety, and even psychosis.[46] Furthermore, online education actually costs more to produce and maintain compared with traditional in-person classroom learning, and in general, it depresses wages for teachers and staff, immiserates working conditions, constrains academic freedom, and negatively filters academic shared governance practices.[47]

Public schooling prior to the pandemic lockdowns was, generally speaking, not good for many kids, but especially bad for a lot of black and brown and poor kids.[48] Public schools have always been a contested terrain marked by public policies geared to reproduce the labor needs of a severely stratified capitalist political economy, on the one hand, and the aspirational labors of young people who hope to transform their circumstances through education, supported by the many "teachers who transgress."[49] Some education scholars have pointed to a "school-to-prison pipeline" as a feature of the prison industrial complex, wherein public schools begin the process of de-skilling, criminalization, and punishment that facilitates black and brown youth's entrance into the criminal justice system.[50] Meanwhile, other scholars argue that the analytic form of the "school-to-prison pipeline" mystifies the root causes of the complex dynamics between public education and the criminal justice system.[51] Either way, the question of how education technology and remote learning undermine learning relationships, violate privacy, and breach personal security assumes a different connotation in black households which historically have never been able to claim integrity in the face of the police power. To question remote learning modalities today for violating student privacy is to formulate policing as merely a matter of tactics: instead of asking, do police officers correctly obtain a warrant or probable cause before entering a home, the question becomes, do technology companies, or the educational institutions relying on their platforms, correctly obtain parental consent to collect student data?

While important, these questions mistake the map for the territory, as Sylvia Wynter puts it.[52] On the contrary, antiblackness as the precondition for society and all of its rules, including constitutional rights to privacy and protection from unwarranted search and seizure, means that the black domestic sphere has always existed in a state of structural vulnerability. Under slavery, the black family and "blood" were functionally outlawed; and the prison industrial complex brought enhanced legal cover for the long-standing practice of police raids on black homes. Asset forfeiture laws, for instance, permit law enforcement to confiscate black property without a criminal conviction or due process.[53] Structurally analogous to the slave quarters, then, black domesticity is neither private nor secure: that there is no sanctuary for black bodies underscores how captivity is a constituent element of black life.[54]

The pandemic's intrusion on privacy, then, does not simply accentuate the unequal application of the law—it exposes the necessity for a complete overhaul in how we understand law in relation to the police power it subtends. Western knowledge systems are rife with the schizoid sensibilities of slaveholding culture. Saying one thing, meaning another; principled on paper, immoral in practice. From the perspective of the black liberation struggle, it is axiomatic to situate the language of the law in subordinate relation to the law in action. It is pointless to debate, for instance, concepts of privacy and rights under the law when everyone knows that they do not apply to black people. When we center our analysis of law in its action context, then, "privacy" and "rights" only cohere as such for non-blacks *as expressions of the structural vulnerability of black people*. In other words, it is not that "privacy" means one thing for whites and another for blacks; if we allow the police power to inform our understanding of legal concepts and the problem of surveillance, then the words do not mean what they purport to mean *for anybody*. This fact is now becoming live reality for non-blacks as well, as everyday activities under pandemic lockdown are forced further into the marketplace of surveillance capitalism.

In the age of big tech, people are not consumers, customers, employees, or even products—they are the raw material for new procedures of manufacturing and sales that define the surveillance economy. The slave as the original fungible object anchors today's surveillance capitalism in a long genealogy of biometric technologies developed to control black people. Enslaved people's bodies were marked and marketed racially and through branding and other techniques of disfigurement.[55] These early forms of biometrics expanded to include lantern laws, pass laws, the pseudo-science of craniometry and criminology, and various use of the enslaved as prototypical research subjects for modern medicine and science.[56] Popular biometric surveillance technologies today include iris and retinal scans, hand geometry, fingerprint data, facial and vascular patterns, and gait recognition. "In simple terms," explains Simone Browne, "biometrics is a technology of measuring the living body. The application of this technology is the verification and identification practices that enable the body to function as evidence."[57] The high tech mechanization of these practices lends a presumption of infallibility and objectivity, an assumption of mathematical precision, without error or bias on the part of the computer programmers who calibrate the search parameters of these machines or on the part of those who read the templates to make decisions regarding which bodies to detain or release, to treat or punish. Surveillance technology thus enjoins scientific discourse that mediates lived experience—but the body made into data is *not* human experience. It is rather an algorithm that extracts behaviors *from* experience, inputs this data into predictive models, and then attaches identities to these predictions of human behavior. It is these moments of observation, calibration, and application that reveal themselves as racializing.[58] The outcomes of this computer modeling, the "truth" of surveillance technologies, are wedded to the cultural production of difference and power. There is a tight seam of connection, then, between the ubiquity of temperature scanners during pandemic lockdowns and the National Guard's attempt to use heat rays in crowd control during protests against policing; between the history of craniometry and AI software that fails to recognize black faces or pulse oximeters that do not recognize dark skin; between new infection contact tracing systems and the data mining capacities central to computer technologies; between identity verification machines and the demand for blood and medical data during vaccination campaigns.[59] The bottom line for the technology industry is the sale of certainty: when you can predict human behaviors, you can sell certainty, and just about every business and state agency wants to buy certainty—banks, insurance, landlords, retailers, education, healthcare, criminal justice.[60] The competition for certainty in human behavior requires large-scale data, subliminal cues, social comparison dynamics, subtle rewards and punishments, and micro-psychological targeting to align behavior with market outcomes and social control. This translates into the construction of populations based on the cultural production and representation of race and myth that reveals "certainty" to be two-sided at all times: which kinds of people you want to include and which kinds you want to exclude.

Surveillance technologies, therefore, have always been central to notions of a body made out of place or threatening or dangerous—a species of racial profiling, in decidedly un-scientific other words. Social media use is a trove of archival material for the police power, with the state-corporate nexus able to both monitor and shape the behaviors of the disenfranchised. Social movements that rely on social media—which is all of them at this point—are thus taking two steps backwards for every arduous forward step they are able to achieve. For every feeling of isolation and despair that is assuaged by social media connection, actual solidarity in action is undermined by the individuation of the digital landscape. Surveillance technologies work to subvert social movement because people engage with technology individually, isolated from the social spaces that foster the relational ethic that can only come from the messiness of simply getting along in person and that facilitate the transference of wisdom that can only occur through passed down experience in relation to others. The irony of the globally connected internet age, then, is that activists find themselves sequestered in their own local vacuums: isolated from generational knowledge that leaves them to reinvent the wheel over and over again; and isolated from the accountability to each other and to the communities in whose name they act which generates the true solidarity and care that people need.[61] In this light, "socially distanced" becomes the supreme irony, a paradoxical pretense for social control. Social change may require total disengagement from social media use, in the least, in order to build the communities of accountability with the consciousness and ethic necessary for self-determination.

Notes

1. Woods, *Blackhood*, 171.
2. See https://abc.com/news/insider/watch-24-hours-assault-on-the-capitol-abc-news-special-streaming-exclusively-on-hulu.
3. See https://www.finance.senate.gov/hearings/hearing-to-consider-the-anticipated-nomination-of-to-be-the-honorable-janet-l-yellen-to-secretary-of-the-treasury.
4. See Kim Amadeo, "How U.S. Treasury Yields Affect the Economy," *The Balance*, August 21, 2020, https://www.thebalance.com/treasury-yields-3305741.
5. Pam Martens and Russ Martens, "Wall Street's Financial Crisis Preceded COVID-19: Chart and Timeline," *Wall Street on Parade*, May 1, 2020, https://wallstreetonparade.com/2020/05/wall-streets-financial-crisis-preceded-covid-19-chart-and-timeline/.
6. Martens and Martens, "Wall Street's Financial Crisis Preceded COVID-19."
7. See https://www.newyorkfed.org/aboutthefed/fedpoint/fed04.html.
8. Martens and Martens, "Wall Street's Financial Crisis Preceded COVID-19."
9. See generally, Linda Evans and Eve Goldberg, *The Prison-Industrial Complex and the Global Economy* (Oakland: PM Press, 2009); Martha L. Olney and Aaron Pacitti, "The Rise of Services, Deindustrialization, and the Length of Economic Recovery," *Economic Inquiry*, 2017, https://eml.berkeley.edu/~olney/olney-pacitti%2004-24-17.pdf; Michael Hudson interview, "Financialization and Deindustrialization," *The Analysis*, November 2, 2020, https://theanalysis.news/interviews/financialization-and-deindustrialization-michael-hudson/.
10. Martens and Martens, "The Fed Has Pumped $9 Trillion into Wall Street Over the Past Six Months, But Mnuchin Says, 'This Isn't Like the Financial Crisis,'" *Wall Street on Parade*, March 14, 2020, https://wallstreetonparade.com/2020/03/the-fed-has-pumped-9-trillion-into-wall-street-over-the-past-six-months-but-mnuchin-says-this-isnt-like-the-financial-crisis/.

11. See Michael Hudson, "The Rentier Resurgence and Takeover: Finance Capitalism vs. Industrial Capitalism," January 27, 2021, https://michael-hudson.com/2021/01/the-rentier-resurgence-and-takeover-finance-capitalism-vs-industrial-capitalism/.
12. Repeal of the Glass-Steagall Act in 1999 by the Clinton Administration largely set the stage for this house of cards economy. Passed in 1933 to prevent another Great Depression, Glass-Steagall ensured hard institutional barriers between the private banking system and the commercial investment institutions on Wall Street. With this regulatory infrastructure dismantled, Wall Street firms were able to turn the private banking system, from personal savings accounts to pension plans to home mortgages, into new financial instruments, and in the process exposed the entire economy to its high-risk casino-style investment practices. Because these new "investments" are now backed by the federal government in the same manner of a traditional depository institution, even though the Wall Street "banks" are not banks in any real sense of the word, the taxpayer is on the hook for all of Wall Street's gambles—such as when JP Morgan Chase, the largest "bank" in the country, was exposed in 2012 for using hundreds of billions of dollars from its federally-insured "bank" to gamble in exotic London derivatives, losing at least $6.2 billion of its depositors' money. The two main outcomes of the post-Glass-Steagall environment is that it requires the federal government to funnel massive amounts of money to Wall Street to keep the entire economy afloat; and secondly, this amounts to a historic wealth transfer upwards as it has enabled Wall Street to create the greatest income and wealth inequality in the United States since the 1920s, prior to Glass-Steagall. See https://wallstreetonparade.com/2019/10/federal-reserve-spokesman-explains-how-it-creates-money-out-of-thin-air-to-pump-out-to-wall-street/.
13. When the stock market crashed on October 29, 1929, the nation's unemployment rate was at 2.2 percent. It took almost two years for unemployment to reach 15.01 percent in August 1931. When the pandemic shutdowns began at the end of February 2020, the unemployment rate was 3.5 percent, and by the end of April it was 14.7 percent. See https://wallstreetonparade.com/2020/05/u-s-

unemployment-reaches-14-57-percent-chart-from-great-depression-shows-risks-ahead/.
14. See https://covidbailouttracker.com/.
15. See https://evictionlab.org/.
16. See https://www.businessinsider.com/countries-offering-direct-payments-or-basic-income-in-corona-crisis-2020-4?op=1#in-the-netherlands-the-government-will-pay-up-to-90-of-workers-salaries-3.
17. Nemoy Lewis, "Anti-Blackness Beyond the State: Real Estate Finance and the Making of Urban Racial Capitalism," *Society and Space*, September 14, 2020, https://www.societyandspace.org/articles/anti-blackness-beyond-the-state-real-estate-finance-and-the-making-of-urban-racial-capitalism.
18. See https://www.bloomberg.com/news/features/2019-10-03/how-private-equity-works-and-took-over-everything.
19. Lewis, "Anti-Blackness Beyond the State."
20. See Ta-Nehisi Coates, "The Case for Reparation," *The Atlantic*, May 2014; Richard Rothstein, *The Color of Law: A Forgotten History of How Our Government Segregated America* (New York: Liveright, 2017); Keeanga-Yamahtta Taylor, *Race for Profit: How Banks and the Real Estate Industry Undermined Black Homeownership, Justice, Power, and Politics* (Chapel Hill: North Carolina, 2019).
21. Edward Baptist, "Toxic Debt, Liar Loans, Collateralized and Securitized Human Beings, and the Panic of 1837," in Michael Zakim and Gary J. Kornblath, eds., *Capitalism Takes Command: The Social Transformation of Nineteenth-Century America* (Chicago: Chicago, 2012), 79.
22. Baptist, "Toxic Debt," 80–82.
23. Baptist, "Toxic Debt," 82.
24. Ian Baucom, *Specters of the Atlantic: Finance Capital, Slavery, and the Philosophy of History* (Durham: Duke, 2005), 66.
25. This paragraph draws from the work of Deep Lab. See http://www.deeplab.net/; Deep Lab's mini-documentary film, https://vimeo.com/116314844.
26. Most countries around the world experienced the same unprecedented collapse in GDP. See, for example, Canada https://www.ctvnews.ca/business/canadian-economy-posted-steepest-decline-on-rec

ord-as-coronavirus-struck-statcan-1.5082814; India https://www.telegraphindia.com/india/economy-steepest-gdp-decline-on-record/cid/1790636; Germany https://www.rt.com/business/498951-german-economy-record-contraction/; U.S. https://finance.yahoo.com/news/us-economy-entering-deepest-recession-on-record-172304066.html.
27. See Naomi Klein, Shoshana Zuboff, and Simone Browne, "Surveillance in an Era of Pandemic and Protest," *The Intercept*, September 11, 2020, https://theintercept.com/2020/09/11/coronavirus-black-lives-matter-surveillance/?utm_campaign=theintercept&utm_medium=social&utm_source=twitter; Zuboff, *The Age of Surveillance Capitalism: The Fight for a Human Future at the New Frontier of Power* (New York: Public Affairs, 2019).
28. Zuboff, "Surveillance in the Era of Pandemic and Protest."
29. See https://www.bloomberg.com/news/articles/2020-04-09/google-widens-lead-in-education-market-as-students-rush-online; https://www.forbes.com/sites/johanmoreno/2020/05/19/downloads-of-googles-zoom-killer-grew-900-since-march/?sh=2d0797fe2868.
30. See https://www.un.org/development/desa/dspd/wp-content/uploads/sites/22/2020/08/sg_policy_brief_covid-19_and_education_august_2020.pdf.
31. Zuboff, "Surveillance in the Era of Pandemic and Protest."
32. See https://www.nytimes.com/2020/02/20/technology/new-mexico-google-lawsuit.html.
33. See https://www.nytimes.com/2019/09/04/technology/google-youtube-fine-ftc.html; https://www.mediapost.com/publications/article/330620/google-urges-judge-to-toss-new-mexico-ags-suit-ov.html; https://www.cnn.com/2020/10/20/tech/doj-google-antitrust-case/index.html.
34. See https://www.washingtonpost.com/news/answer-sheet/wp/2013/03/13/lawsuit-charges-ed-department-with-violating-student-privacy-rights/.
35. Steve Martinot, "The Militarization of the Police," *Social Identities* 9(2) 2003: 217.
36. See https://www.vaccitech.co.uk/about/.

37. See https://medicinewomanscabinet.com/about; https://nypost.com/2020/09/04/pentagon-says-microsoft-won-10b-contract-over-amazon-fair-and-square/.
38. https://www.huffpost.com/entry/nypd-domain-awareness-surveillance-system-built-microsoft_n_1759976.
39. See https://kutv.com/news/local/beyond-the-books-people-who-regulate-charter-schools-also-make-millions-off-them?fbclid=IwAR2yvYrQlE7-EOYEEHlVWjjgIOzZEQiif7PwEPlxTE2S7OKSQRP0KseybaA; https://philanthropynewsdigest.org/news/gates-teacher-effectiveness-initiative-fell-short-study-finds; https://www.gatesnotes.com/2019-Annual-Letter; https://tultican.com/2018/06/27/iready-magnificent-marketing-terrible-teaching/; http://k12education.gatesfoundation.org/what-we-do/networks-for-school-improvement/.
40. See https://harvardpolitics.com/case-standardized-testing/; https://www.huffpost.com/entry/educating-for-democracy-s_1_b_915132; https://truthout.org/articles/the-anti-standardized-testing-movement-claims-a-victory-in-chicago/.
41. See https://www.ed.gov/oii-news/competency-based-learning-or-personalized-learning.
42. See Priscilla M. Regan and Valerie Steeves, "Education, Privacy, and Big Data Algorithms: Taking the Persons Out of Personalized Learning," *First Monday* 24(11), November 4, 2019, https://journals.uic.edu/ojs/index.php/fm/article/view/10094/8152.
43. See Michael W. Apple, *Knowledge, Power, and Education* (New York: Routledge, 2012); John Dewey, *Democracy and Education* (Gorham, ME: Myers Education Press, 2018); Paulo Freire, *Pedagogy of the Oppressed* (New York: Penguin, 2017); Henry A. Giroux, *Teachers as Intellectuals: Toward a Critical Pedagogy of Learning* (Westport, CT: Bergin & Garvey, 1988).
44. Jack Schneider and Jennifer Berkshire, *A Wolf at the Schoolhouse Door: The Dismantling of Public Education and the Future of School* (New York: New Press, 2020), as cited by Thomas Ultican, "Selling Edtech When Disguised as Philanthropy," *Tultican*, November 27, 2020, https://tultican.com/2020/11/27/selling-edtech-when-disguised-as-philanthropy/.

45. https://dianeravitch.net/2020/12/05/tom-ultican-when-tech-philanthropists-support-edtech-beware/.
46. See Jane M. Healy, *Failure to Connect: How Computers Affect Our Children's Minds—And What We Can Do About It* (New York: Simon & Schuster, 1999); Nicholas Kardaras, "Screens in Schools are a $60 Billion Hoax," *Time,* August 31, 2016, https://time.com/4474496/screens-schools-hoax/; Nicholas Kardaras, *Glow Kids: How Screen Addiction Is Hijacking Our Kids—And How to Break the Trance* (New York: St. Martin's, 2016).
47. See https://www.forbes.com/sites/dereknewton/2018/06/25/why-college-tuition-is-actually-higher-for-online-programs/?sh=2b374811f11a; https://sites.google.com/barrerakolb.net/positionpaperfromrank-andfilea/home.
48. For example, Michigan recently settled a federal class action lawsuit brought by Detroit students, acknowledging (1) the students' right to literacy and (2) the state's failure to provide basic minimal conditions for literacy acquisition for Detroit students due to a lack of books and teachers, and to dilapidated school buildings. See https://www.courthousenews.com/michigan-agrees-to-settle-detroit-literacy-rights-case/. We might expect subsequent courts to interpret this historic "right to literacy" in narrowly mechanistic ways, and we can also expect the state to attempt to fulfill its obligation by means of educational technology. On the other hand, activists and their legal support teams might strategize ways of using this decision to push back against "personalized learning" as wholly inadequate for producing literate citizens.
49. bell hooks, *Teaching to Transgress: Education as the Practice of Freedom* (New York: Routledge, 1994).
50. See *Ending the School-to-Prison Pipeline: Hearing before the subcommittee on Constitution, Civil Rights and Human Rights of the Committee on the Judiciary.* Senate. 112th Congress. (2012).
51. Damien M. Sojoyner, "Black Radicals Make for Bad Citizens: Undoing the Myth of the School to Prison Pipeline," *Berkeley Review of Education* 4(2) 2013: 241–263.
52. Sylvia Wynter, "On How We Mistook the Map for the Territory, and Re-Imprisoned Ourselves in Our Unbearable Wrongness of Being,

of *Desetre*: Black Studies Toward the Human Project," in Lewis R. Gordon and Jane Anna Gordon, eds., *Not Only the Master's Tools: African-American Studies in Theory and Practice* (Boulder: Paradigm, 2006), 107–172.
53. See generally, https://www.usmarshals.gov/assets/index.html; Mary Murphy, "Race and Civil Asset Forfeiture: A Disparate Impact Hypothesis," *Texas Journal on Civil Liberties and Civil Rights* 16(1) 2010: 77–100.
54. Frank B. Wilderson, III, *Red, White & Black: Cinema and the Structure of U.S. Antagonisms* (Durham: Duke, 2010), 127.
55. See Christian Parenti, *The Soft Cage: Surveillance in America from Slavery to the War on Terror* (New York: Basic, 2007).
56. See Simone Browne, *Dark Matters: On the Surveillance of Blackness* (Durham: Duke, 2015); Daina Ramey Berry, *The Price for Their Pound of Flesh: The Value of the Enslaved, from Womb to Grave, in the Building of a Nation* (Boston: Beacon, 2017); Rana Hogarth, *Medicalizing Blackness: Making Racial Difference in the Atlantic World, 1780–1840* (Chapel Hill: North Carolina, 2017).
57. Browne, "Digital Epidermalization: Race, Identity, and Biometrics," *Critical Sociology* 36(1) 2009: 134.
58. Browne, "Digital Epidermalization," 133.
59. See https://www.msn.com/en-us/news/world/us-military-officials-considered-using-heat-ray-at-dc-protest/ar-BB199p7G; https://time.com/5520558/artificial-intelligence-racial-gender-bias/; https://www.npr.org/sections/health-shots/2020/12/16/947226068/dark-skin-can-lead-to-errors-with-pulse-oximeters-used-in-covid-19-treatment.
60. Zuboff, "Surveillance in the Era of Pandemic and Protest."
61. Taylor, "Five Years Later," https://www.jofreeman.com/joreen/tyranny.htm; https://www.colorlines.com/articles/ella-taught-me-shattering-myth-leaderless-movement.

5

Evaluating COVID-19 Testing, Infection, Mortality, Treatment, and Vaccines

The police power of finance and technology is highly effective in both creating the conditions for public health policing and for defusing the community capacity to confront its disastrous charade. Attempts to confront health and wellness are undermined before they gain traction on the problems of communal well-being because of the control of thought in the social media age. As the foregoing chapters have endeavored to demonstrate, the police power is at work in all reaches of society; criminal justice is merely symptomatic of a more essential social disposition, but these connections are lost when it is reified as *the* policing problem. It is the police power of antiblackness in all of these diffused and socialized ways that creates the conditions of possibility for law and order in the first place. We now arrive, therefore, at the place where policing today hides itself in plain sight, squarely in the form of the one issue monopolizing everyone's attention during the Pandemic Year: COVID-19 and the police power of medical science. There are numerous ways into this problem, with direct connections both to the finance and technology industries, and to state power, with the politics of disease paralleling the pathologizing of crime. In fact, health care is four hugely profitable industries—insurance, instruments and drugs, doctors, and hospitals—and like all capitalist industries, they seek monopolistic control over markets. My approach to this medical industrial complex, however, will be as previously stated: to read the available evidence at the heart of medical science discourse. The teachings of civil rights leader Ella Baker are instructive here:

> In order for us as poor and oppressed people to become a part of a society that is meaningful, the system under which we now exist has to be radically changed. This means that we are going to have to learn to think in radical terms. I use the term radical in its original meaning—getting down to and understanding the root cause. It means facing a system that does not lend itself to your needs and devising means by which you change that system.[1]

The imperative to understand root causes is not in tension with addressing immediate needs. We can analyze how the structure itself is constituted without minimizing or neglecting its operational dynamics and the suffering it produces. This is especially vital in the time of pandemic when fear, sorrow, and despair in equal measures commingle to produce compliance, silence, and resentment in equally toxic doses. According to my reading of the evidence laid out below, the COVID-19 pandemic is not what it has been made out to be. The state's narrative on public health contorts reality in much the same way that it does with law and order. As we saw in the previous chapters, the state-corporate capture of abolitionist rhetoric presents a new wrinkle in an old dynamic—state power insulating itself against change by incorporating the challenges to it. Based on the widespread reticence to interrogate the paradigm of medical science, public health policing may present an even more challenging problem for abolitionism. Abolitionists have shown that law-and-order policies do not make communities safer; public health policies warrant similar abolitionist attention since they do not produce a public in good health. Both safety and health are socially produced, and the policy failures in these areas indict the various interconnected institutions and complex forces that impinge upon healthy lives. In examining the state's case for a COVID-19 pandemic, we will need to read the scientific studies in light of the analysis of state power and antiblackness established in the preceding chapters.

Is There a Pandemic?

Given that what gets recognized as "truth" is a reflection of power relations and is *not* a gauge of whether something is true or not, nothing can be taken for granted; all received knowledge must be cross-examined.[2] To verify if there is in fact a pandemic—and if so, of what nature—we should interrogate the science subtending four key issues: testing, infection, treatment and prevention, and mortality. Since the known scope of COVID-19 as a public health crisis rests on the authority of test results, the Polymerase Chain Reaction (PCR) test sits at the crux of our problems. The PCR test was invented by Kary Mullis in 1985, for which he was awarded the 1993 Nobel Prize in chemistry. The test swiftly and selectively multiplies, isolates, and mass-produces specific DNA segments. Mullis' invention has enabled a range of scientific inquiry, from detecting hereditary cancers in fetuses, to criminal forensics, to retracing the evolutionary chain itself. For instance, an American soldier in Vietnam was identified more than a generation later by pairing DNA from a lock of his baby hair with a single bone found on the battlefield.[3] The Innocence Project and other legal teams that work to overturn wrongful convictions based on DNA evidence owe their very existence to the PCR test.[4] The PCR test was *not* designed, however, for diagnostic purposes because it measures fractal presence of virus DNA, amplifying fragments that may be present as a result of the immune system having confronted and cleared the virus, or *any* virus that shares DNA with COVID-19 including a panoply of corona and influenza viruses, at any time in the past. Using PCR to diagnose viral infection is analogous to using a highly sensitive breathalyzer test to measure drunk driving. If a breathalyzer were calibrated to levels of sensitivity higher than the legal limit, it might detect the residual presence of alcohol from some point in the past, but without any accuracy as to when the substance was in the body, nor in amounts significant enough to result in impairment. Likewise, when PCR is used to diagnose COVID-19, what it detects does not necessarily equate to illness. Something similar happened when PCR was first applied to HIV research, around 1989. Scientists were suddenly able to see viral particles in quantities they could not see previously. As science journalist Celia Farber noted in her 1994 interview with Mullis:

> Scientific articles poured forth stating that HIV was now 100 times more prevalent than was previously thought. But Mullis himself was unimpressed. "PCR made it easier to see that certain people were infected with HIV," he told Spin in 1992, "and some of those people came down with symptoms of AIDS. But that doesn't begin even to answer the question, 'Does HIV cause it?'".[5]

Noting, as well, that many patients diagnosed with AIDS do not have HIV in their systems, or only a miniscule presence, Mullis would join numerous other prominent scientists in questioning the prevailing medical science discourse on AIDS.

In addition to its own creator's objections to using PCR for diagnosing illness, the CDC itself has acknowledged that the test is not suitable for this purpose. The CDC's instruction manual for administering the PCR Diagnostic Panel features a Limitations section in which it notes the following:

- Detection of viral RNA may not indicate the presence of infectious virus or that 2019-nCoV is the causative agent for clinical symptoms.
- The performance of this test has not been established for monitoring treatment of 2019-nCoV infection.
- The performance of this test has not been established for screening of blood or blood products for the presence of 2019-nCoV.
- This test cannot rule out diseases caused by other bacterial or viral pathogens.[6]

When the test limitations undercut the purpose for administering the test in the first place—to detect the presence of infectious virus and to establish the cause of any clinical symptoms—the efficacy of the test appears nullified. The same manual also includes a section on Performance Characteristics, featuring the following statement:

> Since no quantified virus isolates of the 2019-nCoV were available for CDC use at the time the test was developed and this study conducted, assays designed for detection of the 2019-nCoV RNA were tested with characterized stocks of in vitro transcribed full-length RNA (N gene; GenBank accession: MN908947.2) of known titer (RNA copies/μL) spiked into a diluent consisting of a suspension of human A549 cells and viral transport medium (VTM) to mimic clinical specimen.[7]

The key phrasing here is "since no quantified virus isolates ... were available" in December 2020 when this document was published. Every object that exists can be quantified or measured. Medical science must isolate a specimen of the virus in order for it to be identified and verified as existing. Without first extracting, purifying (separating the pathogen from everything else), and isolating the virus, diagnostic tools and vaccines cannot be created with any accuracy. Since the CDC has not isolated a virus specimen, it presents PCR as a diagnostic tool for finding RNA which it merely *presumes* to come from a virus which it has not yet confirmed in the laboratory. Needless to say, science is not supposed to be based on assumptions.

We face no less than six ramifications of using PCR to test for COVID-19. First, with no actual COVID-19 virus isolated in the laboratory, PCR cannot confirm that what it says it finds is in fact the virus. Moreover, PCR cannot reliably ascertain the presence of *active* virus in the body. A positive test result may refer to detected RNA fragments from earlier viral exposure or from a related virus. The sensitivity of PCR is set by cycle thresholds. At a cycle threshold of 25, 70 percent of PCR "positives" are not "cases" because the virus cannot be cultured.[8] If the virus cannot be cultured in the laboratory, then it is dead, and there is no risk of contagion. Most PCR testing for COVID-19, however, is done at cycle thresholds greater than 30, which means the percentage of dead virus can be as high as 90 percent, with the likelihood of a false positive even greater than at lower cycle thresholds.

Second, as a result of the reliance on PCR, the public health establishment has created a scenario whereby it grossly over exaggerates the problem at hand. One researcher has estimated that PCR establishes a benchmark that is between ten and 20 times the actual prevalence of the disease.[9] Third, medical science has abandoned the established clinical basis for establishing a medical "case" that has been in practice since the time of Hippocrates in ancient Greece. A medical case has always been defined in relation to the presence of illness: signs (that which a medical professional recognizes) and symptoms (that which the patient also recognizes). The CDC specifies that a case definition should be no less than a set of standard criteria for classifying whether a person has a certain disease, syndrome, or other health condition.[10] There is great variance internationally, including between the World Health Organization (WHO) and its member nations, as to the clinical features of COVID-19, but in every instance a positive laboratory test trumps clinical diagnosis. At best, we have a problematic conflation between a clinical case definition applied to an individual presenting for health care, and a surveillance definition used to collect information for epidemiological purposes.[11] Fourth, the use of PCR to override or displace clinical diagnosis not only means that we have disconnected a medical "case" from actual illness but it also marks the complete shift into biotech-driven medicine or laboratory result medicine. This development has been underway for quite some time, but COVID-19 marks biotech's saturation point. The dramatic difference between biotech medicine and clinical medicine can be described thusly:

> "You have to have a whopping amount of any organism to cause symptoms. Huge amounts of it," Dr. David Rasnick, bio-chemist, protease developer, and former founder of an EM lab called Viral Forensics told me. "You don't start with testing; you start with listening to the lungs. I'm skeptical that a PCR test is ever true. It's a great scientific research tool. It's a horrible tool for clinical medicine. 30% of your infected cells have been killed before you show symptoms. By the time you show symptoms … the dead cells are *generating* the symptoms."[12]

The PCR may be good enough to confirm a clinical diagnosis of a patient with symptoms. It is not up to the task, however, that is currently being asked of it, namely, to estimate the number of infectious people currently in the community.[13]

The fifth problem arising from reliance on PCR is that if it can produce a COVID-19 "case" without virus or illness, then we are seeing COVID-19 "deaths" declared without causation because the test does not verify the presence of virus. The COVID Tracking Project uses algorithmic modeling to turn PCR-based data into a statistical portrait of the pandemic. The entire liberal spectrum of media distribution is using the same data source platform, licensed by *The Atlantic* Foundation and supported by the Gates, Bloomberg, and Zuckerberg foundations.[14] This means most of the mainstream media is reproducing the same information based on the same unsound PCR foundation. This skewed information acts as "common sense" about the virus, and any dissenting knowledge is vigorously "fact-checked" and "proven" wrong. The PCR test situation, however, suggests that we do *not* have a viral pandemic, but rather a public health situation of another order produced by the medical industrial complex.

The sixth issue with the PCR test is perhaps the most consequential of them all. Even more serious than the exaggerated statistical portrait of the pandemic that PCR enables is the problem with how the PCR test for COVID-19 signals the subordination of the scientific method to the political agenda of the medical industrial complex. The most commonly used test, the RT-PCR, was created as a result of the publication of instructions for how to test for SARS-CoV-2 "without having virus material available," as the authors put it, and instead using the Chinese scientists' genetic sequence published on the Internet.[15] The paper was published by a team of German scientists *twenty-four hours* after submission to *Eurosurveillance*, thus evading peer review, but was quickly accepted as the worldwide testing standard when it was adopted by WHO. In late November 2020, an international group of 22 scientists published a critique of the *Eurosurveillance* study, identifying ten "fatal" empirical and methodological errors.[16] The *Eurosurveillance* study was published long before COVID-19 had even shown up in Europe, and the review paper shows how without actual virus isolated from a patient the "viral morphology" of the test is an artifice, a construct of laboratory science. One of the authors of the review paper offered the following analogy:

> In the fish market, it's like giving you a few bones and saying that's your fish. It could be any fish. Not even a skeleton. Here's a few fragments of bones. That's your fish. Listen, the Corman/Drosten paper, there's nothing from a patient in it. It's all from gene banks. and the bits of the virus sequence that weren't there they made up. They synthetically created them to fill in the blanks. That's what genetics is; it's a code. So its ABBBCCDDD and you're missing some what you think is EEE so you put it in. It's all synthetic. You just manufacture the bits that are missing. This is the end result of the geneticization of virology. This is basically a computer virus.[17]

This loose and artificial construct for viral morphology directly leads to the high false positive test results—which, in turn, have been used to conjure the misleading notion of "asymptomatic transmission." The entire premise for the pandemic crumbles when the faulty foundation of the PCR test is revealed for what it is.

Integrating a variety of data points strongly suggests that the COVID-19 virus is unremarkable in its evolution and spread throughout the human population. Research studies have now established that at least 30 percent of our population already had immunological recognition of this new virus *before* it even arrived.[18] In other words, COVID-19 may be new, but coronaviruses are not, with at least four well-characterized family members which are endemic and cause some of the common colds we experience.[19] Cross-immunity in this case, then, means that our immune systems memorize pieces of whatever virus we are exposed to so the right cell types can multiply and protect us if we get a related infection. This immune response to COVID-19 has been shown in dozens of blood samples taken from donors *prior to* the arrival of the new virus.[20] Similar findings from Germany, Sweden, and the U.S. confirm that this pre-immunity is geographically widespread and prevalent within each population studied.[21] The existence of this cellular memory is why the maintenance of antibodies to every pathogen to which we have been exposed is unnecessary for an effective immune response. The virus thus moves through the population as viruses have always done, affecting the most susceptible harshly and leaving the rest unaffected or recovered. This is also why it does not seem to matter much what kinds of public health protocols are implemented (such as lockdowns, school closures, social distancing, mask-wearing, and so forth), countries, states, and regions with different policies return the same data profile—suggesting that claims of virus variants, spikes, or second waves are likely artifacts of increased PCR testing.[22] Scientists have explained, moreover, why it is that children appear to be the least affected by the virus. In order to do us harm, viruses need to penetrate into our cells; and to do that, they have to utilize receptors on the outside of those cells. In the case of COVID-19, the key receptor is an enzyme called ACE2. It turns out that the levels of ACE2 are highest in adults and much lower in children, with the levels becoming progressively lower in the younger the child.[23] This is why it is highly unlikely for children to be vectors for disease, despite the paranoia, fearmongering, and scapegoating of young people putting their more vulnerable elders at risk—and why it would be unadvisable to vaccinate children against COVID-19 (when such a vaccine is approved for children under 12 years, which it will eventually). The important point here is to reiterate that infection does not mean illness, it simply means the beginning of an immune response (and, in fact, the immune system includes multiple preemptive barriers like skin, mucous, and the gut that work to prevent an antigen from even getting to the internal organs and tissues where infection can occur).

All of which points to the fallacy of asymptomatic transmission. It has been a long-standing tenet of infectious disease that the presence of clinical symptoms indicates when a patient is infected by a live virus and may pose a risk of transmission to other people. The converse—no symptoms = no live virus = no transmission risk—has long informed the basic common sense that you need to stay home from work or school only when you feel unwell so as not to spread whatever affliction you may be coming down with. This is why, pre-COVID-19, we never quarantined the healthy, and why face masks have only ever been recommended for sick people *alone*. With COVID-19, however, we have been told that even if you are not sick and have no symptoms, you could still have the disease and spread it to people who could get sick and die. The idea of asymptomatic transmission began to appear in the media in March 2020, trailed off for a few months, and then spiked up across all media platforms in June 2020, after months of lockdowns and economic shutdowns had taken their toll with no appreciable positive impact on the pandemic.[24] On June 7, 2020, WHO informed us that according to all known research up to that point in time, asymptomatic spread was "very rare."[25] WHO quickly succumbed to political pressure, asserting that "much is still unknown."[26] A COVID-19 screening study conducted in Wuhan, however, has given us the latest scientific confirmation that asymptomatic spread is largely a myth. The study was conducted after lockdown restrictions were lifted in summer 2020 and involved almost ten million city residents. From the original hotspot of the pandemic, the study *did not uncover one single incidence* of asymptomatic transmission.[27]

But what about illness? COVID-19 has indeed made many thousands of people very sick and a portion of those people have succumbed to their illness. The infection mortality rate (IMR) measures the rate at which people who are infected end up dying. The most reliable study of IMR (because it relied upon serology rather than simply PCR test results) was published by WHO in October 2020. By assessing serological data from across the world, this study estimates that the IMR ranged between 0 and 1.63 percent, with a median figure of 0.27 percent. The big range in mortality is affected by a variety of local factors including age profile, treatments, different methods of recording deaths, and pre-existing immune defenses. The study notes that the data was heavily skewed toward locations with much higher IMR than the global average, warning that "most locations probably have an infection fatality rate less than 0.20 percent and with appropriate, precise non-pharmacological measures that selectively try to protect high-risk vulnerable populations and settings, the infection fatality rate may be brought even lower."[28] Moreover, the study shows that this disease "has a very steep age gradient for risk of death," with the median IMR for the under-70 age group coming out at only 0.05 percent.[29] How does the IMR for COVID-19 compare with the annual death rates for influenza? The latest CDC figures from the 2016 to 2017 influenza season in the United States show an IMR of between 0.1 and 0.2 percent.[30] In short, COVID-19 is definitely dangerous for people over 70 years old. For everyone else, it is proving to be on par with the seasonal flu.[31] By comparison, the top infectious disease killer is tuberculosis. WHO reports that ten million people fell ill with TB in 2018, with a mortality rate of three percent—figures that dwarf COVID-19 in every way, but with no commensurate public outcry or public health mobilization, let alone attempts to shut down schools and economic activity.[32]

Getting an accurate aggregate portrait of how COVID-19 illnesses are being treated is difficult. Despite the obsessive focus on vaccination as the only viable solution to COVID-19, numerous effective and cost-efficient treatments are available, backed up by both scientific studies and emergent clinical evidence.[33] With the understanding that specific patient care protocols are case contingent, I simply list here some of the treatment options discussed in the scientific literature, including azithromycin, bromhexine, heparin, intravenous ascorbic acid (quercetin and vitamin C), ivermectin, nitric oxide nasal spray, thiamine, vitamin D, steroids, and zinc, among others.[34] One of the most salient treatment issues for our investigation here of the pandemic police power is hydroxychloroquine (HCQ). Dr. Anthony Fauci, Director of the National Institutes of Allergy and Infectious Diseases (NIAID), told the nation in May 2020 that HCQ was not effective in treating COVID-19, while some European nations moved to ban its use altogether.[35] At the same time, Trump was touting the drug's effectiveness, saying that he used it successfully to treat his infection.[36] The official opposition of most Western governments to treating COVID-19 with HCQ is curious given the drug's long-standing use (it has been approved by the FDA and in widespread use worldwide since the 1950s) as an effective and cost-efficient treatment for a range of both autoimmune diseases and viral infections that impact the upper respiratory system. In 2005, for instance, a study funded by Fauci's NIAID found the drug to be a "potent inhibitor of SARS coronavirus infection and spread," and findings from 2020 show fewer hospitalizations for patients treated with HCQ.[37]

Despite this proven track record, there appears to be a concerted effort to dissuade use of the treatment. Two scientific articles were hurriedly published claiming that HCQ does not work in treating COVID-19—only to be swiftly retracted when the studies were subsequently shown to be erroneous.[38] Nevertheless, the fact that the fallacious studies were published in the world's two most prominent medical science journals, *The New England Journal of Medicine* and *The Lancet*, garnering extensive media attention, combined with the schizoid Janus Head leadership from the U.S. government, seems to outweigh the preponderance of scientific findings showing that HCQ does work. Needless to say, the media hardly covered the studies' retraction, the fraudulent research methods employed, and the scandalous rush to publication by the two leading scientific literature outlets. Then in January 2021, right after the U.S. presidential election of Joe Biden, the *American Journal of Medicine* recommended HCQ, along with azithromycin and zinc, for the treatment of COVID-19.[39] HCQ is merely one among a whole host of effective and inexpensive treatment options, but the way it has been suppressed illustrates how basic medical care is being impacted by the many political interests entangled in the medical industrial complex.

The way ivermectin has been handled by the public health establishment also illustrates how patient treatment is compromised by the medical industrial complex. Dr. Pierre Kory, one of the physician founders of the Front-Line COVID-19 Critical Care Alliance of experienced clinicians, testified before Congress on two occasions during 2020 regarding the efficacy of ivermectin. In addition to reviewing the clinical and research evidence demonstrating the excellent results doctors have obtained treating COVID-19 patients with ivermectin, Dr. Kory reminded Congress that discovery of the drug was awarded the Nobel Prize in medicine in 2015, only the first time the Nobel Committee had recognized advances in infectious disease control in over a half-century.[40] The Nobel Committee saluted ivermectin because it dramatically changed the treatment of infectious diseases throughout the Global South. For decades, some 250 million people annually have been taking ivermectin successfully to ward off a broad spectrum of diseases common throughout the Global South, from parasites to malaria, sleeping sickness, asthma, epilepsy, RNA viruses like Zika, dengue, yellow fever, West Nile, and HIV.[41] In other words, ivermectin directly addresses the disease profiles typical of formerly colonized societies that have been unable to correct the infrastructure depletion caused by over a century of imperial forms of extraction. In the absence of reliably safe drinking water, sanitation, housing, and nutrition, ivermectin fulfills a critical stop-gap measure by mitigating the harmful effects of this colonial legacy.

Dr. Kory suggests that ivermectin can have a similarly game-changing impact on the treatment of COVID-19, and the preponderance of evidence from around the world that he entered into the Congressional record during his testimony on December 8, 2020 backs up his optimism.[42] It is nothing short of scandalous censorship and medical malpractice, therefore, that public health officials have slandered Dr. Kory, the FLCCC, and ivermectin itself. The inadvertent overdoses due to incorrect dosages would have been easily prevented if the drug therapy were not heavily censored.[43] The censorship of ivermectin especially aims to undermine health care throughout the Global South, and connects to the long-standing eugenicist practices by Western medical science in Asia and Africa, as the following chapter examines more closely.[44] It is clear that the viability of treatments for COVID-19 like HCQ and ivermectin thwart the medical industrial complex's agenda. The presence of these therapies undermines the basis for emergency use authorization for the COVID-19 shots and for mandatory vaccination; it also means that the pharmaceutical companies' new upcoming anti-viral drugs for COVID-19 will have to compete with far more cost-effective options like HCQ and ivermectin. Merck, the company whose former patent on ivermectin has expired, recently announced the development of a new anti-viral drug for COVID-19 treatment.[45] Due to the mass censorship from the medical industrial complex, there are websites tracking scientific research studies worldwide that document the effectiveness of COVID-19 treatments like HCQ, ivermectin, and vitamin D.[46]

The primary method promoted for preventing COVID-19 transmission, face masks, is another example of how the pandemic police power flaunts scientific reason. In many places, it is perfunctory to have to wear masks whenever you are in public or around anyone outside of your family. Some people even wear masks when alone in their own cars. In other places, masks are relatively uncommon. While many people have taken to heart the messaging that masks prevent transmission of the virus, many other people wear masks simply because of the social pressures to do so. Mask-wearing is the perfect example of how science takes a backseat to politics and cultural constructs in the COVID-19 response.[47] At different points in the Pandemic Year, Fauci, then U.S. Surgeon General Dr. Jerome Adams, the White House Coronavirus Task Force, WHO, the CDC, and the *Journal of the American Medical Association* all urged healthy people to *not* wear masks; and the messaging was rarely consistent, with Fauci later advocating mask-wearing for all, while the CDC and WHO were still saying masks only for sick people and their caretakers.[48] Through it all, science has never changed. It is becoming more widely known that the masks most people are wearing are ineffective in preventing viral transmission, for the simple fact that the virus particles are so small that they easily go through and around the masks. Coronaviruses and influenza viruses are approximately 0.12 microns, while even the heavy-duty medical N-95 masks are only tested effective to 0.3 microns. While there remains debate as to whether the virus size is the only factor that matters, this debate is largely fueled by opinions, not by research findings.[49] As for the scientific data, a review of the research literature, including 17 of the best studies, found that "None of the studies established a conclusive relationship between masks/respirator use and protection against influenza infection."[50] Additional studies corroborate this finding, confirming that hygiene, face masks, and respirators are ineffective in protecting against common cold viruses, influenza, and COVID-19.[51] Absent a sound scientific basis, then, it would appear that mask mandates are naked social control measures that fuel paranoia and social disconnection.

The data reviewed here shows that the COVID-19 pandemic is not what it has been made out to be. If COVID-19 illness has been grossly overestimated due to the fallacies of PCR testing; if a significant percentage of the population already has natural immunological recognition of the virus; if the virus is no more dangerous a health risk than annual influenza, with 99.95 percent of infected people surviving; and if numerous effective and low-cost treatment options exist, then why is there a need for vaccination?

Why or Why Not Vaccines?

Based on the analysis in the preceding section, the pandemic lockdowns have nothing to do with public health needs. Lockdowns themselves are incredibly immune suppressive for a whole host of reasons, not the least of which are the toxic effects of stress, hunger, isolation, fear, inactivity, homelessness, poverty, and anxiety. People with co-morbidities, those deemed most vulnerable to the virus, are harmed the most by these lockdown toxicities. The promotion of vaccination as the solution to the pandemic, and thus the means by which the poison of lockdown will be ended, is therefore a fraught and multi-layered problem central to how the pandemic police power works. No topic is perhaps more convoluted politically, with anti-vaccination positions more commonly associated with the so-called Right's anti-big government skepticism (at least regarding social policy as opposed to financial or foreign policy), while the so-called Left promotes vaccination as vital to public health and smears its critics as "conspiracy theorists" or "anti-vaxxers."[52] Since the arrival of COVID-19, however, room for critical thought on vaccines appears to have shrunk even further. For instance, the socialist organization Science for the People's position on COVID-19 vaccines amounts to: we need them, and they should be available to all free of charge.[53] For a group with origins in the radical anti-war movement of the 1960s that sought to contest the military industrial complex's control over scientific inquiry, #FreeTheVaccine is a shockingly shallow position to take on one of the most salient issues in contemporary science.[54]

The polarity of vaccine discourse, of course, is wholly unproductive—but then that is precisely the point of the pandemic police power. State power loves a dichotomy because it divides people and facilitates social control. In the interest of busting up dichotomous thinking and establishing the case for vaccine mandates as unconstitutional, I explore three questions about vaccines that have been largely swept aside in the current pandemic climate. First, what is a vaccine and how does it work? Of particular importance here is the role of zoonotic diseases, xenotransplantation and chimeric research, and retroviruses in vaccine production. Secondly, the development of vaccines leads immediately into the question of what kind of medical and public health model relies on vaccination to solve health problems? Like everything else in medical science these days, vaccines are lucrative features of the medical industrial complex, and as such, arise at a particular historical moment as an expression of the relations of power seeking to shape the social order. Subtending the production of vaccines, then, is a confrontation between Western culture's attempt to manipulate nature to control humankind's interaction with some of the viruses and bacteria that share our world. Third, what is a COVID-19 injection and what unique challenges does this new form of vaccination present to immunological health?

Western science's notion that germs are enemies to be fought at all costs led to the concept of a "germ-free" body, with an immune system that functions to repulse invading microbes through effective immune reactions. In part, vaccines are the product of this way of thinking. Over the years, science learned what the ancients already knew, that the notion of "germ-free" is both erroneous *and* harmful to our health. Moreover, a healthy host does not always fight germs but instead lives symbiotically with many of them.[55] The concept of symbiosis between host and microbes was first accepted for bacteria (the "microbiome") and more recently has been applied to viruses as well (the "virome").[56] The body is thus a medium for microbes to maintain themselves, but more to the point, these germs also shape our physiology, especially the immune system.[57]

> In a healthy human body, microbes live in a dynamic equilibrium with the host []. Each new invading microbe—in particular, a virus (or viruses) —resets this balance in an attempt to create favorable conditions for its own existence, leading to beneficial or detrimental conditions for other microbes. In response to some invading microbes, however, the host fails to reset this equilibrium, and such microbes become pathogens. From this perspective, the difference between "symbiotic" and "pathogenic" microbes is related to their ability to establish a new equilibrium with the host rather than to inherited "pathogenic" or "nonpathogenic" features. For a particular microbe, this ability may also depend on the body compartment. Nevertheless, some microbes are never capable of establishing such an equilibrium and are invariably harmful, whereas others are harmless under most conditions. Because the establishment of such an equilibrium is evolutionarily beneficial, human pathogens often become less pathogenic with time.[58]

The corona and influenza viruses are naturally occurring organisms that have coexisted with humans for millennia. The fact of co-existence tells us that these particular viruses are not killers because they need humans to survive; they have developed in a way that they do not kill their hosts. Exposure to such viruses, in fact, enhances the chances of human survival by strengthening our immune responses to the environment. It is not a parasitic situation. On the contrary, there is a dialectical relationship between viruses and the human immune system, with each developing through its interaction with the other.

In theory, a vaccine can be prophylactic to maintain equilibrium in the body's virome and to mitigate viral spread throughout a community. In practice, however, a vaccine disrupts the natural occurring symbiotic system in two ways. First, vaccination itself is a challenge to the immune system because it introduces a weakened version of the virus, or its blueprint, into the body. The problem is that the vaccine enables the virus to bypass some of the normal protective features of the body's immune system. The equilibrium is disrupted as the body reacts to the vaccine, but without its full complement of resources; and if the vaccine introduces multiple viruses at once, the disequilibrium is compounded. More to the point, since vaccination is *not* the same thing as viral infection, it does not produce a natural immune response. The vaccine compels the body to reset the balance with its virome, but in so doing, detrimental conditions are created for other microbes that were previously in equilibrium with the host environment. In other words, viruses, bacteria, or toxins that were not a problem to the body prior to the vaccine may become a problem after vaccination due to the uncontrolled replication of previously symbiotic microbes. Immunologists analogize the immune system in this situation to an orchestra without its conductor. The conductor is not one entity that serves as the operator of the system; rather, the conductor is the dynamic between the body and its natural exposure to the environment, which includes viruses. When this natural dynamism is interrupted—when the orchestra loses its conductor—the music continues, but it will be off-key and out of sync or the wrong melody: "the immune system continues to play out a chaotic and ineffective attack against microbes."[59]

Researchers are only beginning to understand the differences between a vaccine-boosted immune system and naturally acquired immunities. It is clear, however, that not only do natural exposures produce life-long immunity, unlike the short-lived boost of a vaccine, but it also tunes the system to make it less vulnerable to health problems down the road, whereas the vaccinated system continues down an out-of-tune pathway with its inevitable associated health issues. We are now seeing how these basic precepts of the human immune system play out with COVID-19. In late 2021, data is emerging confirming that natural acquired immunities are stronger than vaccinated immunity. A study of healthcare workers by the Cleveland Clinic showed that not one of the previously infected and unvaccinated workers got reinfected by the Delta variant, leading researchers to conclude that persons with naturally acquired immunities to COVID-19 are unlikely to benefit from vaccination.[60] We are also seeing that the death rate from the Delta variant is significantly higher for vaccinated persons than it is for unvaccinated people. Early data out of England in August 2021 shows that vaccinated persons died from COVID-19 infection at five times the rate of unvaccinated people.[61] While the key variable here is the COVID shot itself, which as we will see below could be a significant debilitating factor, this evidence clearly supports what we already know about the importance of acquired immunities compared with vaccinated immunity. The England data also conforms to the statistical profile from Israel on "breakthrough" infections, where the most vaccinated populace on the planet is also experiencing a surge in new cases that outpaces the rate of infection from 2020.[62] The best protection from the Delta variant, in other words, and from all subsequent seasonal variants of COVID-19 that we are likely to see appearing in coming years, is natural environmental exposure rather than vaccination.

The second way vaccines disrupt the body's equilibrium is because of what they contain. All vaccines introduce elements that would not otherwise be entering the human body. A recent inquiry in December 2018 by the Italian laboratory Corvela on the GlaxoSmithKline vaccine Priorix Terta enumerated the various ingredients.

We continued the investigation, both chemical and biological, on the Priorix Tetra, quadrivalent against measles, rubella, mumps and varicella . . . we have found . . .Proteobacteria, Platyhelminthes worms and Nematoda, 10 more ssRNA viruses, Microviridae (bacterial viruses or phage) and numerous retroviruses including endogenous human and avian retroviruses, avian viruses, human immunodeficiency virus and immunodeficiency virus of monkey (if inserted into the database turn out to be fragments of HIV and SIV), murine virus, horse infectious anemia virus, lymphoproliferative disease virus, Rous sarcoma virus . . . alphaendornavirus, hepatitis b virus, yeast virus.[63]

To this list, we can add the various metals, toxins, and chemical preservatives and adjuvants (elements designed to prime the immune response) that have been proven to be harmful.[64] To weaken a virus so that a human will produce an effective immune response to protect the host rather than injure or kill the host requires passing the virus isolate repeatedly through animal tissue in the laboratory until it becomes tolerable. When viruses cross species, their genetic structure undergoes changes that can make them either more benign or more lethal. The problem is that in trying to conquer one disease, research scientists may inadvertently create another. Scientists became aware of this potential problem as early as the 1950s. At the time, the yellow fever vaccine had been in use for over a decade and the polio vaccine was still in development. A Rockefeller Institute researcher investigating efforts to lower the virulence of the yellow fever vaccine made a presentation to WHO in 1953 in which he noted the following:

> [T]wo main objections to this vaccine have been voiced, because of the possibility that: (i) the mouse brains employed in its preparation may be contaminated with a virus pathogenic for man although latent in mice … or may be the cause of demyelinating encephalomyelitis; (ii) the use, as antigen, of a virus with enhanced neurotropic properties may be followed by serious reactions involving the central nervous system[.][65]

Every species has its own virome, and in animals like mice, monkeys, and humans—the most commonly interacting species in the laboratory environment—viruses ensconce themselves into tissues. When these tissues (mouse brain tissue, in the case of the early yellow fever virus above) are used to create vaccines, viruses extant in the tissues also enter the vaccine. The Rockefeller scientist noted that although the virus existed in equilibrium with mice, it can produce disease and autoimmune dysfunction in humans. Demyelinating encephalomyelitis is the degradation of the myelin sheaths which coat neurons, leading to brain and spinal cord inflammation. Multiple sclerosis is the most common manifestation of encephalomyelitis, but myelitis is also linked to autism spectrum disorder.[66] The Oxford-AstraZeneca COVID-19 vaccine trial was twice halted because trial subjects developed the serious side effect of transverse myelitis, featuring inflammation on both sides of the spinal cord that potentially causes paralysis.[67] Moreover, the Rockefeller scientist noted the possibility that the vaccine, precisely because of the compounded viral load it contains, might make the body overreact, provoking autoimmune disease in which the body attacks not an invader, but rather turns on itself.[68]

Vaccine development continued undeterred, however, with the polio vaccine becoming the most prominent and prolific disseminator of animal viruses. The science is still unfolding in this area, probably disincentivized by the considerable financial and political weight behind vaccination, but there is enough evidence to point to connections between vaccinations and myalgic encephalomyelitis (ME), more commonly mis-labeled as "chronic fatigue syndrome," the emergence of "stealth adapted viruses," HIV, autism, and cancer.[69] The known cause of ME is xenotropic murine retrovirus (XMRV). Xenotropic refers to the replication of cells in tissue of an organism other than its normal host—such as in the production of vaccines wherein murine (mouse) tissues are introduced into humans. A retrovirus is a virus that evades the immune system and lodges itself into the body's tissues. When the immune system is activated at some later point—as a result of vaccination, for instance—the retrovirus is activated, either sending the immune system into overdrive, as in ME, or suppressing its functioning, as with HIV. Since XMRV is known to be the result of viral transmission from mouse to human, and humans and mice have coexisted for thousands of years without direct transmission, it seems most likely that it is the result of laboratory-created biological products, which has only occurred since the 1930s and the steady expansion of Western medicine's vaccination program in the late twentieth and early twenty-first centuries.[70] Between 1989 and 2008, every known outbreak of Ebola virus was connected to laboratories experimenting with monkeys.[71] Similarly, HIV is known to be derived from SIV, simian immunodeficiency virus, and is usually attributed to Africans hunting and eating chimpanzees, combined with African promiscuity and bestiality. The classic antiblack racism of this colonial discourse remains largely taken for granted to this day.[72] The more likely explanation of the jump from monkeys to humans came during the polio vaccine campaigns in the Belgian-controlled Congo from 1957 to 1960 in which more than 500 chimpanzees and bonobos (pygmy chimpanzees) were slaughtered to harvest their kidney cells and sera to grow the oral polio vaccine.[73]

Much of this information is not widely known by the public that must make regular decisions about whether to vaccinate or not. The polarity of the vaccine debate largely devolves into its connection to autism. The 2008 Nobel Prize winner for his discovery of HIV, Luc Montagnier has noted, "Many parents have observed a *temporal* association, which does not mean causation, between a vaccination and the appearance of autism symptoms." "Presumably," he continues, "vaccination, especially against multiple antigens, could be a trigger of a pre-existing pathological situation in some children."[74] Given the ubiquity of xenotropic viruses, retroviruses, and numerous other toxins introduced into humans via vaccination, autism need not be directly caused by a vaccine jab in order for it to be causally connected. For some children who develop autism, the immune challenge of vaccination could have activated a retrovirus from hiding; for others, it could have been activated by a fever; a similar immune challenge to the mother during pregnancy could have also stimulated a retrovirus to rampage and affect the child from birth.[75]

The problem with vaccines, in sum, is the problem of xenotransplantation, the transplantation of living cells from one organism to another. The result of xenotransplantation is a chimera, named after the Greek mythological hybrid monster usually depicted as a lion with the head of a goat protruding from its back and a snake for a tail. Vaccines are chimeras, and as the non-human RNA combines with human DNA, vaccines produce human chimeras. As we will see momentarily, the

COVID-19 vaccines are certainly chimeras in that they rely entirely on biotechnology to approximate virus RNA, since there is no virus isolate available.[76] The dangers of xenotransplantation have been widely shared within the medical research community, to little effect.[77] In fact, the state drives chimeric research through the public health establishment's opaque relationship to the Defense Department, illuminating a key backstory for COVID-19. The Army's premier biological laboratory at Ft. Detrick, MD has been at the heart of the U.S. bioweapons program from 1943 to 1969 and is now the center of its "biodefense" program. Central to so-called biodefense is "gain-of-function" research, where scientists attempt to increase the virulence, ease of spread, or host range of dangerous pathogens. Safety concerns led the CDC to close gain-of-function research on anthrax and influenza at Ft. Detrick and its Atlanta laboratories twice in the past seven years after accidents.[78] Indeed, it was Ft. Detrick that supplied virus samples for a NIAID-funded study, under Fauci's direction, of bat coronaviruses. The research team included U.S.-based scientists and researchers from the Wuhan Institute of Virology in China, and in both 2013 and 2015, it announced its success in creating a chimeric virus, a hybrid microorganism based on a bat coronavirus and an adapted SARS virus, that proved capable of infecting human cells.[79] This record of U.S.-China collaboration in bioengineering with coronaviruses, combined with the conveniently unavailable COVID-19 isolate, raises as yet unanswerable questions as to what the COVID-19 virus really is.[80] But in the least, it exposes the duplicity of the public health establishment. What does it mean that Fauci oversaw the gain-of-function research that allowed the corona virus to jump from bats to humans—and now oversees the development and dissemination of its vaccine?

In the wake of the COVID-19 pandemic, there should be a moratorium on all "gain-of-function" research, at minimum. When the Bush Administration's torture regime in Abu Ghraib, Guantanamo, and other unnamed CIA-operated black sites came to light, there was intense pressure put on the lawyers and psychologists who played critical roles in legitimating torture. Deputy Assistant Attorney General John Yoo, Assistant Attorney General Jay Bybee, and Acting Assistant Attorney General for the Office of Legal Counsel Steven Bradbury, supported by

White House Counsel Alberto Gonzales, authored the notorious "torture memos" used to bypass both international treaty prohibiting torture and federal anti-torture law to create a legal scaffolding under which detainees could be tortured without calling it torture. Despite the outcry from within the legal community and from the general public, the authors of the torture memos, like their superiors in the Bush Administration, were never held accountable, despite an internal Justice Department investigation by an Obama Administration that was in the midst of its own equally invidious circumlocution of international and federal laws in order to prosecute its unprecedented drone killing program around the world.[81] Today, Yoo enjoys a successful career at UC Berkeley School of Law, Bybee is a federal judge on the U.S. Court of Appeals for the Ninth Circuit, Bradbury served in various high-level positions in the Trump Administration, and Gonzales became Attorney General under Bush and is currently Dean of Belmont University College of Law. More importantly, however, the Bush lawyers cited each of the Supreme Court's seven Eighth Amendment decisions between 1976 and 1994 as laying the legal foundation for the U.S.'s treatment of detainees—*and* Guantanamo and the many CIA black sites continue to operate with impunity to this day.[82] In other words, the lawyers only had to rely upon the Supreme Court's own evisceration of the meaning of "cruel and unusual punishment" across its Eighth Amendment corpus to justify torture. It was psychologists, however, who devised many of the torture methods that the lawyers' creative terminology of "enhanced interrogation" tried to obfuscate. The American Psychological Association and its member psychologists faced intense scrutiny, but no accountability, for their role in crafting and implementing torture techniques at Abu Ghraib and Guantanamo—not to mention culpability for their decades-long collaboration with the CIA going back at least to the early Cold War.[83]

The point here is that once abuse of power is institutionalized by the state, no matter the disciplinary fields from which it issues, it becomes nigh-impossible to eradicate. The Bush Administration's controversial warrantless surveillance program is now, for all intents and purposes, effectively insulated from scrutiny (and now wholly devoid of controversy) through the Foreign Intelligence Surveillance Court.[84] In the biological sciences, "gain-of-function" is a post-Cold War euphemism for bioweapons research and if the COVID-19 pandemic does not provide sufficient justification to shut it down entirely, then we are in for much worse to come. Fauci's blatant lie to Congress while testifying under oath on July 20, 2021 that the NIAID has not supported "gain-of-function" research remains remarkable not for the intended deceit, but for the impunity with which it was expressed.[85] The NIAID's record, going back at least to its funding of research resulting in the 2013 and 2015 publications, is incontrovertible as to its support of "gain-of-function" studies. It remains to be seen what kind of accountability key figures in the medical industrial complex such as Fauci will face, if any.

We will consider in due course some provisional answers to the question of how Fauci can support "gain-of-function" bioengineering on coronaviruses, and at the same time, oversee (and hold patents on) biotechnology developed to inoculate against same said viruses. But now we arrive at the second problem for the pandemic police power that is raised by vaccines, which is the kind of public health model that relies upon vaccination. As the foregoing analysis demonstrates, vaccination itself presents numerous serious costs to public health. What does this tell us about the approach to public health that we are facing? The pandemic police power rests on the so-called germ theory of disease, in which disease is understood as the result of random attacks on the body by external agents—germs, bacteria, and viruses.[86] From this perspective, disease indicates a dangerous environment, and the antidote requires an external intervention: vaccines, drugs, and surgery. This approach has its roots in the rise of Western science and was given its specific elevation by the findings of Louis Pasteur, the nineteenth-century French chemist who demonstrated the existence of microorganisms and claimed that they were pathogenic. Blaming germs for illness was coincident with the rise of the medical profession, and we largely turned over responsibility for our health to modern medicine.

Ironically, Western science has always had a dissenting vein, and it was a contemporary of Pasteur's, Antoine Béchamp, who found that germs change from one type of organism to another depending on their conditions, leading to the understanding that the conditions are more important than the germs themselves.[87] Or as Florence Nightingale is supposed to have said, "There are no specific diseases, there are [only] specific disease conditions."[88] Today this is referred to as the terrain theory of disease. According to the germ theory, the fish tank is dirty so we must vaccinate the fish; whereas the terrain theory says, if the tank is dirty, then clean the tank and the fish will be healthy. Bruce Lipton's early research with stem cells verified and extended this finding that the environment controls the behavior and physiology of cells, rather than genes possessing fixed characteristics that hard-wire cells to behave in a certain fashion. Lipton showed that environmental factors turn genes off or on, and in so doing, define how cells actually read genetic coding. These findings have lent further support to the science of epigenetics, the recognition that our lives are not determined by our genetic make-up at birth, but instead that human behavior can alter our genes.[89]

The dissenting voice in modern medicine included the persistence of ancient knowledge that had to be controlled in order that the medical model could fully take over. Biomedical advancement at the turn of the twentieth century proceeded apace with capitalist expansion, and in particular, innovations in petroleum industry derivatives—pharmaceuticals and plastics. The encroachment of capitalist technological advancements exerted tremendous and comprehensive pressures on how medicine was practiced in the early part of the century. These pressures were encapsulated in the 1910 publication of *Medical Education in the United States and Canada,* which came to be known as the Flexner Report after its author Abraham Flexner. The Flexner Report did not create the germ theory of disease nor was it primarily responsible for disseminating it; but it was instrumental in institutionalizing the germ theory in the form of research science-based medicine.[90] Commissioned by the Carnegie Foundation, the Flexner Report sought to align medical education under a set of norms based on laboratory research and on patenting the medical innovations it produces. The consequences for health care were manifold, including the underdevelopment of patient care. Reflecting at the Flexner Report's centennial, Thomas Duffy of the Yale School of Medicine observed:

> There was maldevelopment in the structure of medical education in America in the aftermath of the Flexner Report. The profession's infatuation with the hyper-rational world of German medicine created an excellence in science that was not balanced by a comparable excellence in clinical caring. Flexner's corpus was all nerves without the life blood of caring. Osler's warning that the ideals of medicine would change as "teacher and student chased each other down the fascinating road of research, forgetful of those wider interests to which a hospital must minister" has proven prescient and wise.[91]

This is classic economic-scientific overdevelopment and politico-cultural underdevelopment.[92] As racism and capitalism produced increasingly unhealthy environments to live in, modern medicine touted treatments for the symptoms of this lifestyle, which in turn produced a new set of symptoms requiring further treatment. The stage was thus set for the re-education of the American public, "with a view to turning it into a population of drug and medico dependents, with the early help of the parents and the schools, then with direct advertising and, last but not least, the influence the advertising revenues had on the media-makers."[93] This is the policing power of the nascent medical industrial complex.

In addition to disempowering patients, professionalizing biomedicine, and promoting pharmacological intervention, the coup de grace of the medical model's maldevelopment of clinical care was to render natural medicine marginal and illegitimate.[94] In the mid-nineteenth century, homeopathic practitioners outnumbered allopathic doctors almost two to one, with the various disciplines of what today would be called alternative medicine taught at most medical schools. The Flexner Report marked a drastic reversal in all of this. Any methods not based on Western scientific research, and that did not advocate vaccines as treatment, were construed as quackery and charlatanism. Schools were forced to drop the non-allopathic programming and eventually most closed their doors altogether. In 1906, there were 162 medical schools; after the Flexner Report, the number was reduced by 50 percent. As a result, naturopathy, holistic, integrative, or alternative medicines are entirely segregated from the professionalized teaching of medical care. The ancient healing arts and their integration with modern science yield a uniquely balanced, perceptive, and effective methodology for health care—especially for poor and oppressed communities without access to health insurance.

The Flexner Report was equally destructive to non-white doctors. Five of the seven black medical schools were forced to shut their doors, leaving thousands of black medical students with no viable alternative. It is estimated that as many as 35,000 black medical doctors would have entered the workforce during the century between the closing of these schools and today were the black medical schools not forced to close.[95] The Report also further entrenched racist stereotypes about black people, both as patients and as healthcare professionals.[96] The institutionalizing force of the Report lay in its control over pedagogy, and the simultaneous expulsion of blacks and naturopathy from medical education under the guise of scientific professionalization pathologized the former and made out the latter to be the province of the uncivilized. The groundwork for today's racist healthcare system was effectively enhanced.

At the risk of understatement, the transformations in health care since the early twentieth century have been extraordinary—but the costs of these changes, including what has been lost in terms of knowledge, have been equally remarkable. There are many ways of measuring the high costs of modern medicine, but one of the more invisible costs is "iatrogenic death," modern medicine *as the cause of death*. A *Journal of the American Medical Association* article in 2000 revealed that iatrogenic death is easily the third leading cause of death, behind heart disease and cancer with 225,000 total in-patient deaths annually. The breakdown is as follows:

- *12,000 deaths/year from unnecessary surgery*
- *7000 deaths/year from medication errors in hospitals*
- *20,000 deaths/year from other errors in hospitals*
- *80,000 deaths/year from nosocomial infections in hospitals*
- *106,000 deaths/year from non-error, adverse effects of medications*[97]

To what extent has modern medicine already contributed to COVID-19 deaths in the Pandemic Year, and how much more death in the years to come will be linked to the new vaccine created to combat the virus? One example is the inappropriate but widespread use of mechanical ventilators for hospitalized COVID-19 patients, with an almost 90 percent mortality rate for ventilated patients.[98]

In response to the disastrous results of initial COVID-19 treatments, and in the face of federal public health and hospital-level "supportive care only" directives that restricted the use of proven therapies such as corticosteroids, HCQ, ivermectin, and azithromycin, the Front-Line COVID-19 Critical Care Alliance (FLCCC) clinicians created a treatment protocol for hospitalized patients based on the core therapies of methylprednisolone (steroid), ascorbic acid (quercetin and vitamin C), thiamine (vitamin B_1), heparin (anti-coagulant), and co-interventions (MATH+).[99] In their research and clinical rationale published in late 2020 in the *Journal of Intensive Care Medicine*, the FLCCC reviews the published in vitro, pre-clinical, and clinical data in support of each medicine in their recommended protocols, with a special emphasis on studies supporting their use in the treatment of patients with viral syndromes and COVID-19 specifically. They find that the MATH+ outcomes compare favorably with published multi-national COVID-19 mortality data. After Indian doctors began implementing MATH+ protocols with dramatic success, the Indian health ministry recommended in April 2021 the use of HCQ and ivermectin treatments.[100] Despite preliminary evidence of precipitous declines in COVID-19 cases with the new treatments, WHO pressured the Indian government to rescind its guidelines.[101] It is telling that Merck, the pharmaceutical company that once owned the now-expired patent on ivermectin, says that the drug should not be used in COVID-19 treatment, falsely claiming that there is "no meaningful evidence" and "no scientific basis" for its clinical efficacy.[102]

The foregoing analysis amplifies what it means to say that comorbidity has been the key in COVID-19-related deaths and that since an agent cannot be causative of disease unless every case with the infected agent gets the disease, people are dying *with* COVID-19 (at best), not *of* it. Or, in terms of the equilibrium discussed earlier, comorbidities are simply manifestations of an out-of-balance immune system. Again, it is the plethora of environmentally induced underlying conditions that lead to the fatal cases, not the virus itself, as is also the case with influenza and coronaviruses generally. In this light, COVID-19's greatest service will hopefully be to shed light on how vaccination has become a costly all-or-nothing approach to public health in an era where a large percentage of the global population is not in good health, does not live in healthy conditions, or does not have healthy practices. Since the virus is actively mutating as it progresses through the global population, the effectiveness of any vaccine now being developed will be limited by the time it is available, thus necessitating constant updates. Indeed, the state-corporate public health discourse is already shifting toward preparing the populace for annual "boosters." From the standpoint of the pharmaceutical industry, constant updates plus the negligible efficacy of many vaccines equates to constant demand. A good year for the flu shot is only a 45 percent effective rate, and studies show that the influenza vaccine actually *increases* the rate at which recipients are affected by upper respiratory diseases.[103] As noted earlier, provisional evidence from 2021 also suggests a similar profile for the COVID-19 shots: people who have received the COVID-19 shots appear more likely to be infected by the latest coronavirus variant, and to become more ill, than people who have not taken the shots and have developed their own natural immunities. This should be unsurprising given the foregoing analysis in which comorbidities are the lynchpin between, on the one hand, infection and an effective immune response, or on the other hand, infection and disease: a vaccine for influenza means injecting a person with a live upper respiratory infection, and therefore, vaccination is less likely to work in people vulnerable to upper respiratory infection—in short, in the very people presenting with the various key comorbidities. As we will see in a moment, on top of the fact that they were never intended to prevent transmission, the COVID-19 shots present a uniquely debilitating challenge to long-term immune health, much like the flu shots and other vaccines before them.

Nonetheless, in 2019 WHO defined anti-vaccination as one of the top ten gravest threats to global health.[104] It also asserted that vaccination is one of the most cost-effective ways of avoiding disease. In light of the dynamics noted above, this claim should be read as only applying to the individual, not to the collective. This is an example of how neoliberalism contorts social thinking and policy: public health only has meaning at the level of society, not the individual, and at the social level the focus on vaccination over healthy environments should be seen as both costly and ineffective, as the current pandemic is bearing out. COVID-19 mortality, inflated statistics aside, is an expression of a public health model that produces unhealthy environments, both in our communities and in people's bodies. The zeal for vaccine solutions to social problems is no more glaring than in Fauci's plan to develop a vaccine to "treat opioid disorder."[105] Again, our standard should be not what is good for the healthy and wealthy, but rather what is good for all, including the millions of people around the world who face structural impediments to enjoying health and wealth. Vaccines may sometimes aid the former, but the costs of our lack of investment in healthy environments are disproportionately borne by the latter. Ironically, anti-vaccination has become associated with a far-right or religious fundamentalist fringe: "anti-vaxxers" is used as a slur construing all resistance to, or even critical inquiry into, vaccination as sociopathic.[106] Unfortunately, this dogmatic treatment of questions about state power reinforces shoddy science and neoliberal social policy which leaves us all less safe.

COVID-19 Vaccines

The third matter for examination regarding vaccination is, what exactly is the COVID-19 vaccine and what are the issues it raises? Everything and anything said at this point—*by anybody*—about the COVID-19 vaccine must be taken as preliminary and conditional. Since the vaccines have only been in existence for less than a year, let alone in use, there has not been *nearly* enough time and data to make solid claims about their efficacy or safety. Typical vaccines take ten to 15 years of development and testing before they become FDA-approved. Despite the FDA approval for the Pfizer shot on August 23, 2021, the remaining COVID-19 vaccines are being used under emergency use authorization (EUA) because they have not been sufficiently studied and verified as efficacious and safe. As we will see in the following chapter on the law, the experimental status of these vaccines *alone* means they cannot be mandated. But the provisional data examined in the remainder of this section strongly suggests that the potential harmful effects of this new vaccine outweigh the potential harmful effects from acquiring the disease. To be clear, given the data on COVID-19 infection, treatment, and mortality reviewed in the previous sections, which shows that infection and mortality rates are commensurate with annual influenza, and that fairly simple, effective, and cost-efficient treatments are widely available, a COVID-19 vaccine is unnecessary. Any such vaccine would therefore need to be bulletproof, with 100 percent certainty of preventing disease infection, death, and spread, with no harmful effects. Of course, no vaccine can offer that degree of guaranteed efficacy, but this context is important to keep in mind while reviewing the following provisional data because it makes the case against a COVID-19 vaccine mandate a slam dunk. There is simply no reasonable justification to require people to take the chance of incurring the variety of potential problems posed by this vaccine.

In evaluating the COVID-19 vaccine, we need to examine three issues. First, how this vaccine works differently from all other vaccines; second, the potential modes of injury this unique biotechnology presents; and third, the early warning signs provided by the vaccine's injury data profile, less than six months into widespread usage. The preceding part of this chapter analyzes the problems associated with the history of vaccines. This problematic history is what passes for "normal" vaccine production. In other words, until 2020, all vaccines were based on injecting a foreign matter in the form of a minor disease course to stimulate the body's production of antibodies, but not enough virus is injected to cause the disease. This attenuated form of the actually occurring virus, or viral bits, is meant to trigger the body's immune response to generate antibodies that ward off the immune challenge of the virus contained in the vaccine, and that promote the cellular memory that protects the body if and when it encounters the virus "in the wild," as it were, through a normal environmental encounter with the pathogen. In short, a normal vaccine is expected to (1) develop antibodies that give immunity to the virus being vaccinated against; (2) protect against getting infected by the virus; (3) reduce the number of deaths from that virus; (4) reduce circulation of the virus; and (5) reduce transmission or spread of the virus.

According to these standards, the COVID-19 injections are not vaccines because they are a genetic manipulation tool that do not follow any of the criteria for vaccines. Most astonishingly, they were not even *designed* to address any of the above-noted criteria for effective vaccines. The vaccine manufacturers do not claim that the shots will prevent transmission, produce immunity, or reduce circulation of the virus.[107] They did not test for reduced hospitalizations, disease severity, or deaths. The drug companies only sought to create a product that would mitigate the severity of the symptoms of COVID-19 infection. But to measure symptomology, the minimum qualification for a case of COVID-19 was merely a positive PCR test and one or two mild symptoms, such as headache, fever, cough, or mild nausea. In other words, the trials tested the prevention of common cold symptoms. As William Haseltine put it in *Forbes* in late 2020, "It appears that these trials are intended to pass the lowest possible barrier of success."[108]

Using attenuated virus in the shots is not possible since the virus has not been isolated in the laboratory (at least as far as the public has been made aware). The COVID-19 injections, therefore, use an mRNA platform that has never before been used in human subjects on a global scale for the purpose of inoculation against viral infection. DNA serves as the basis for life, its blueprint if you will, and it gets transcribed into mRNA which then translates into proteins, which are described as the building blocks of life. The new COVID-19 biotechnology utilizes this system within our host cells. The mRNA template in the shot is allegedly encoded for the spike protein that the body would encounter if infected by COVID-19 virus. We must say "allegedly" here because the pharmaceutical companies will not release the sequence of these synthetic mRNAs so we do not know what they will actually encode in our bodies. We do know with certainty, however, that the mRNA is synthetic for two reasons. First, the drug companies and the government have both applied for patents for these new biologicals, and it is illegal to patent nature; they can only patent the technology if it is not naturally occurring. In fact, the technology used to create the COVID-19 shots is based on earlier technologies which are patented by various biotech firms, universities, governments, and researchers, and sublicensed to the developers of the COVID-19 biologicals. For instance, 2017 filings with the Securities and Exchange Commission indicate that the University of Pennsylvania exclusively licensed their mRNA patents to RiboTherapeutics, which then sublicensed them to its affiliate CellScript, which in turn, sublicensed the patents to Moderna and BioNTech.[109] Secondly, mRNAs are unstable, especially in aqueous solution, meaning that they have limited lifetimes in which to alter protein synthesis. The pharmaceutical companies have all disclosed that their products utilize a modified spike protein developed by the National Institutes of Health (NIH) geared to stabilize the mRNAs.[110]

The mRNAs are delivered in the shot wrapped in lipid nanoparticles to enable them to get into the cells and attached to polyethylene glycol to protect them. In certain cells, the mRNA then gets released from its package and is translated into the spike protein that ostensibly registers as the COVID-19 virus to the body's immune system. The body becomes the manufacturing site for this exogenous protein, which will then resemble, at least in theory, an actual spike protein from wild COVID-19 virus such that if you meet this antigen protein in the future, your body will recognize it. Again, because this mRNA technology has never before been used to function like a vaccine, there is no evidence that it will meet the five aforementioned criteria by which we have come to recognize something as a vaccine. As noted above, the pre-market trials did *not* test to see if the mRNA injections will reduce deaths from COVID-19, and they did *not* test to see if the shots will reduce the circulation of the virus or its spread throughout the population. The trials also did *not* include people with existing immune deficiencies or autoimmune conditions, children, women who are breastfeeding or pregnant, people with cancer, the elderly, people with comorbidities, and so forth—the trial exclusion list was lengthy.

The list of concerns with this new technology continues with the fact that there is no actual virus isolated in any laboratory anywhere (again, as far as we have been told). Without virus isolate, not only is there no actual virus in the shot but the synthetic spike protein is not coded to the actual COVID-19 virus. This may or may not be a problem. One potential risk is that the similarities in proteins between the synthetic spike protein and the antibody that is made, and those in organ tissues throughout the body, may lead the body to not only mount an immune response against the synthetic spike protein but also against tissue that is very similar to it in the lungs, kidneys, brain, heart, and reproductive system. This situation is known by a number of terms that are more or less synonymous, such as "cytokine storm" or "pathogenic priming." Pathogenic priming is marked by a dangerous and uncontrolled increase in inflammation and the potential for autoimmune dysfunction. Ironically, this potential situation mirrors an observable clinical effect of COVID-19 infection itself.[111] A possible explanation for this situation lies with the potential for the anti-spike protein to damage the body's anti-inflammatory responses, an effect observed with severe acute respiratory syndrome coronavirus (SARS-CoV) and Middle Eastern respiratory syndrome (MERS-CoV).[112] Recent findings also inform the concern that the cross-reaction between the anti-spike proteins and human tissue can lead to multi-systemic disorders and autoimmune disease.[113]

Finally, there is potential for harmful reactions to the polyethylene glycol (PEG) and to the flagellin adjuvant used in the shot. PEG has never before been used in a vaccine and therefore there is no safety data. Allergic reactions to the COVID-19 shots may be due to the PEG.[114] Severe allergic reactions to the Moderna shot led California to temporarily suspend injections in January 2021.[115] Adjuvants are added to vaccines for the purpose of increasing immune response.[116] Flagellin is an "entirely novel protein" and has never been tested in humans.[117] The only existing trials have been in chicken vaccines. The chicken trials have shown flagellin increases cytokines, which given the above-noted limiting effect of the anti-spike protein on the body's anti-inflammatory response, could be a serious source of harm to recipients of the COVID-19 shots. There is no way of knowing how long the synthetic proteins will remain in the body and to what effect.

While these concerns are scientifically founded, based as they are on pre-existing studies and clinical data, they nonetheless remain suggestive until fully investigated. The Vaccine Adverse Event Reporting System (VAERS), however, exists to signal potential problems with the COVID-19 shots. VAERS is operated jointly by the CDC and the FDA, and serves as a "national early warning system to detect possible safety problems in U.S.-licensed vaccines."[118] An adverse event (AE) is defined as any unfavorable medical occurrence, including any abnormal physical exam or laboratory finding, symptom, or disease, temporally associated with the person's vaccination. A serious or severe adverse event (SAE) is defined as any adverse event that results in death, is life-threatening, or places the person at immediate risk of death from the event, requires prolonged hospitalization, causes persistent or significant disability or incapacity, results in congenital anomalies or birth defects, or is another condition which investigators judge to represent significant hazards.[119] According to the VAERS handbook, on average approximately 15 percent of reported AEs are classified as severe.[120] It is a passive reporting system in that it relies on people who have experienced an adverse event from vaccination to report their experience. Anyone can file a report, but healthcare professionals and vaccine manufacturers are required to report events that come to their attention. CDC and FDA officials review and investigate reports; only a fraction of all reports to VAERS get recorded as official adverse events in the database, and studies have shown that only one to ten percent of all adverse events are actually reported. While VAERS data is likely a significant underestimation of adverse events with vaccines, it can illuminate possible trends that may signal problems with the vaccines or with the vaccination process (who receives it and when).

The only comprehensive analysis to date of the VAERS database reveals a strong signal of caution regarding the safety of the mRNA shots. Twenty percent of all VAERS reports for the entirety of 2020 were COVID-19-related, despite the shot only being administered 14 days of the year (beginning December 17th). As of early May 2021, the data files for COVID-19-related AEs almost surpass that for all vaccines for all of 2020.[121] This reflects the high numbers of COVID-19 injections compared with all other vaccines, and the accordingly increased overall number of adverse events. The exponentially larger *rate* of incidence compared with all other previous vaccines, however, is a serious red flag. In terms of serious or severe adverse events (SAEs) for the COVID-19 shots, SAEs account for 26 percent of all AEs, which is almost twice the normal estimate in the VAERS handbook.[122] The VAERS data as of May 14, 2021 is 182,559 total AE reports, including 4015 deaths, 12,000 hospitalizations, and 24,000 emergency room visits. When the

AEs are grouped into categories, the VAERS data reveals 31,400 cardiovascular events, 20,000 neurological events, and 68,836 immunological events. Spontaneous abortions, which are not counted as deaths, total 138 thus far, and there have been 843 anaphylaxis reactions to the shot. A "breakthrough infection" is when a vaccinated person becomes infected with the virus against which they had been previously vaccinated. The VAERS data shows 3317 people received the COVID-19 injection, and subsequently became infected with the virus. Of those breakthrough infections, 179 people died.[123]

The VAERS site warns the public not to conclude that the adverse event reports are causally connected to the vaccines, and yet analysis of the time duration between vaccination date and onset of symptoms provides strong evidence for causation. For every single category of AE, the average time frame post-vaccination is between day 0 and day 1. If there was no causation, the adverse events reported would not systematically cluster around day 0–1. For instance, if the deaths following COVID-19 injections were not causally linked, the reported percentages of deaths should be equally distributed across the days after the vaccination date.[124] Most reports were thus made right away, and strongly correspond to the traditional epidemiological standards for gauging causality.[125]

An immunological event in the context of a treatment or vaccination is an important sign, and the fact that immunological AEs occur with the COVID-19 biologicals at over twice the rate of other kinds of events raises serious concerns about the injection's safety. Pathogenic priming may explain the high number of immunological AEs. A 2012 study of the trial vaccine developed in response to SARS-CoV found that the vaccine induced antibody responses in mice and protection against infection.[126] But the mice also developed diseased lungs within two days of vaccination, demonstrating the pathogenic priming risk of such vaccines. In other words, the vaccine "worked," but the antibody-dependent response it created killed the mice. These findings have thwarted the successful development of a vaccine for coronaviruses. A recent study from April 2020 verifies this data, finding that one-third of the immunogenic proteins in the SARS and MERS viruses have potentially problematic homology to proteins key to the human adaptive immune system, confirming the reason for the failures of the SARS and MERS vaccines.[127] This may be the reason behind some of the COVID-19 injection deaths and the numerous immunological AEs. In order to meet minimal medical ethics requirements, consequently, researchers are calling for clarifying informed consent disclosures for the public that the mRNA products may worsen COVID-19 disease upon exposure to challenge or to circulating virus post-vaccination.[128]

Given the extremely high numbers of people who have received the COVID-19 products thus far, the incidence of AEs recorded in the VAERS database is small in terms of a percentage of the overall injected population. However,

> [t]he weekly releases of VAERS data do not include all of the reports made to date—they are all the reports the CDC has processed to date—and the backlog is likely to be staggering. Thus, due to both the problems of under-reporting and the lag in report processing, this analysis reveals a strong signal from the VAERS data that the risk of suffering an SAE following injection is significant and that the overall risk signal is high. Analysis suggests that the vaccines are likely the cause of reported deaths, spontaneous abortions, and anaphylactic reactions in addition to cardiovascular, neurological, and immunological AEs. Based on the precautionary principle, since there is currently no precedent for predictability with regards to long-term effects from mRNA injections, extreme care should be taken when making a decision to participate in this experiment. mRNA platforms are new to humans with regard to mass injection programs in the context of viruses. There is currently no way to predict potential detrimental outcomes with regards to SAE occurrences in the long-term. Also, with regards to short-term analysis, this data is limited based on reporting that likely significantly underestimates actual events.[129]

Behind each statistic, moreover, is a life irreparably altered or prematurely ended unnecessarily. Three healthcare workers, Shawn Skelton, Angelia Desselle, and Kristi Simmonds were among the earliest to receive mRNA injections. Within days of their shots, each of them became wrought by full-body, uncontrollable convulsions.[130]

Three themes emerge from these women's stories: each woman lost her job; each woman was met with medical professionals who sought to suppress the fact of her mRNA injection injury, and who claimed that her condition was psychological, not physiological; and each woman discovered that the medical profession has no clue how to treat serious adverse effects from the COVID-19 shots. These themes resonate with the experiences of people injured by other vaccines. The mRNA products are meant to prevent or mitigate harm from COVID-19, but it appears from this analysis they are, in fact, doing more harm than good when considering the early trends in the data. The *maximum* observation period for safety assessment of these products before receiving FDA emergency use authorization was six months—and in only *two* months, we have seen all of the above-noted damage. If any other product caused this much damage in the first two months of being on the market, it would surely be pulled from use. People should weigh the evidence and the risks very carefully before making their decisions. At the very least, the decision to get the shot or not should not be mandated.

Notes

1. Cited in Barbara Ransby, *Ella Baker and the Black Freedom Movement: A Radical Democratic Vision* (Chapel Hill: North Carolina, 2003), 1.
2. See Michel Foucault, "Power/Knowledge: Selected Interviews and Other Writings, 1972–1977 131–33," Colin Gordon, ed. (1988).
3. See Celia Farber, "AIDS: Words from the Front," *VirusMyth*, July 1994, http://virusmyth.com/aids/hiv/cfmullis.htm.
4. See Rory O'Sullivan, "The Innocence Project: A Short History Since 1983," *BlackPast*, March 8, 2018, https://www.blackpast.org/african-american-history/perspectives-african-american-history/innocence-project-short-history-1983/ (detailing how the Innocence Project used DNA tests that utilized the PCR method to launch their services in 1992). See generally "What Is DNA?" *Innocence Project News*, March 2, 2007, https://innocenceproject.org/what-is-dna/ (listing Short Tandem Repeat testing as the

current standard of DNA testing, which includes elements of the PCR method).
5. Farber, 19.
6. See "CDC 2019-Novel Coronavirus (2019-nCoV) Real-Time RT-PCR Diagnostic Panel," *CDC* 40, December 1, 2020, https://www.fda.gov/media/134922/download.
7. "CDC 2019-Novel Coronavirus (2019-nCoV) Real-Time RT-PCR Diagnostic Panel," 42.
8. Rita Jaafar et al., "Correlation Between 3790 Quantitative Polymerase Chain Reaction–Positives Samples and Positive Cell Cultures, Including 1941 Severe Acute Respiratory Syndrome Coronavirus 2 Isolates," *Clinical Infectious Diseases* 1 (2020).
9. Michael Yeadon, "Lies, Damned Lies, and Health Statistics—The Deadly Danger of False Positives," *Lockdown Sceptics*, September 20, 2020, https://lockdownsceptics.org/lies-damned-lies-and-health-statistics-the-deadly-danger-of-false-positives/.
10. See "Principles of Epidemiology in Public Health Practice, Third Edition an Introduction to Applied Epidemiology and Biostatistics," *CDC*, May 18, 2012, https://www.cdc.gov/csels/dsepd/ss1978/lesson1/section5.html.
11. See Elizabeth Spencer et al., "When Is COVID, COVID?" *Centre for Evidence-Based Medicine*, September 11, 2020, https://www.cebm.net/covid-19/when-is-covid-covid/.
12. See Celia Farber, "Was the COVID-19 Test Meant to Detect a Virus?" *UncoverDc*, April 7, 2020, https://uncoverdc.com/2020/04/07/was-the-covid-19-test-meant-to-detect-a-virus/.
13. See Paul Kirkham et al., "How Likely Is a Second Wave?" *Lockdown Sceptics*, September 8, 2020, https://lockdownsceptics.org/addressing-the-cv19-second-wave/.
14. See The COVID Tracking Project, https://covidtracking.com/ (last visited May 30, 2021).
15. Victor M. Corman et al., "Detection of 2019 Novel Coronavirus (2019-nCoV) by Real-Time RT-PCR," *Eurosurveillance* 25(3) (January 2020), https://www.eurosurveillance.org/content/10.2807/1560-7917.ES.2020.25.3.2000045.
16. Pieter Borger et al., "External Peer Review of the RTPCR Test to Detect SARS-CoV-2 Reveals 10 Major Scientific Flaws at the

Molecular and Methodological Level: Consequences for False Positive Results," November 30, 2020, https://cormandrostenreview.com/report/.
17. Celia Farber, "Ten Fatal Errors: Scientists Attack Paper That Established Global PCR Driven Lockdown," *Uncoverdc*, December 3, 2020, https://uncoverdc.com/2020/12/03/ten-fatal-errors-scientists-attack-paper-that-established-global-pcr-driven-lockdown/.
18. See Alba Grifoni et al., "Targets of T Cell Responses to SARS-CoV-2 Coronavirus in Humans with COVID-19 Disease and Unexposed Individuals," *Cell* 181(1489), 2020: 1498. See generally Julian Braun et al., "Presence of SARS-CoV-2 Reactive T Cells in COVID-19 Patients and Healthy Donors," *Medrxiv*, April 22, 2020, https://doi.org/10.1101/2020.04.17.20061440; Nina Le Bert et al., "SARS-CoV-2-Specific T cell Immunity in Cases of COVID-19 and SARS, and Uninfected Controls," *Nature* 584(457) (2020).
19. These isolated coronavirus families are: 229E, NL63, OC43, and HKU1.
20. See Jose Mateus et al., "Selective and Cross-Reactive SARS-CoV-2 T Cell Epitopes in Unexposed Humans," *Science* 89(370) 2020.
21. See Herb F. Sewell, "Cellular Immune Responses to Covid-19," *BMJ* 1(370), July 31, 2020.
22. Kirkham, et al.
23. K. Lingappan et al., "Understanding the Age Divide in COVID-19: Why Are Children Overwhelmingly Spared?" *American Journal of Physiology Lung Cellular & Molecular Physiology* 39(319) 2020: 40–41.
24. See Jeffrey A. Tucker, "Asymptomatic Spread Revisited," *The American Institute for Economic Research* (November 22, 2020), https://www.aier.org/article/asymptomatic-spread-revisited/.
25. See Will Feuer and Noah Higgins-Dunn, "Asymptomatic Spread of Coronavirus Is 'Very Rare,' WHO Says," *CNBC*, June 8, 2020, 1:05 PM, https://www.cnbc.com/2020/06/08/asymptomatic-coronavirus-patients-arent-spreading-new-infections-who-says.html.
26. See Berkeley Lovelace et al., "WHO Walks Back Comments on Asymptomatic Coronavirus Spread, Says Much Is Still Unknown,"

CNBC, June 9, 2020, 10:07 AM, https://www.cnbc.com/2020/06/09/who-scrambles-to-clarify-comments-on-asymptomatic-coronavirus-spread-much-is-still-unknown.html.
27. See Shiyi Cao et al., "Post-Lockdown SARS-CoV-2 Nucleic Acid Screening in Nearly Ten Million Residents of Wuhan, China," *Nature Communications* (November 20, 2020), https://www.nature.com/articles/s41467-020-19802-w.
28. See John P. Ioannidis, "Infection Fatality Rate of COVID-19 Inferred from Seroprevalence Data," *WHO*, October 14, 2020, https://www.who.int/bulletin/online_first/BLT.20.265892.pdf.
29. Ioannidis, "Infection Fatality Rate."
30. See "Past Seasons Estimated Influenza Disease Burden," *CDC*, October 1, 2020, https://www.cdc.gov/flu/about/burden/past-seasons.html.
31. Much has been made of the effect of co-morbidities, or the various factors compromising immune system efficacy—and rightly so. Comorbidities play crucial roles in health outcomes—this goes for any disease, COVID-19 is not unique in this way. But it is important to recognize here that these infection mortality rates for COVID-19 and influenza are aggregate statistics, which means that are *inclusive* of all the various comorbidities in the population. And still the IMR for people under 70 years old with COVID-19 is essentially the same as that for seasonal influenza.

    "People at High Risk for Flu Complications," *CDC*, February 11, 2021, https://www.cdc.gov/flu/highrisk/index.htm; "People with Certain Medical Conditions," *CDC*, April 29, 2021, https://www.cdc.gov/coronavirus/2019-ncov/need-extra-precautions/people-with-medical-conditions.html [hereinafter *Certain Medical Conditions*].
32. See "Global Tuberculosis Report 2019," *WHO*, https://www.who.int/teams/global-tuberculosis-programme/tb-reports/global-report-2019 (last visited May 30, 2021); "Global Health Observatory (GHO) Data," *WHO*, https://www.who.int/gho/tb/epidemic/cases_deaths/en/ (last visited May 30, 2021); Devan Cole, "Fauci: Science Shows Hydroxychloroquine Is Not Effective as a Coronavirus Treatment," *CNN*, May 27, 2020, 3:43 PM, https://www.

cnn.com/2020/05/27/politics/anthony-fauci-hydroxychloroquine-trump-cnntv/index.html.

33. See "Frontline COVID-19 Critical Care Alliance," *FLCCC Alliance*, https://covid19criticalcare.com/ (last visited May 30, 2021) (providing resources on treatment protocols supported by scientific literature and clinical evidence).

34. See Pierre Kory et al., "Review of the Emerging Evidence Demonstrating the Efficacy of Ivermectin in the Prophylaxis and Treatment of COVID-19," *FLCCC Alliance*, January 16, 2021, https://covid19criticalcare.com/wp-content/uploads/2020/11/FLCCC-Ivermectin-in-the-prophylaxis-and-treatment-of-COVID-19.pdf; see also Yaseen M. Arabi et al., "The Ten Reasons Why Corticosteriod Therapy Reduces Mortality in Severe COVID-19," *Intensive Care Medicine* 46(2067) 2020: 2067–2070; Ruben Manuel Luciano Colunga Biancatelli et al., "Quercetin and Vitamin C: An Experimental, Synergistic Therapy for the Prevention and Treatment of SARS-CoV-2 Related Disease (COVID-19)," *Frontiers in Immunology* 11(1451) (2020), https://www.frontiersin.org/articles/10.3389/fimmu.2020.01451/full; Ning Tang et al., "Anticoagulant Treatment Is Associated with Decreased Mortality in Severe Coronavirus Disease 2019 Patients with Coagulopathy," *Journal Thrombosis and Haemostasis* 18(1094) 2020: 1094–1099; Ali Daneshkhah et al., "The Possible Role of Vitamin D in Suppressing Cytokine Storm and Associated Mortality in COVID-19 Patients," *Medrxiv*, May 18, 2020, https://www.medrxiv.org/content/10.1101/2020.04.08.20058578v4; "New Nasal Spray Proven to Kill 99.9% of the Coronavirus that Causes Covid-19 Is Being Trialled in the UK," *Royal Holloway University of London*, January 12, 2021, https://www.royalholloway.ac.uk/research-and-teaching/departments-and-schools/biological-sciences/news/new-nasal-spray-proven-to-kill-999-of-the-coronavirus-that-causes-covid-19-is-being-trialled-in-the-uk/; Ari Moskowitz and Michael W. Donnino, "Thiamine (Vitamin B1) in Septic Shock: A Targeted Therapy," *Journal of Thoracic Disease* 12(S78) 2020: S78–83; Aartjan J. W. te Velthuis et al., "Zn(2+)

Inhibits Coronavirus and Arterivirus RNA Polymerase Activity In Vitro and Zinc Ionophores Block the Replication of These Viruses in Cell Culture," *PLOS Pathogens* (November 4, 2010), https://journals.plos.org/plospathogens/article?id=10.1371/journal.ppat.1001176; Peter A. McCullough, "Pathophysiological Basis and Rationale for Early Outpatient Treatment of SARS-CoV-2 (COVID-19) Infection," *American Journal of Medicine* (2020), https://aapsonline.org/mccullough-protocol-3-page.pdf.
35. Cole, "Fauci."
36. See Nikki Carvajal and Kevin Liptak, "Trump Says He Is Taking Hydroxychloroquine Though Health Experts Question Its Effectiveness," *CNN*, May 19, 2020, 4:58 AM, https://www.cnn.com/2020/05/18/politics/donald-trump-hydroxychloroquine-coronavirus/index.html.
37. See Andrew Mark Miller, "Study Finds 84% Fewer Hospitalizations for Patients Treated with Controversial Drug Hydroxychloroquine," *Wash Examiner*, November 25, 2020, 3:02 PM, https://www.washingtonexaminer.com/news/study-finds-84-fewer-hospitalizations-for-patients-treated-with-controversial-drug-hydroxychloroquine. See generally Martin J. Vincent et al., "Chloroquine is a Potent Inhibitor of SARS Coronavirus Infection and Spread," *Journal of Virology* 2(69) (August 22, 2005). For effectiveness of HCQ in treating influenza, see generally Eng Eong Ooi et al., "In Vitro Inhibition of Human Influenza A Virus Replication by Chloroquine," *Virology Journal* 3(39) (May 29, 2006). For effectiveness on a range of viral infections, see also *id.*; Andrea Savarino et al., "Effects of Chloroquine on Viral Infections: An Old Drug Against Today's Diseases?" *Lancet Infectious Disease* 11(722) (2003); "Real-Time Database and Meta Analysis of 322 COVID-19 Studies," *COVID-19 Studies*, https://c19study.com/ (last visited May 30, 2021) (tracking global HCQ COVID-19 treatment studies).
38. See Alexandre B. Cavalcanti et al., "Hydroxychloroquine With or Without Azithromycin in Mild-to-Moderate Covid-19," *The New England Journal of Medicine* 383, 2041 (November 19, 2020); Sarah Boseley and Melissa Davey, "Covid-19: Lancet Retracts

Paper That Halted Hydroxychloroquine Trials," *The Guardian*, June 4, 2020, 3:43 PM, https://www.theguardian.com/world/2020/jun/04/covid-19-lancet-retracts-paper-that-halted-hydroxychloroquine-trials; Daniel Espinosa, "Lancetgate: Why Was This "Monumental Fraud" Not a Huge Scandal?" *Dissident Voice* (August 20, 2020), https://dissidentvoice.org/2020/08/lancetgate-why-was-this-monumental-fraud-not-a-huge-scandal/.

39. See "The American Journal of Medicine Now Recommends HCQ for COVID19," *Principia Scientific International* (January 26, 2021), https://principia-scientific.com/the-american-journal-of-medicine-now-recommends-hcq-for-covid19/.

40. A. D. Santin et al., "Ivermectin: A Multifaceted Drug of Nobel Prize-Honoured Distinction with Indicated Efficacy Against a New Global Scourge, COVID-19," *New Microbes and New Infections* 43 (August 3, 2021): 100924, https://www.ncbi.nlm.nih.gov/pmc/articles/PMC8383101/.

41. Andy Crump, "Ivermectin: Enigmatic Multifaceted 'Wonder' Drug Continues to Surprise and Exceed Expectations," *The Journal of Antibiotics* 70 (2017): 495–505.

42. Testimony of Pierre Kory, MD, *Homeland Security Committee Meeting: Focus on Early Treatment of COVID-19*, December 8, 2020, https://www.hsgac.senate.gov/imo/media/doc/Testimony-Kory-2020-12-08.pdf.

43. Vanessa Romo, "Poison Control Centers Are Fielding a Surge of Ivermectin Overdose Calls," *National Public Radio*, September 4, 2021, https://www.npr.org/sections/coronavirus-live-updates/2021/09/04/1034217306/ivermectin-overdose-exposure-cases-poison-control-centers. On August 21, 2021, the FDA provided one of the more patronizing mis-directions in a Pandemic Year full of subterfuge and deceit by telling the public, via Tweeter no less, not to use ivermectin to treat COVID-19: "You are not a horse. You are not a cow. Seriously, y'all, stop it." https://twitter.com/US_FDA/status/1429050070243192839.

44. Andy Crump and Satoshi Omura, "Ivermectin, 'Wonder Drug' from Japan: The Human Use Perspective," *Proceedings of the Japan Academy, Series B, Physical and Biological Sciences*, 87(2)

February 10, 2011: 13–28, https://www.ncbi.nlm.nih.gov/pmc/articles/PMC3043740/.
45. Virginia Langmald, "What Would an Antiviral Pill Mean for the Fight Against COVID-19?" *CNN*, October 2, 2021, https://www.cnn.com/2021/10/02/health/antiviral-pill-covid-19-explainer/index.html.
46. See https://c19hcq.com/, https://c19ivermectin.com/, https://c19vitamind.com/.
47. See Christine Favocci, *Confusion: WHO Disagrees with CDC Recommendations, Says No Need for Healthy People to Wear Masks*, W. J. (June 1, 2020, 1:05 PM), https://www.westernjournal.com/confusion-disagrees-cdc-recommendations-says-no-need-healthy-people-wear-masks/ (showing examples of the many contradictions and reversals regarding mask-wearing).
48. Favocci, *Confusion*.
49. See Eric Litke, "Fact Check: No, N95 Filters Are Not Too Large to Stop COVID-19 Particles," *USA Today* (June 12, 2020, 11:36 AM), https://www.usatoday.com/story/news/factcheck/2020/06/11/fact-check-n-95-filters-not-too-large-stop-covid-19-particles/5343537002/.
50. See Faisal Bin-Reza et al., "The Use of Masks and Respirators to Prevent Transmission of Influenza: A Systematic Review of the Scientific Evidence," *Influenza Other Respiratory Viruses* 4(257), 257 (June 6, 2012).
51. See Joshua L. Jacobs et al., "Use of Surgical Face Masks to Reduce the Incidence of the Common Cold Among Health Care Workers in Japan: A Randomized Controlled Trial," *American Journal of Infection Control* 37(417) (June 3, 2009); Vittoria Offeddu et al., "Effectiveness of Masks and Respirators Against Respiratory Infections in Healthcare Workers: A Systematic Review and Meta-Analysis," *Clinical Infectious Disease* 11(1934) (November 17, 2017); Christopher R. Friese et al., "Respiratory Protection Considerations for Healthcare Workers During the Covid-19 Pandemic," *Health Sec* 3(237) (April 22, 2020); B. J. Cowling et al., "Face Masks to Prevent Transmission of Influenza Virus: A Systematic Review," *Epidemiology & Infection* 138(449) (January 22, 2010).

52. See generally Jonathan M. Berman, *Anti-vaxxers: How to Challenge a Misinformed Movement* (2020).
53. See Nafis Hasan, "#FreeTheVaccine to End the Pandemic," *Science for the People*, June 25, 2020, https://magazine.scienceforthepeople.org/?s=vaccine.
54. I would argue that racism, capitalism, state power, and cultural chauvinism are the problems with science. But in terms of the world's most pressing issues involving science today, a good starting list might be: environment and energy, food-water-seed justice, vaccines, internet and social media, and war.
55. See Andrea Lisco et al., "War and Peace Between Microbes: HIV-1 Interactions with Coinfecting Viruses," *Cell Host & Microbe* 6(403) 2009: 403.
56. See generally Herbert W. Virgin et al., "Redefining Chronic Viral Infection," *Cell* 13830 (2009).
57. See Erik S. Barton et al., "Herpesvirus Latency Confers Symbiotic Protection from Bacterial Infection," *Nature* 447(326) 2007: 329. See generally Katie L. Mason et al., "Overview of Gut Immunology," in 635 GI Microbiota and Regulation of the Immune System (Advances in Experimental Medicine and Biology), Gary B. Huffnagle and Mairi C. Noverr, eds., 2008; Emil R. Unanue, "Viral Infections and Nonspecific Protection—Good or Bad?" *The New England Journal of Medicine* 357(1345) 2007.
58. Lisco et al., 403.
59. Lisco et al., 403.
60. Nabin K. Shrestha et al., "Necessity of COVID-19 Vaccination in Previously Infected Individuals," June 1, 2021, preprint https://www.medrxiv.org/content/10.1101/2021.06.01.21258176v3; "Cleveland Clinic Statement on Previous COVID-19 Infection Research," updated August 16, 2021, https://newsroom.clevelandclinic.org/2021/06/09/cleveland-clinic-statement-on-previous-covid-19-infection-research/.
61. Public Health England, *SARS-CoV-2 Variants of Concern and Variants Under Investigation in England—Technical Briefing 20*, August 6, 2021, https://assets.publishing.service.gov.uk/government/uploads/system/uploads/attachment_data/file/1009243/Technical_Briefing_20.pdf.

62. Benedict Brook, "Israel Fighting Record Breaking Surge in COVID-19 Cases Despite High Levels of Vaccination," *News.com.au*, September 4, 2021, https://www.news.com.au/world/coronavirus/global/israel-fighting-record-breaking-surge-in-covid19-cases-despite-high-levels-of-vaccination/news-story/3445287a9c46e8712574da2316bd3ee1.
63. See "Metagenomic Analysis Report on Priorix Tetra," *Corvela*, December 24, 2018, https://www.corvelva.it/en/speciale-corvelva/vaccinegate-en/metagenomic-analysis-report-on-priorix-tetra.html.
64. See generally Neil Z. Miller, "Aluminum in Childhood Vaccines Is Unsafe," *Journal of American Physicians and Surgeons* 21, 109 (2016).
65. See G. Stuart, "The Problem of Mass Vaccination Against Yellow Fever," *WHO*, August 20, 1953, https://apps.who.int/iris/bitstream/handle/10665/75301/WHO_YF_20_eng.pdf.
66. See BaDoi N. Phan et al., "A Myelin-Related Transcriptomic Profile is Shared by Pitt-Hopkins Syndrome Models and Human Autism Spectrum Disorder," *Nature Neuroscience* 23(375) 2020: 384.
67. See Jackie Salo, "What Is Transverse Myelitis? The Illness That Halted AstraZeneca Vaccine Trial," *New York Post*, September 9, 2020, 4:23 PM, https://nypost.com/2020/09/09/transverse-myelitis-the-illness-that-halted-astrazeneca-vaccine-trial/.
68. See Kent Heckenlively and Judy Mikovits, *Plague: One Scientist's Intrepid Search for the Truth About Human Retroviruses and Chronic Fatigue Syndrome (ME/CFS), Autism, and Other Diseases* (New York: Skyhorse, 2014).
69. See Heckenlively and Mikovits, *Plague* (providing a comprehensive analysis of the links between ME, XMRV, autism, and vaccinations). On "stealth adapted viruses" and the vaccination connection, see generally W. John Martin, *Stealth Adapted Viruses; Alternative Cellular Energy (ACE) & KELEA Activated Water: A New Paradigm of Healthcare* (2014). On the connection between the polio vaccine and cancer, see also generally Eric A. Engels, "Cancer Risk Associated With Receipt of Vaccines Contaminated With Simian Virus 40: Epidemiologic," *Research Anticancer Research* 19 1999: 2173; Hillary Johnson, *Osler's Web:*

Inside the Labyrinth of the Chronic Fatigue Syndrome Epidemic (1996) (regarding the history of myalgic encephalomyelitis); Annie Jacobsen, *The Pentagon's Brain: An Uncensored History of DARPA, America's Top-Secret Military Research Agency* (2015); Steve Haltiwanger et al., "Stealth Viruses: The Hidden Epidemic," *Pulsed Tech.'s Research*, July 15, 2001, http://www.pulsedtechresearch.com/wp-content/uploads/2013/04/Stealth-Viruses-Hidden-Epidemic-Haltiwanger-Martin-Kholos.pdf.
70. See Antoinette Cornelia van der Kuyl et al., "Of Mice and Men: On the Origin of XMRV," *Frontiers in Microbiology* 1(1) 2011: 4–5.
71. See Suresh Rewar and Dashrath Mirdha, "Transmission of Ebola Virus Disease: An Overview," *Annals of Global Health* 80(444) 2014: 446. See generally Judy Mikovits and Kent Heckenlively, *Plague of Corruption: Restoring Faith in the Promise of Science* (New York: Skyhorse, 2021).
72. See Richard Knox, "Origin of AIDS Linked to Colonial Practices in Africa," *NPR*, June 4, 2006, 8:00 AM, https://www.npr.org/templates/story/story.php?storyId=5450391.
73. See Edward Hooper, "The Origins of the AIDS Pandemic: A Quick Guide to the Principal Theories and the Alleged Refutations," *AIDS Origins*, April 25, 2012, http://www.aidsorigins.com/the-origins-of-the-aids-pandemic/#more-200. See generally Hooper, *The River: A Journey to the Source of HIV and AIDS* (New York: Penguin, 2000).
74. See Declan Butler, "Nobel Fight Over African HIV Centre," *Nature* 486(301) 2021: 301–302.
75. See generally Mikovits and Heckenlively, *Plague of Corruption*.
76. See "Understanding mRNA COVID-19 Vaccines," *CDC*, March 4, 2021, https://www.cdc.gov/coronavirus/2019-ncov/vaccines/different-vaccines/mrna.html.
77. See Jonathan P. Stoye and John M. Coffin, "The Dangers of Xenotransplantation," *Nature Medicine* 1(1100) 1995: 1100.
78. See Denise Grady, "Deadly Germ Research Is Shut Down at Army Lab Over Safety Concerns," *New York Times*, August 5, 2019, https://www.nytimes.com/2019/08/05/health/germs-fort-detrick-biohazard.html; Donald G. McNeil, Jr., *C.D.C.* "Closes Anthrax

and Flu Labs After Accidents," *New York Times*, July 12, 2014, https://www.nytimes.com/2014/07/12/science/cdc-closes-anthrax-and-flu-labs-after-accidents.html.
79. Vineet D. Menachery et al., "A SARS-Like Cluster of Circulating Bat Coronaviruses Shows Potential for Human Emergence," *Nature Medicine* 21(1508) 2015: 1508. This was actually the *second* successful gain-of-function collaboration between U.S. researchers and the Wuhan lab to show bat coronavirus can be made adaptable to humans. See Ge Xing-Yi et al., "Isolation and Characterization of a Bat SARS-Like Coronavirus That Uses the ACE2 Receptor," *Nature* 503, 535 (2013).
80. See Declan Butler, "Engineered Bat Virus Stirs Debate Over Risky Research," *Nature*, November 12, 2015, https://www.nature.com/news/engineered-bat-virus-stirs-debate-over-risky-research-1.18787.
81. See Richard A. Serrano, "Waterboarding Memo Authors Committed No Misconduct, Report Says," *Los Angeles Times*, February 20, 2010, 12:00 AM, https://www.latimes.com/archives/la-xpm-2010-feb-20-la-na-interrogation-memo20-2010feb20-story.html; see also Christopher Anders, "Obama's Drone Killing Program Slowly Emerges from the Secret State Shadows," *ACLU*, March 28, 2013, 11:11 AM, https://www.aclu.org/blog/national-security/targeted-killing/obamas-drone-killing-program-slowly-emerges-secret-state.
82. These cases, which decided when punishments are judged as cruel and unusual, are *Estelle v. Gamble* 429 U.S. 97 (1976); *Rhodes v. Chapman* 452 U.S. 337 (1981); *Whitley v. Albers* 475 U.S. 312 (1986); *Wilson v. Seiter* 501 U.S. 294 (1991); *Hudson v. McMillian* 503 U.S. 1 (1992); *Farmer v. Brennan* 511 U.S. 825 (1994); *Hope v. Pelzer* 536 U.S. 730 (2002).
83. See Gregg Levine, "Psychologists Worked with CIA, Bush Administration to Justify Torture," *Al Jazeera America*, April 30, 2015, 5:14 PM, http://america.aljazeera.com/blogs/scrutineer/2015/4/30/psychologists-worked-with-cia-bush-administration-to-justify-torture.html; see also Alfred W. McCoy, "The CIA's Secret History

of Psychological Torture," *Salon*, June 11, 2009, 2:15 PM, https://www.salon.com/2009/06/11/mccoy/.
84. See Charlie Savage, "Court Approves Warrantless Surveillance Rules While Scolding F.B.I.," *The New York Times*, September 5, 2020, https://www.nytimes.com/2020/09/05/us/politics/court-approves-warrantless-surveillance-rules-while-scolding-fbi.html.
85. Sharon Lerner et al., "NIH Documents Provide New Evidence U.S. Funded Gain-of-Function Research in Wuhan," *The Intercept*, September 9, 2021, https://theintercept.com/2021/09/09/covid-origins-gain-of-function-research/.
86. See generally Joshua Lederberg, *Encyclopedia of Microbiology*, M. Alexander et al., eds., 2d ed. 2000.
87. See Keith Manchester, "Antoine Béchamp: Père de la Biologie. Oui ou Non?" *Endeavour* 25, 68(70), 72 (June 1, 2000).
88. See Joe Dubs, "The Fallacious Germ Theory," $\sqrt{\phi\sum}DUBS$, April 24, 2013, https://joedubs.com/the-fallacious-germ-theory/.
89. See Bruce Lipton, *The Biology of Belief: Unleashing the Power of Consciousness, Matter, and Miracles* (New York: Hay House, 2016).
90. See Abraham Flexner, "Medical Education in the United States and Canada; a Report to the Carnegie Foundation for the Advancement of Teaching," *Carnegie Found* (1910), http://archive.carnegiefoundation.org/publications/pdfs/elibrary/Carnegie_Flexner_Report.pdf.
91. See Thomas P. Duffy, "The Flexner Report—100 Years Later," *Yale Journal of Biology* 84(269) 2011: 275–276.
92. See James Boggs, *Racism and The Class Struggle: Further Pages from a Black Worker's Notebook* (New York: Monthly Review, 1970).
93. See Hans Ruesch, "The Truth About the Rockefeller Drug Empire: The Drug Story," *Whale*, http://www.whale.to/b/ruesch.html (last visited May 30, 2021).
94. See generally Frank W. Stahnisch and Marja Verhoef, "The Flexner Report of 1910 and Its Impact on Complementary and Alternative Medicine and Psychiatry in North America in the 20th Century," *Evidence-Based Complementary and Alternative Medicine* (2012).
95. See Elizabeth Hlavinka, "Racial Bias in Flexner Report Permeates Medical Education Today," *MedPageToday*, June 18, 2020, https://

www.medpagetoday.com/publichealthpolicy/medicaleducation/87171.
96. See Elizabeth Hlavinka, "Study Backs Flexner Report's Negative Impact on Black Physicians," *MedPageToday*, August 20, 2020, https://www.medpagetoday.com/publichealthpolicy/medicaleducation/88176/.
97. See Barbara Starfield, "Is U.S. Health Really the Best in the World?" *American Medical Association* 284 2000: 483–484.
98. See Robert "Preidt, Study: Most N.Y. COVID Patients on Ventilators Died," *WebMD*, https://www.webmd.com/lung/news/20200422/most-covid-19-patients-placed-on-ventilators-died-new-york-study-shows#1 (last visited May 30, 2021).
99. See Pierre Kory et al., "Clinical and Scientific Rationale for the "MATH+ " Hospital Treatment Protocol for COVID-19," *Journal of Intensive Care Medicine* 36(135) 2021: 135–156.
100. See "Revised Guidelines for Home Isolation of Mild/Asymptomatic COVID-19 Cases," *Covid Blog*, April 28, 2021, https://thecovidblog.com/wp-content/uploads/2021/05/Revised-India-COVID-guideline.pdf.
101. See Tamil Nadu, "Ivermectin Dropped as COVID-19 Drug," *Hindu*, May 14, 2021, https://www.thehindu.com/news/national/tamil-nadu/tn-drops-ivermectin-as-covid-19-drug/article34561235.ece; see also "WHO Warns Against the Use of Ivermectin a Day After GOA Approves Use for Treating COVID-19," *MoneyControl News*, May 11, 2021, 4:36 PM, https://www.moneycontrol.com/news/trends/who-recommends-against-the-use-of-ivermectin-says-chief-scientist-soumya-swaminathan-6880501.html.
102. See "Merck Statement on Ivermectin Use During the COVID-19 Pandemic," *Merck*, February 4, 2021, 11:45 AM, https://www.merck.com/news/merck-statement-on-ivermectin-use-during-the-covid-19-pandemic/.
103. See generally Fatimah S. Dawood et al., "Interim Estimates of 2019–20 Seasonal Influenza Vaccine Effectiveness—United States, February 2020," *Morbidity Mortality Weekly Report* 69(177) 2020; Greg G. Wolff, "Influenza Vaccination and Respiratory Virus Interference Among Department of Defense Personnel During the 2017–2018 Influenza Season," *Vaccine* 38(350) 2020.

104. See "Ten Threats to Global Health in 2019," *WHO*, https://www.who.int/news-room/spotlight/ten-threats-to-global-health-in-2019 (last visited May 30, 2021).
105. See "A Shot Against Opioids," *National Health Institute* (October 20, 2020), https://heal.nih.gov/news/stories/OUD-vaccine.
106. See Jason Wilson, "U.S. Was Warned of Threat from Anti-Vaxxers in Event of Pandemic", *The Guardian*, April 27, 2020, 6:30 AM, https://www.theguardian.com/us-news/2020/apr/27/us-warning-pandemic-anti-vaxxers.
107. William A. Haseltine, "COVID-19 Vacccine Protocols Reveal That Trials Are Designed to Succeed," *Forbes*, September 23, 2020, https://www.forbes.com/sites/williamhaseltine/2020/09/23/covid-19-vaccine-protocols-reveal-that-trials-are-designed-to-succeed/?sh=4588bc815247.
108. Haseltine, "COVID-10 Vaccine Protocols."
109. The patent numbers are redacted on the SEC filings, however, making it impossible to specify the technology contained in the COVID-19 products. See Mario Gaviria and Burcu Kilic, "A Network Analysis of COVID-19 mRNA Vaccine Patents," *Nature Biotechnology* 39(546) 2021: 546–548.
110. Gaviria and Kilic, "A Network Analysis."
111. See Mehmet Soy et al., "Cytokine Storm in COVID-19: Pathogenesis and Overview of Anti-Inflammatory Agents Used in Treatment," *Clinical Rheumatology* 39(2085) 2020: 2085–2094.
112. See generally Li Liu et al., "Anti-Spike Igg Causes Severe Acute Lung Injury by Skewing Macrophage Responses During Acute SARS-Cov Infection," *JCI Insight* 4(1) (2019).
113. See Aristo Vojdani et al., "Reaction of Human Monoclonal Antibodies to SARS-CoV-2 Proteins with Tissue Antigens: Implications for Autoimmune Diseases," *Frontiers in Immunology* (January 19, 2021), https://www.frontiersin.org/articles/10.3389/fimmu.2020.617089/full.
114. See Tom Shimabukuro, "Allergic Reactions Including Anaphylaxis After Receipt of the First Dose of Moderna COVID-19 Vaccine—United States, December 21, 2020—January 10, 2021," *CDC*, January 29, 2021, https://www.cdc.gov/mmwr/volumes/70/wr/mm7004e1.htm; Tom Shimabukuro, "Allergic Reactions

Including Anaphylaxis After Receipt of the First Dose of Pfizer-BioNTech COVID-19 Vaccine—United States, December 14–23, 2020," *CDC*, January 15, 2021, https://www.cdc.gov/mmwr/volumes/70/wr/mm7002e1.htm.
115. Catherine Ho, "Allergic Reactions at One San Diego Site Led State To Shelf 330,000 Vaccine Doses," *San Francisco Chronicle*, January 18, 2021, 8:53 PM, https://www.sfchronicle.com/bayarea/article/Allergic-reactions-that-caused-state-to-halt-15879657.php.
116. See "Adjuvants and Vaccines," *CDC*, August 14, 2020, https://www.cdc.gov/vaccinesafety/concerns/adjuvants.html.
117. Zaria Gorvett, "The Surprising Ingredients Found in Vaccines," *British Broadcasting*, October 27, 2020, https://www.bbc.com/future/article/20201027-what-is-added-to-vaccines.
118. About "VAERS," *The Vaccine Adverse Event Reporting System*, https://vaers.hhs.gov/about.html (last visited May 30, 2021).
119. See "NIA Adverse Event and Serious Adverse Event Guidelines," *National Institute on Aging*, https://www.nia.nih.gov/sites/default/files/2018-09/nia-ae-and-sae-guidelines-2018.pdf (last visited May 30, 2021).
120. See "VAERS Data Use Guide," *The Vaccine Adverse Event Reporting System*, https://vaers.hhs.gov/docs/VAERSDataUseGuide_November2020.pdf (last visited May 30, 2021).
121. Jessica Rose, "A Report on the U.S. Vaccine Adverse Event Reporting System (VAERS) of the COVID-19 Messenger Ribonucleic Acid (mRNA) Biologicals," *Science, Public Health Policy and the Law* 2(59) 2021: 60, 64.
122. Rose, 120. Rose reports that AEs for COVID-19 biologicals are increasing by as much as thirty-six percent *each week* (VAERS data is updated each Friday). This means that the data from early April contained in her peer-reviewed journal article published in mid-May significantly understates the current statistical portrait of adverse events. Rose has given interviews and presentations on VAERS that present more current data, and I cite to those sources as well as to her published article. Her interviews and presentations are summaries of her published article, only with the most up-to-date data. While only the published article has been peer-reviewed,

readers of this article should follow up on this data using her talks as supplements to the article. For a presentation of the same graphs contained in her article, but with updated data, see Mordechai Sones, "Study: Analysis Suggests the Vaccines Are Likely Cause of Reported Deaths, Spontaneous Abortions, Anaphylactic Reactions, Cardiovascular, Neurological, and Immunological Adverse Events," *America's Frontline Dr.*, May 19, 2021, https://www.americasfrontlinedoctors.org/frontline-news/study-analysis-suggests-the-vaccines-are-likely-cause-of-reported-deaths-spontaneous-abortions-anaphylactic-reactions-cardiovascular-neurological-and-immunological-adverse-events; and for her most recent interview, see also "The Gary Null Show – 05.19.21," *Progressive Radio Voices*, https://prn.fm/gary-null-show-05-19-21/ (last visited May 30, 2021).
123. For the statistics in this paragraph as reported by Rose, see *Progressive Radio Voices*, at 07:35.
124. See Rose, 69–71.
125. See Michal Shimonovich et al., "Assessing Causality in Epidemiology: Revisiting Bradford Hill to Incorporate Developments in Causal Thinking," *European Journal of Epidemiology* (December 16, 2020), https://doi.org/10.1007/s10654-020-00703-7.
126. See Chien-Te Tseng et al., "Immunization with SARS Coronavirus Vaccines Leads to Pulmonary Immunopathology on Challenge with the SARS Virus," *PLOS One* (April 20, 2012), https://doi.org/10.1371/journal.pone.0035421.
127. See James Lyons-Weiler, "Pathogenic Priming Likely Contributes to Serious and Critical Illness and Mortality in COVID-19 Via Autoimmunity," *The Journal of Translational Autoimmunity* (April 9, 2020), https://doi.org/10.1016/j.jtauto.2020.100051.
128. See Timothy Cardozo and Ronald Veazey, "Informed Consent Disclosure to Vaccine Trial Subjects of Risk of COVID-19 Vaccines Worsening Clinical Disease," *International Journal of Clinical Practice* (October 28, 2020), https://doi.org/10.1111/ijcp.13795.
129. Rose, 73.
130. See "They Don't Want to See People Like Us," *The Highwire*, April 30, 2021, https://thehighwire.com/videos/they-dont-want-to-see-people-like-us/.

6

Efficacy, Eugenics, and Law in the Modern Vaccine Regime

Pandemic Police Power develops the historical principle that policing precedes law, that law conforms to the police power in every area of society. The pandemic police power would therefore drive law as it pertains to public health protocols, not the other way around. Indeed, a review of vaccination law and legal discourse during the Pandemic Year affirms the essential alignment between legal and medical discourse. This assessment may seem simplistic or reductive to both lawyers and medical professionals, both of whom are well versed in the ways in which the day-to-day job of healthcare provision takes place within a highly technical legal universe. The standard employed in this book, however, is that police power is essential to the reproduction of a society structured in dominance.[1] An evaluation of the legal discourse regarding vaccination, therefore, will be useful for illuminating the structure of dominance that vaccine law is meant to fortify.

Two problems come into view when we track both the jurisprudence on public health law and the discourse among legal scholars surrounding it. First, the law effectively shrouds the speciousness of vaccine efficacy. The leading public health discourse maintains that the dawn of vaccine development spelled the end of the historical scourge of viral epidemics. The historical record has been much more complicated and dubious and does not, in fact, bear out this heroic portrait of medical science. The preceding chapter discussed the collateral problems intrinsic to vaccines as biotechnology, and analyzed the shortcomings of a public health model dependent upon vaccination. The open-minded reader, nevertheless, might still reply that, despite its attendant problems, vaccination has been instrumental in eradicating a number of catastrophic illnesses from the industrialized societies of the Western world. The present chapter presents historical evidence that this notion is inaccurate as well. If indeed vaccines have not been the central factor in the eradication of certain diseases that they have been purported to be, then compulsory vaccination under the law appears far more oppressive than it would otherwise seem. In other words, in this chapter, we come to see how vaccination further crystallizes as more *political* than medical or scientific, as an expression of power relations organized to reproduce certain hierarchies in the society.

Secondly, the political essence of the vaccination regime is most readily apparent in its connections with eugenics. The leading narrative regarding eugenics is that it was a corruption of modern science by racist ideology during the first half of the twentieth century, with Naziism and the Jewish Holocaust as the pinnacle of eugenicist practices. Eugenics was thus closely tied to early twentieth century fascism, so the story goes, and therefore also crumbled in the face of democratic culture's reassertion in the post-war period. The fallacy of this narrative is robust and easily dismissed with recourse to slavery as the original eugenicist project. The slaveholding culture sustained eugenicist notions of relative human value, and continues to rely upon a bio-epistemology of symbolic life and death in which some humans are made to appear naturally selected for life and prosperity while other human groups are construed as naturally marked out for death and suffering. In other words, eugenicist ideology is central to the functioning of contemporary society and remains alive and well in the twenty-first century. A political reading of vaccination can divulge the connections between racist violence and the vaccine regime. In other words, a reading that does not sideline the power dynamics that gained expression as compulsory vaccination will permit understanding vaccines as one facet of larger bio-medical racism that remains in full effect today.

Finally, it is a constituent phenomenon of policing that the police power spawns its own resistance, and vaccine law as a key component of the police power has resulted in mounting legal challenges. The point here, again, is to demonstrate law's purpose *within* the pandemic police power, not external to it or in any way a check on it. It is necessary to both analyze how vaccine law contradicts its own legal and scientific framework *and* to suggest how trapped legal discourse is within this paradigm. There is an important role for law in protecting people from vaccine mandates and unraveling the harms associated with the medical industrial complex, but ultimately the turn toward actual healthy publics will originate from elsewhere, beyond law and the state-corporate structure. This finding parallels the abolitionist approach to the prison industrial complex. Abolishing the medical industrial complex does not mean getting rid of medicine, science, or public health; it does not mean doctors, nurses, and scientists are inherently bad. It simply means that the present structure of healthcare is fatally compromised by state power, the profit motive, and the social control function of racism. This chapter uses vaccine law to expose some key dimensions of this problem.

As with science, so too with law: both are intrinsically open-ended and subject to constant evaluation and revision. The problem with "consensus" in science has its parallel with "settled" law. Nevertheless, currently, there is very little debate within the legal community regarding vaccination. The Supreme Court's 1905 decision in *Jacobson v. Massachusetts* is widely regarded as establishing the states' police powers to include compulsory vaccination.[2] In challenging a Massachusetts smallpox vaccine mandate, Jacobson argued that "compulsion to introduce disease into a healthy system is a violation of liberty."[3] But the Court held that the police power includes a community's "right to protect itself against the epidemic of disease which threatens the safety of its members." The Court would go on to analogize compulsory vaccination to the military draft, arguing that just like a citizen "compelled, by force if need be, against his will and without regard to his personal wishes" to serve in the army and "risk the chance of being shot down in its defense," so too may such a citizen forfeit "control of one's body upon his willingness to submit to reasonable regulations established by the constituted authorities... for the purpose of protecting the public collectively against such danger."[4] The decision galvanized the formation of the Anti-Vaccination League of America under the principle that "'health is nature's greatest safeguard against disease and that therefore no State has the right to demand of anyone the impairment of his or her health,'" and it aimed "'to abolish oppressive medical laws and counteract the growing tendency to enlarge the scope of state medicine at the expense of the freedom of the individual.'"[5] Similar organizations had formed in Europe with the attempted introduction of compulsory vaccination programs there.[6] Although these organizations are portrayed as anti-science by contemporary historians, they were in fact merely resistant to what they perceived as the state's misuse of power.[7] Their stance against science, therefore, is properly understood not as anti-science per se, as it is usually depicted by contemporary scholars and observers, but rather as a critique of science as a discourse of state power. It is this dissenting take on science, nature, and production that the Carnegies, Rockefellers, and Morgan's sought to overcome through the Flexner Report, as discussed in the previous chapter.

Harvard Law Review published a *Note* in 2008 that argued *Jacobson* was no longer relevant to today's needs.[8] It did not, interestingly, pin *Jacobson*'s irrelevance on the fact that the Court's analogy to the military draft was outdated. Instead, it asserted that vaccination campaigns today are no longer focused on infectious viruses, arguing that *Jacobson* provides little guidance on the controversial hepatitis B and HPV vaccines. *HLR* suggested that vaccine law distinguishes between vaccines that are medically necessary (for which there is no alternative) and those that are practically necessary (viable alternatives exist but are not taken up by most people). Presumably, *HLR* was eating its words during the Pandemic Year, not because we are now faced with a serious public health threat from an infectious virus, which as we have seen in the preceding chapter is not in fact the case—but rather because the current season of vaccination is showing that there is no real difference between "medical necessity" and "practical necessity" when it comes to the state's promotion of vaccines and the restrictions placed on how society functions. *HLR*'s assessment of vaccine law typifies legal discourse in the matter in that the politics of science are taken at face value, leaving the problem with vaccination as state power beyond the grasp of most legal scholars.

In 2014–2015 there was a minor outbreak of measles in southern California, centered at Disneyland.[9] California responded in June 2015 by passing more stringent compulsory vaccination laws, eliminating personal and religious belief exemptions for children enrolled in school or daycare.[10] Under California's SB 277, parents can decline to vaccinate their children only if the child is enrolled in a home-based private school or off-campus independent study program. Moreover, unvaccinated children can utilize their exemptions obtained before 2016 until they enter either kindergarten or the seventh grade, depending on their age. Additionally, parents may still obtain medical exemptions for their children and the law permits doctors to take family history or sibling health into account in deciding whether to issue a medical exemption. California's SB 277 survived its first legal challenge, with the Second Appellate District's Court of Appeals upholding the law in July 2018.[11]

The events of 2014–2015 spawned a response of their own from legal scholars. Although my review was not exhaustive, I did not find any legal analysts arguing against compulsory vaccination, only different takes on how to utilize the law to achieve vaccine compliance.[12] Erwin Chemerinsky and Michele Goodwin, for instance, argue that the new California law does not go far enough.

> Our position is that every state should require compulsory vaccination of all children, unless there is a medical reason why the child should not be vaccinated. In other words, there should be no exception to the compulsory vaccination requirement on account of the parents' religion or conscience or for any reason other than medical necessity. Simply put, the government's interest in protecting children and preventing the spread of communicable disease justifies mandatory vaccinations for all children in the United States.[13]

Goodwin and Chemerinsky even go so far as to suggest that parents who do not vaccinate their children should be charged with criminal negligence.[14] Who gets to decide "medical necessity?" In a world governed by the police power of the medical industrial complex, biotechnology, and medical science's germ theory, presumably, the answer would be the public health establishment. At some point, people outside of medical science will have to study the science for themselves. Instead of independently evaluating the science on their own, however, Chemerinsky and Goodwin rely on CDC claims that vaccination prevented the deaths of 732,000 U.S. children between 1994 and 2014.[15] These statistics are spurious on their face because they are entirely based on a hypothetical world, and as such, the numbers of children saved by vaccines can be neither verified nor definitively impugned. More importantly, referencing the CDC as the authority on vaccine safety and efficacy is like going to the Department of Justice for the final word on whether or not there is a crime problem and to verify how many lives have been saved by putting more police on the streets and locking people up in prisons and jails. Indeed, it is precisely the hypothetical of preemptive incapacitation that justified the notorious "three strikes" sentencing laws passed in the 1990s that sent third-time felony offenders to prison for life without the possibility of parole, regardless of the offense.[16] Lock them up forever to prevent future crime and mayhem, was the argument at the time. The state has been thoroughly exposed over the past couple of decades for its use of criminology discourse to legitimate law-and-order policies that have built a massive prison industrial complex; it is time that the state be similarly exposed for its use of immunology discourse to legitimate public health policies that have built a massive medical industrial complex. The former has conjured problems in order to fit its preferred solutions of policing, punishment, and incapacitation; with those kinds of solutions, the range of permissible questions is severely restricted. The latter similarly conjures problems that fit its preferred solutions of vaccination, drug intervention, and health disempowerment; these kinds of solutions, again, are meant to keep people from asking the questions that could actually produce healthy lives in the long run. As we will see below, the presumption of vaccine efficacy and safety cannot be taken for granted any more than the fallacious notion that mass incarceration is causally linked to increased safety and crime control.

Chemerinsky and Goodwin illustrate how the state's narrative of public health is advanced through the legal and medical literature. They claim that the science on vaccinations is air tight:

> Strong and irrefutable medical and scientific evidence demonstrates that there is no less restrictive alternative except to require every person to be vaccinated. Only vaccinations can protect children from communicable diseases. Only by vaccinating every child who medically can be inoculated, can there be protection for those who cannot be vaccinated, whether by reason of being too young or it being medically inadvisable.[17]

If it is irrefutable, then it is not science; that would be faith or myopia, which are intrinsically uncontestable because they are not formed through reason. Or, as the preferred term these days regarding public health decisions would have it, the "scientific consensus."[18] The late Michael Crichton once had this to say about scientific consensus:

> I want to pause here and talk about this notion of consensus, and the rise of what has been called consensus science. I regard consensus science as an extremely pernicious development that ought to be stopped cold in its tracks. Historically, the claim of consensus has been the first refuge of scoundrels; it is a way to avoid debate by claiming that the matter is already settled. Whenever you hear the consensus of scientists agrees on something or other, reach for your wallet, because you're being had.[19]

The work of science has nothing to do with consensus. Chemerinsky and Goodwin arrogantly endorse the general elitist dismissal of the many people concerned about vaccine safety and efficacy by stating that the evidence in support of vaccines is "irrefutable." Since science, by definition, must be subject to constant challenge, critique, and revision, the best the law could do is to state *for now* vaccinations are scientifically valid, or *until competing evidence emerges*—which, as we have seen, it already has.

We can go to the experts in law and medicine for the legal and medical arguments for vaccination, but in so doing, we must check two things at the door. First, we must set aside our knowledge that state power is never benign because it is a social control apparatus. Second, we must suspend our awareness of the fact that the scientific and medical establishments are comprised of institutions that *are* the state, and as such, they present agendas that compete with and sometimes directly conflict with scientific inquiry and medical health. Setting aside our knowledge of these two things, however, is itself costly to our health. Since we are aware of how both of these forces are driving the suppressed history of vaccination, as the preceding pages have sought to illuminate, we have to read legal scholars like Chemerinsky and Goodwin as disseminating state narratives.

As of the time of my writing, the COVID-19 shots are not mandated at a federal or state level, despite some calls to make them so.[20] The Australian Prime Minister proclaimed that the vaccine "would be as mandatory as you can possibly make it," before he had to walk back that statement.[21] A new law in Israel allows the Health Ministry to share the personal info of people who decline the vaccine.[22] And already the use of "vaccine passports" is in the works in the United States[23] Except for the Pfizer shot, these new vaccines have only received emergency use authorization from the FDA (an issue to which we will return shortly), and a nationwide adult vaccine mandate would be the first of its kind. *Jacobson* only upheld a local vaccine mandate with conditions, and it is not clear that the case would support a broad law mandating compulsory vaccination nationwide, especially if lesser measures were not tried first. Compulsory vaccination is more likely to come through tailored local, institutional, or employer-based mandates, much like the targeted vaccination laws for schoolchildren, military personnel, and healthcare workers.[24] Depending on which state they are located in, many universities and colleges have already announced that students must receive a COVID-19 injection in order to return to campus in the fall, and numerous employers are also requiring their employees to receive the shot in order to keep their jobs. Health insurers are already ending cost-sharing waivers for COVID-19 treatment while covering vaccine costs in full. At the same time, there are increasing reports of health care workers opting out of the shot. In Los Angeles County, up to forty percent of frontline healthcare workers have refused the COVID-19 injections, while sixty percent of homecare workers in Ohio have declined.[25] As one nurse put it, "I am not an anti-vaxxer, I have every vaccine known to man, my flu shot, I always sign up right there, October 1, jab me. But for this one, why do I have to be a guinea pig?"[26] Many nurses are choosing to leave their jobs rather than accept the shot, going from "frontline heroes" in 2020 to unemployed pariahs in 2021, leading to staffing shortages in the nation's healthcare system.[27] Indeed, the long-term effects of the COVID-19 injections will not be known for years, and its development timeline was unprecedented, something that did not play out well at all the last time such a tactic was attempted.[28]

Jacobson has been interpreted by the courts in ways that may lend support for the implementation of a limited vaccine mandate. In *Zucht v. King*, the Court held that vaccination of schoolchildren is justified even if there is no immediate threat, as there supposedly was with smallpox in *Jacobson*.[29] In the recent case of *Workman v. Mingo County Board of Education*, the U.S. Court of Appeals for the Fourth Circuit upheld as constitutional a West Virginia law requiring all schoolchildren to be vaccinated, with no exemption for religious reasons.[30] In its decision, the appeals court cited a prior holding by the Supreme Court that religious freedom must yield to the compelling state interest of preventing disease: "[t]he right to practice religion freely does not include liberty to expose the community or the child to communicable disease or the latter to ill health."[31] The argument that compulsory vaccination violates parents' constitutional right to control the upbringing of their children may have a stronger foundation than free exercise claims, but even there the courts have found that parental rights are not absolute and the state can interfere to protect the interests of the child.[32]

Despite the lack of debate in the legal community regarding vaccine law, *Jacobson* raises four serious objections with respect to COVID-19. First, when we examine more closely the claims that vaccines have saved scores of lives in the two centuries since their development, a decidedly different portrait of disease mitigation emerges.[33] While health in eighteenth century Western society was dominated by disease epidemics and shortened life expectancy relative to today, the nineteenth century saw progressive improvements in health such that by the first half of the twentieth century complete suppression of the major infectious disease killers of the previous century was expected. Rapid urbanization and industrialization in the late eighteenth and early nineteenth centuries created cities marked by residential density, inadequate housing, and poor sanitation and public hygiene. Working conditions for the average worker at the time ranged from unhealthy to life-threatening, both in terms of workplace hazards and the poverty-level wages that left most people in a constant state of nutritional lack. In sum, the conditions were ripe in two important ways for the devastation of bacterial and viral diseases: most cities were in effect human and animal waste cesspools for the cultivation and spread of illness, and most people encountered these living conditions with immune systems already compromised by poverty. To make matters worse, medical practitioners themselves were instigators of disease during this time (foreshadowing the serious problem with iatrogenesis today, death by medical practice, as noted in the previous chapter). For instance, puerperal fever is a deadly infection that affected many mothers and infants in the immediate post-partum period, with as many as 50 percent of mothers giving birth in a Paris hospital in 1746 dying.[34] But mothers tended by medical doctors (always men at this point) had more than three times the rate of death compared with those tended by midwives. When doctors were directed to disinfect their hands prior to touching women, the maternal mortality rate went from a high of 32 percent down to zero.[35] Many doctors resented the implication that they were the cause of harm, and were arrogant enough to continue to ignore the often fatal consequences of their unsanitary practices up until the 1940s when antibiotics were invented.[36] Maternal death directly jeopardizes children's health: infants whose mothers died around childbirth had a four times higher risk of dying, most commonly from infections.

In most cases, the dramatic increases in life expectancy in the second half of the nineteenth century and into the early twentieth were attributable more to improvements in sanitation, hygiene, housing, and working conditions, and overall nutrition, and not to advancements in medical science, including vaccines. For instance, scarlet fever deaths plummeted in the second half of the nineteenth century. No vaccine for scarlet fever was ever successfully developed, and the dramatic decrease in mortality occurred by the early 1900s, long before the advent of antibiotic therapies.[37] In other words, nothing had been eradicated, other than the pathogenic social conditions for disease. Even today, the bacterial organisms most associated with scarlet fever colonize 15–20 percent of school children and harmlessly remain ever-present because most people's immune systems today can handle it: health is *social*, not simply individual. In fact, antibiotics may actually increase the toxin release from the bacteria, reminding us that suppression of the naturally occurring biome can unsettle the body's equilibrium that is so essential to proper immune system functioning.[38]

The threat of death from all infectious diseases in the Western world had faded to insignificance by the mid-1900s. Mortality from pertussis (whooping cough) had been falling steeply for over seventy years before the vaccine came into widespread use in the 1950s.[39] The story is similar for measles. In the years 1807–1812, measles accounted for eleven percent of all deaths in Glasgow. Case fatalities were very high: data from a Paris orphanage shows that 49 percent of the children who developed measles died between 1867 and 1872. The measles vaccine was not introduced until 1968, but by 1960 notification of childhood measles in England and Wales was only 2.4 percent and mortality had fallen to 0.030 percent, which is 1:200 of the 1908 Glasgow mortality rate.[40] The fact that babies were no longer dying of poverty-related ailments like diarrhea was a major factor in the overall improved life expectancy during the twentieth century. From 1900 to 1940, deaths from diarrhea declined from 143.7 to 9.4 per 100,000—a 93.5 percent decrease—all before the introduction of antibiotics.[41]

That improvements in living conditions, not vaccines or medicines, inaugurated the overall decline in disease mortality is confirmed by the return of these same diseases in societies that experience dramatic declines in living conditions, despite high rates of vaccination. Russia in the 1990s provides one such case study. A sharp deterioration in Russian life expectancy during the period included a diphtheria outbreak, with over 2500 cases in St. Petersburg in 1994 alone, despite a highly vaccinated population.[42] The persistence of high mortality rates and infectious diseases in various places in the non-Western world, amidst high rates of poverty and inadequate infrastructure, suggests that clean drinking water and improved sanitation alone would do more to increase life expectancy and suppress disease than the billions of dollars currently being invested in vaccination programs in the so-called developing world. Child mortality due to measles is 200–400 times greater in malnourished children than those with adequate nutrition levels; as nutrition improves, complications from measles diminish until the disease largely disappears altogether.[43]

The smallpox vaccine, the first of its kind developed against an infectious disease, has a particularly dubious history. Introduced in 1796, there was great debate and dissension regarding the vaccine throughout the nineteenth century, leading directly to the *Jacobson* decision in 1905. In a remarkable 1889 article published in the *Westminster Review*, the author observed that "compulsory or non-compulsory vaccination was among the most important questions engaging the attention of thoughtful men," and proceeded to elaborate how beginning "[f]rom 1804, reports of failures in vaccination began to multiply."[44] Early medical journals detailed how smallpox could still infect and even kill those who were vaccinated. In 1810, the *Medical Observer* featured details of 535 cases of smallpox after vaccination in London, 97 fatal cases, and 150 cases of vaccine injuries.[45] Eighteen years after smallpox vaccination became mandatory in England, *The Lancet* noted the desultory failure of universal vaccination:

> The deaths from small-pox have assumed the proportions of a plague. Over 10,000 lives have been sacrificed during the past year in England and Wales. In London, 5641 deaths have occurred since Christmas. Of 9932 patients in the London small-pox hospitals, no less than 6854 have been vaccinated—nearly 73 per cent. Taking the mortality at 17.5 per cent of those attacked and the deaths this year in the whole country at 10,000, it will follow that more than 122,000 vaccinated persons have suffered from small-pox! This is an alarming state of things. Can we greatly wonder that the opponents of compulsory vaccination should point to such statistics, as evidence of the failure of the system? It is necessary to speak plainly on this important matter.[46]

As it became increasingly irrefutable that the smallpox vaccine was unable to prevent disease, the medical profession adjusted by claiming that it produced milder disease. This claim also proved unfounded. In the 1844 smallpox epidemic, about one-third of the vaccinated contracted a mild form of smallpox, but roughly eight percent of those vaccinated still died, and nearly two-thirds had severe disease.[47]

The failures of vaccination yielded greater dissension from the practice, which in turn led to compulsory vaccination laws. Massachusetts passed a set of comprehensive vaccination laws in 1855. Following the

1855 mandates, there were smallpox epidemics in 1859–1860, 1864–1865, 1867, and 1872–1873. Not only did strict vaccination laws have no beneficial effect, but more people died from smallpox in the twenty years *after* compulsory laws were instituted than in the twenty years prior, with the same pattern repeated throughout highly vaccinated populations across the Western world.[48] Objections to vaccine safety, effectiveness, and government infringement on personal liberty culminated in the Great Demonstration in Leicester, England in 1885. Leicester diverged from the compulsory vaccination approach to disease mitigation in effect throughout England, relying instead on quarantine of smallpox patients and thorough disinfection of their homes. The method immediately vindicated itself as superior to vaccination when smallpox mortality in Leicester during the 1893 outbreak was 32 times lower than in the surrounding well-vaccinated districts.[49] Over the years, Leicester's death rate from smallpox declined even further:

> Leicester's small-pox history, and her successful vindication of sanitation as a small-pox prophylactic, will bear the closest scrutiny. Each successive epidemic since vaccination has decreased, with a larger proportion of unvaccinated population, furnishes a still lower death-rate. [*sic*][50]

Leicester proved that more effective, less costly, and safer methods than vaccination could bring infectious disease under control. The reason Leicester's methods were successful, we now know, is because they were aligned with the historical trend toward improved sanitation and nutrition that would largely end the scourge of infectious disease in Western societies by the mid-twentieth century—without the assistance of medicines and vaccines. Indeed, the historical downward trajectory of smallpox almost perfectly mirrors that of scarlet fever, for which there has never been a vaccine developed. Medical science's false narrative that the introduction of vaccines directly led to the dramatic reductions in the late nineteenth and twentieth centuries in disease epidemics closely mirrors the false narrative of criminal justice in the late twentieth century. As noted in the second chapter, the claim that the massive build-up in the criminal justice system beginning in the 1980s was a response to an increase in property crimes, drug crimes, and violence, and is responsible for reducing crime thereafter, is false. In both cases, the reality was that the incidence of infectious disease and of all kinds of crime declined precipitously *before* the state began to introduce mass vaccination and incarceration, respectively.

As also noted in the second chapter, the fact that mass incarceration has failed to increase safety and eradicate crime, while fomenting bloat and corruption throughout the criminal justice system, and destruction and rage across the most impacted communities, has increasingly led to agreement across the political spectrum that mass incarceration has been an unmitigated failure. Similar data from measles research points to a mirror charade with respect to vaccine efficacy and safety. Although mortality remains very low, outbreaks in the 1980s and 1990s suggest that measles is becoming a disease of the vaccinated. The CDC concluded the following about an outbreak in Illinois in 1984:

> This outbreak demonstrates that transmission of measles can occur within a school population with a documented immunization level of 100 percent. This level was validated during the outbreak investigation. Previous investigations of measles outbreaks among highly immunized populations have revealed risk factors such as improper storage or handling of vaccine, vaccine administered to children under one year of age, use of globulin with vaccine, and use of killed virus vaccine. However, these risk factors did not adequately explain the occurrence of this outbreak.[51]

A 1994 study lends further weight to the conclusion that vaccination is not the most effective means of disease prevention, showing that multiple measles outbreaks have occurred in school populations in which 71 percent to 99.8 percent of the student body had been vaccinated appropriately.[52] In other words, the same problems that generated mass resistance to vaccination in the late nineteenth and early twentieth centuries, led to the Leicester Demonstration, and spawned the *Jacobson* case remains very much in effect today. Whereas resistance to the criminal justice disaster of the prison industrial complex took less than fifty years to produce rhetorical, if not actual, commitments to end mass incarceration, the medical industrial complex has endured for over two centuries.

When Henning Jacobson challenged the Massachusetts vaccine mandate in court, he was well aware not only of vaccination's dubious track record, but also of the potential harms associated with the vaccine. Jacobson was born in Sweden in 1856 and received smallpox vaccination at age six under Sweden's compulsory program. Jacobson's children, in turn, were vaccinated when they reached school age as a result of the Massachusetts law requiring vaccination of all school children. Jacobson and one of his sons had bad reactions to the vaccine. Although the nature of the Jacobsons' adverse experiences with vaccination is unclear, it is well documented that smallpox vaccination caused deaths, and based on the documented appearance of severe jaundice following vaccination, may have also been the means by which other diseases such as hepatitis, tuberculosis, and syphilis were transferred to vaccine recipients.[53] According to a 2002 report from researchers at the University of Michigan, the dangers of eczema vaccinatum, postvaccinial encephalitis, and progressive vaccinia, all of which can be fatal and have dogged the vaccine since the beginning, remain statistical likelihoods if the United States were to resume routine smallpox vaccination (which ended in 1972) due to the impurity and contamination of the vaccine stock. The researchers estimate that a smallpox campaign in the United States would lead to 285 deaths and 4600 serious adverse events—and that is *after* excluding 25 percent of the population that would have to avoid the shot because of high risk for adverse events for themselves or their close contacts.[54] Other researchers found that the main smallpox vaccine in use since the late 1800s, Dryvax, is of "quasispecies" origin so complex that they were unable to isolate the diversity of viruses contained in the vaccine.[55] In 2008, after more than a century of use, the CDC called for the quarantine and destruction of all remaining Dryvax, but replaced it with "a live vaccinia virus derived from plaque purification cloning from Dryvax." With no apparent irony, the CDC assures the public that the safety data for this updated version of the vaccine indicates a "similar safety profile to Dryvax."[56]

At the time he resisted the Massachusetts vaccinators when they came to his door, Jacobson also would likely have been familiar with the related outbreaks in New England in 1902–1903 of foot-and-mouth disease associated with the production of smallpox vaccine. The smallpox vaccine was manufactured by growing the virus seed in cows and harvesting the resultant infectious cowpox pus to create the smallpox vaccines for humans. Any germs or diseases in the cow will therefore also go into the vaccine, and vice versa. Subsequent vaccine virus was also passed through rabbits, mice, goats, horses, sheep, and human tissues. As detailed in the previous chapter, this is the problem of zoonotic diseases intrinsic to all vaccine production. The vaccine virus propagated by the manufacturer in New England was contaminated with foot-and-mouth disease, leading to an epidemic that lasted six months, infected 244 herds of cattle, and ultimately led to the slaughter of 3872 cattle, 360 hogs, and 220 sheep.[57] Not only were humans who came into contact with the contaminated animals (especially butchers, farmers, tanners, blacksmiths, and others who worked with animal products) infected with foot-and-mouth disease, but just prior to the 1902 outbreak a serious and sometimes fatal skin malady called pemphigus appeared in people who had recently received the contaminated smallpox vaccine.[58] The possibility of vaccines introducing new diseases into previously healthy persons compounds the problem of vaccine ineffectiveness—which was precisely the argument that Jacobson made against the Massachusetts compulsory vaccination law, and brings us to the second issue with the *Jacobson* decision.

Second, the suspect effectiveness and safety record of vaccination, combined with the immunological evidence reviewed in the previous chapter, reveals how profoundly out of sync *Jacobson v. Massachusetts*—the holding precedent in U.S. public health law—is with emergent science. Henning Jacobson argued that vaccinations could be harmful and that it would be impossible to tell in an individual case whether vaccination would be beneficial at all. The Court held that because Jacobson "was himself in perfect health and a fit subject of vaccination," his argument was not persuasive.[59] The *Jacobson* Court simply dismissed the scientific and medical evidence that Jacobson presented which demonstrated the smallpox vaccine's lack of efficacy and its risks, including for otherwise apparently healthy individuals. What the Court could not have known, but what the scientific evidence now strongly suggests, is that the negative effects of vaccination may not be immediately apparent. The consequences of vaccination can take a variety of forms down the road, from autoimmune dysfunction to neurological disorder to cancer. In the 1960s, the effort to learn why the new measles vaccine sometimes had the effect of *causing* illness rather than protecting people from it led to the discovery of "recovery without antibodies" and "antibody dependent enhancement" (ADE). Children with congenital agammaglobulinaemia do not produce antibodies, and yet they recovered from measles just as well as normal antibody producers.[60] If the antibody part of immunity is not always necessary for clearing infection, then innate immunity assumes an even larger importance. Innate immunity does not require cellular memory or prior exposure or pre-formed specific antibodies. Instead, it involves the activation of white blood cells, T lymphocytes, and various cytokines (the immune system proteins discussed in the previous chapter). The innate immunity response is present regardless of vaccination, but is highly dependent on nutritional health. In other words, immunological science since *Jacobson* has learned that the part of the immune system that vaccination is designed to activate is not as essential to a successful response to an immune challenge as is the part of the system unaffected by vaccination. This helps to explain the scenario wherein healthy unvaccinated people do not get sick while unhealthy vaccinated people still come down with the illness that they have been immunized against. Nothing can replace or supersede the body's nutritional needs at the cellular level. Although scientific evidence of the historical relationship between sanitation, nutrition, and disease (as in the Leicester example) was available to (and ignored by) the *Jacobson* Court, contemporary science has deepened our understanding tenfold.

Antibody-dependent enhancement is when antibodies actually *increase* the ability of viruses to infect their target cells.[61] Scientists have documented the fact that measles vaccines have led to this antibody-dependent enhancement, although the precise mechanisms by which it occurs remain somewhat elusive.[62] What does seem clear, however, is that contemporary science is learning how much it does not yet understand about the immune system. The implications for vaccine science are paradigm-shifting:

> [I]t is increasingly apparent that, rather than being inherently good or bad, the effects of Abs (antibodies) are either beneficial or deleterious in a host, depending on the type of microbe-host interaction, including the setting in which damage occurs as a function of the host immune milieu and response. A logical extension of this concept is that an Ab that is protective in one host may not be protective in another if the nature of their immune responses to the relevant agent places them on different parts of the damage response curve. These concepts have important ramifications for vaccine design since vaccine efficacy could depend on enhancement of the immune response for those with weak immune responses, but enhanced responses could be detrimental in those who naturally generate strong immune responses.[63]

In other words, a vaccine-mediated response to an immune challenge *may* be supportive for people with otherwise weak immune health, but it *may* lead to antibody-dependent enhancement in healthy individuals. But how can we know which outcome will occur under which circumstance in order to make a decision to vaccinate or not?

> Considering that the immune response to pathogenic microbes includes Abs to many Ags (antigens) differing in the predominant isotype and amount, one can easily envision unfathomable complexity that becomes even more daunting if one considers host genetic variation... Clearly, defining protective efficacy of an Ab molecule in a predictive fashion is currently beyond the state of immunological science and may not be possible with current reductionistic approaches to scientific problems.[64]

Despite their sobering findings regarding the present unknowns in vaccine science, the authors of the two passages cited above go on to express their optimism that what we do not presently know can be shortly uncovered through better predictive algorithms and more, not less, vaccination. These scientists are well-ensconced in the medical science model of health, in which present setbacks are only interpreted as calls for further investment in biotechnology. In this framework, if one vaccine cannot adequately encompass the diversity of host genetic variation, then two or more vaccines will be required. This is the police power of the medical industrial complex firing on all cylinders. Alternatively, given the ground covered thus far in the previous and present chapters, I suggest that the above findings mean that immunological knowledge *within the present germ theory paradigm* is insufficient to predict the antibody characteristics that will be protective in a given individual at a given moment in time. Therefore, what the *Jacobson* Court could not have known is that science now finds its predictive capacity severely, if not fatally, incapacitated by advances in knowledge. In this advanced state, the understanding is now available to us, in the least, that compulsory vaccination's universalizing approach to the "unfathomable complexity" at the heart of individual immune responses is guaranteed to create harms that are commensurately immeasurable.

The third problem arising from *Jacobson* is that while the state has an interest in preventing disease outbreaks, compulsory vaccination traverses multiple constitutional rights, as well as some that are yet to be specified. Does it implicate the right to procreate, especially given the alarming number of spontaneous abortions, miscarriages, and reports of disrupted menstrual cycles in women from the COVID-19 shots, and who knows yet what kinds of consequences for male fertility? Is it a feature of the right to control the raising of children? Is it connected to the right to privacy, similar to that which begets the right to abortion? Is it more closely related to the right to refuse medical treatment? Is it connected to the right to practice a trade or to education, given that employer or school mandates stand in the way of these things? Does the validity of the law depend on the actual efficacy of vaccination, or merely that some "common belief" holds it does, as *Jacobson* states? The kind of right in question with vaccine mandates determines the level of constitutional scrutiny that courts must apply. The right to refuse medical treatment is unclear, and the right to work and education are fundamental rights that require a rational basis test. The other rights mentioned above require a strict scrutiny analysis, the highest standard of review. Strict scrutiny requires the state to show that vaccination is the least restrictive means for accomplishing this goal. In order for a law to pass strict scrutiny, it must advance a "compelling governmental interest," and there must not be any alternate and less restrictive way of achieving the same ends. It flies in the face of the extensive scientific evidence reviewed in *Pandemic Police Power* to maintain that there is no less restrictive alternative to injecting people with chimeric biotechnology and its panoply of zoonotic diseases, bacteria, retroviruses, and toxins, let alone with the experimental mRNA product. The legal scholarship on vaccine law does not acknowledge, let alone factor into its analysis, the long history of vaccine ineffectiveness and injury, nor does it consider the dangers of xenotransplantation—such as when the CDC responded to the 1976 swine flu outbreak by swiftly producing a vaccine that was administered to fifty million Americans and resulted in at least six hundred cases of paralysis, seventy-four deaths, and a cascade of lawsuits.[65]

What about investing in nutrition, clean air and water, healthy homes and communities, universal healthcare, and medicine uncoupled from the profit motive? These measures would be less restrictive and guaranteed to produce genuine and enduring positive public health outcomes compared with vaccination. As demonstrated in the previous chapter, the reliance on vaccination is a sign of a public health *failure*. At best, vaccination is a stop-gap measure propping up the medical industrial complex: vaccination as public health funnels resources away from actual healthy publics, pulling us deeper into biotech-driven medicine that leaves us communally un-well by suppressing knowledge crucial for strong cellular immune health. For instance, the "anti-infective" properties of vitamin A have been known to science for quite some time, and measles researchers have shown that low vitamin A levels correlate with low measles-specific antibodies and increased morbidity; that vitamin A reduces mortality in hospitalized measles cases by 60–90 percent; and that vitamin A supplementation during acute measles illness leads to significant drops in both adverse outcomes and death.[66] Poor nutritional values translate into weak cellular immunity, which leaves the body susceptible to infections, which in turn deplete the body's store of essential infection-fighting vitamins and minerals such as vitamin A.[67]

Vaccination can play a detrimental role in this vicious cycle of ill-health: naturally acquired measles infections *and* high-titer measles vaccines *both* impair cell-mediated immunity, in part because of vitamin A depletion in both processes.[68] The typical diet in the United States leaves the average child vitamin A deficient; the situation is even more severe in parts of the world where acute malnutrition predominates.[69]

This means that vaccination itself can increase children's susceptibility to other infections:

> High titre vaccines, like natural measles, cause long term disruption of immune function, including an imbalance in the type of helper T cell response…The message is clear. Strategies involving vaccination in infants with maternal antibody, or new measles vaccines, must be tested in randomized trials in which the end point is mortality and not a surrogate effect such as measles antibody titre.[70]

In short, vaccines are not simply a poor substitute for natural cellular immune health; they can also undermine it to the extent that vaccination itself becomes a risk factor for other infectious illnesses. These findings mean that instead of protecting against illness, vaccination can make a person susceptible to it. There is no shortcut to public health; vaccination is not only *not* the least restrictive means, as would be required under strict scrutiny review, it is part of the overall problem.

If vaccination at its best attempts to plug some of the holes in the public's health as a result of the medical industrial complex, then at its worst, vaccination covers up for inappropriate and ineffective medical treatment combined with the poisonous effects of industrial society. The case of polio stands out in this regard. Polio is held up as another vaccine success story, but the reality is far more tragic. Poliovirus in the wild has always circulated through humans for centuries without ever causing paralysis until the early twentieth century, at which point the paralytic disease showed up only in the industrialized Western societies, not in those parts of the world where the virus was equally endemic.[71] In the advanced capitalist societies, diets of refined and processed foods with the resultant lack of vitamins, environmental and agricultural poisons, and specific invasive medical procedures contributed to the rise of paralytic polio diagnoses. Diets high in refined sugars and flour feature harsh chemicals that contribute to the synergy between an otherwise innocent virus and the sugar.[72] The first modern synthetic pesticide, DDT, was developed in the 1940s and comprehensively applied not simply on agriculture but also on clothing, bedding, houses, children's lunches, public beaches, and directly onto children. The stated logic of this practice was that flies and mosquitoes transmitted viruses like polio and therefore it was thought that widespread consumption of the insecticide would prevent illness. Exposure to DDT *alone*, however, induced symptoms that were largely indistinguishable from poliomyelitis, even in the absence of a virus. Moreover, the chemical toxin was also found to increase the susceptibility to viral infection because poliovirus is able to live in pesticide-treated cells.[73]

In places like India today, which is one of four countries that still manufactures DDT and remains the chemical's largest consumer, claims of eradicating polio are contradicted by the continuing high incidence of symptoms virtually identical to polio: the clinical syndrome "acute flacid paralysis" and its various instigating conditions, Guillain–Barre Syndrome (GBS), transverse myelitis, traumatic neuritis, and post diphtheritic neuropathy.[74] It appears that over-vaccination of oral polio vaccine in India may be a factor, conjoined with environmental toxins like DDT, in perpetuating polio-by-other-names.[75] While there have been no positives for polio in India since 2012, a recent study there suggests that oral polio vaccine has been responsible for inducing paralysis at rates as high as 30 per 100,000 persons because "repeated doses of the live virus vaccine delivered to the intestine may colonize the gut and alter the viral microbiome of the intestine."[76] When the vaccine causes the illness that it ostensibly inoculates against, we have the worst kind of public health methods. On top of all this, the treatments for polio—in mid-twentieth century United States and today in places like India, Nigeria, and Gaza—have been found to be responsible for much of the residual paralyses, deformities, and lingering stiffness associated with polio and its related diseases. Immobilizing limbs for three to six months will lead to dysfunction regardless of whether or not the virus is present.[77] All in all, the preoccupation with vaccination continues to divert attention from the extensive environmental toxicities that continue to create favorable conditions for viral infections and poor health outcomes.

The fourth objection to *Jacobson* is that the landmark decision in vaccine law undermines the status of scientific evidence altogether. The

Court held that vaccine skepticism by individuals or medical professionals was not grounds for voiding the mandatory law as long as it was the "common belief" of other people that vaccines are safe and do effectively prevent disease. In rejecting Jacobson's arguments against vaccination, the Court elevated what we might call "official knowledge":

> Those offers in the main seem to have had no purpose except to state the general theory of those of the medical profession who attach little or no value to vaccination as a means of preventing the spread of smallpox, or who think that vaccination causes other diseases of the body. What everybody knows the court must know, and therefore the state court judicially knew, as this court knows, that an opposite theory accords with the common belief, and is maintained by high medical authority.[78]

"What everybody knows" is a decidedly unscientific basis for knowledge about medical science. Evidence-based objections to the science of vaccination, the Court is saying, are insufficient. The objections must also be grounded in "what everybody knows." Going back to flat Earth theory and the Church's efforts to suppress the Copernican Revolution, human history is replete with the gross scientific errors of "common belief." The Court essentially endorses group-think and the "tyranny of the majority":

> A common belief, like common knowledge, does not require evidence to establish its existence, but may be acted upon without proof by the legislature and the courts…The fact that the belief is not universal is not controlling, for there is scarcely any belief that is accepted by everyone. The possibility that the belief may be wrong, and that science may yet show it to be wrong, is not conclusive; for the legislature has the right to pass laws which, according to the common belief of the people, are adapted to prevent the spread of contagious diseases. In a free country, where the government is by the people, through their chosen representatives, practical legislation admits of no other standard of action, for what the people believe is for the common welfare must be accepted as tending to promote the common welfare, whether it does in fact or not.[79]

Indeed, on this score *Jacobson* could not have been more prescient for our Pandemic Year: whether there is in fact a pandemic or not, whether there is a public health crisis or not, whether lockdowns and quarantines are warranted or not, whether school closures are justified or not, whether vaccines are safe, effective, and sound public health policy or not—if "common belief" holds that they are, then so be it.

What qualifies as "common belief" is political, of course, and indicts untoward uses of majoritarian power. As legal scholar Lani Guinier explained almost thirty years ago with respect to representative democracy, voting rights are null and void if the minority is structurally prevented from achieving electoral representation. In *Tyranny of the Majority: Fundamental Fairness in Representative Democracy*, which curates her major law review articles on the subject, Guinier shows how minorities are effectively disenfranchised, despite the trappings of equal citizenship, because they cannot elect what voting rights law calls "representatives of their choice."[80] The tensions between procedural fairness and whether or not minorities have a fair chance to have their policy preferences satisfied remain hotly contested and underwrite the myriad attempts at voter suppression today. The lessons from voting rights point to the anti-democratic and anti-scientific tenets of the *Jacobson* decision. Unsurprisingly, the decision let loose this "tyranny of the majority" in short order. In the 1927 case of *Buck v. Bell*, the Court upheld a Virginia law permitting compulsory sterilization of persons who state officials deemed "feebleminded."[81] Feeblemindedness, or imbecility, was turn-of-the-century scientific discourse for cognitive impairment. State science at the time of *Buck* claimed that heredity played a key role in the spread of cognitive impairment, social unfitness, and insanity. The Court relied upon its ruling in *Jacobson* to reason that if states could vaccinate against viruses like smallpox, then they could "immunize" against social traits like intergenerational poverty. Justice Oliver Wendell Holmes concluded, "It is better for all the world, if instead of waiting to execute degenerate offspring for crime, or to let them starve for their imbecility, society can prevent those who are manifestly unfit from continuing their kind…Three generations of imbeciles are enough."[82]

For Goodwin and Chemerinsky, *Buck* "offers a chilling glimpse into the extremes of protecting the public's health in times of perceived crisis."[83] But Goodwin and Chemerinsky are at once retroactively imputing twenty-first-century sentiment onto a prior historical context that was saturated with eugenicist ideology and policies, and obfuscating the ongoing role of eugenics in the medical industrial complex. Six states had already passed compulsory sterilization legislation for the "mentally unfit" by 1911; after *Buck*, twenty states instituted eugenicist sterilization laws, resulting in as many as 100,000 sterilizations by 1950.[84] Both Ellis Island on the East Coast and Angel Island on the West Coast functioned as eugenicist immigrant filters. The point is that law is never extreme at the time; *Buck* is merely an acute expression of the early twentieth century scientific racism from which vaccination emerges. Medical science had long sought to control black, American Indian, Mexican, and Puerto Rican reproduction. In 1903, the influential physician Charles S. Bacon advocated that "the Black Belt will be defined by the government as a negro reservation similar to Indian reservations…the plan that has worked so well in its treatment of the Indian question until it has practically eliminated the question with the race."[85] Eugenics was the unifying discursive thread connecting questions of race, health, poverty, welfare, intelligence, crime, and immigration throughout much of the twentieth century. Margaret Sanger, perhaps the most famous American eugenicist (and founder of the organization that would become Planned Parenthood), strategically enlisted prominent black leaders such as W. E. B. DuBois, Charles S. Johnson, and Adam Clayton Powell, Jr. for her Negro Project aimed at reducing the black population. Black elite complicity in eugenicist policy is a testament (in the least) to the hegemony of science as an objective and rational form of knowledge. Sanger noted, "The most successful educational approach for the Negro is through a religious appeal…We do not want the word to get out that we want to exterminate the Negro population, and the minister is the man who can straighten out that idea if it occurs to any of their more rebellious members."[86]

The practice of rendering black women infertile without their knowledge during other surgery was so common that the procedure was called a "Mississippi appendectomy," although it was equally prevalent in the North and West up through the 1980s. Between 1930 and 1970, nearly one-third of all Puerto Rican women and a quarter of indigenous women were forcibly sterilized.[87] Throughout the 1970s, 1980s, and 1990s, poor women of color were subjected to the toxic contraceptives Depo-Provera and Norplant, and black women in particular continue to face coerced sterilization and other forms of reproductive control as condition for welfare, probation, or parole.[88] A 1977 class action lawsuit originating from Alabama found that an estimated 100,000 to 150,000 poor women, half of whom were black, had been sterilized annually under federally funded programs, a rate of sterilization on par with the Nazi program of the 1930s.[89] California alone estimates that over 20,000 female inmates in its state prison system were forcibly sterilized without their consent or knowledge while undergoing medical procedures up through 2010.[90] Recent whistleblower allegations of forced sterilization at ICE detention facilities confirm that these long-standing eugenicist practices are not over.[91]

Eugenics, like slavery, is not an artifact of a white supremacist past nor a racist fringe of modern science. It is a feature of slaveholding culture's present that occupies the center of mainstream science in multiple ways, and as such, it exposes the racism intrinsic to the vaccination imperative. The contraceptive implant Norplant was finally taken off the U.S. market in 2002 after fifty thousand women joined class action lawsuits against device manufacturer Bayer and the doctors who prescribed it, citing a range of side effects including severe depression, extreme nausea, scalp-hair loss, ovarian cysts, migraines, and excessive bleeding, in addition to the difficulties in getting the implants removed.[92] Norplant is now promoted throughout Africa through a collaboration between the Gates Foundation, the U.S. Agency for International Development (USAID), and EngenderHealth.[93] Formerly named the Sterilization League for Human Betterment, EngenderHealth's original eugenicist mission statement was "to improve the biological stock of the human race."[94] Depo-Provera, the injectable contraceptive manufactured by Pfizer, is part of recent developments in biotechnology best understood as "contraceptive vaccines" that aim to regulate reproduction by manipulating the body's immune responses to shut down some bodily functions necessary for pregnancy. Just like typical vaccines, these fertility regulating technologies use antibodies to thwart the development of reproductive hormones, eggs, sperm, or the early embryo.[95]

As with the COVID-19 biotechnology, the triggered antibodies in these contraceptive vaccines can cause a range of autoimmune dysfunction.

Although contraceptive vaccines are marketed as a way for women to take control over their fertility, in reality the semi-permanent nature of the injectables affords women the least reproductive choice possible short of actual sterilization.[96] The Gates Foundation and USAID are heavily funding distribution of Depo-Provera throughout Africa, India, and Bangladesh. Reproductive choice became a major investment for philanthropy and the government as an outgrowth of eugenicist fears about population growth among communities of color in the United States and across the Global South. Around the same time that Carnegie was funding the Flexner Report to shut down black medical schools and promote medical science at the expense of naturopathy in medical education in the early twentieth century, the Rockefeller Foundation was beginning to invest in eugenics. By the 1950s it had established the Population Council to promote the idea that "overpopulation" posed a catastrophic obstacle to global development.[97] Western economic planners claimed that overpopulation was a primary cause of poverty and suffering. In reality, capital was less concerned about poverty than it was with how the growth of an impoverished population throughout the formerly colonized Global South might foment greater opposition to Western plans for the neocolonial era. India became ground zero for capital's eugenicist population control efforts, with the Ford Foundation, USAID, and the Population Council coordinating to produce a brutal sterilization campaign in the name of "family planning" that forcibly vasectomized 6.2 million men and killed at least 1770 during the 1970s.[98] As Mahmood Mamdani explained in his 1972 study of an Indian village, however, children become more essential *because of* poverty, not despite it—in other words, poverty causes population growth, not the other way around.[99] As noted earlier, the rise of living standards throughout the West after the Industrial Revolution were the result of improved sanitation, drinking water, and nutrition, rather than medical advances, but it was also highly dependent on the transfers of wealth to these Western metropoles from the colonies that they controlled at the time. Imperialist forms of production made life more stable and predictable throughout the West, but they were disastrous socially and economically for the colonized. As Jacob Levich explains in the *Palgrave Encyclopedia on Imperialism and Anti-Imperialism*,

> Imperialism "brought down death rates through modern technology but ... could not bring down birth rates because [it] increased social inequality and undermined the economic security and self-sufficiency of the masses." Ironically, then, the West was able to complete demographic transition only through a system of exploitation that relied on the prevention of a similar transition in the South.[100]

By the time the Gates Foundation picked up the baton and revived the discredited notion of overpopulation in 2012, the global population growth rate was at an all-time postwar low of 1.17 percent.[101] Nonetheless, Gates somehow made population control appear both legitimate and urgent again, putting contraception, of all things, at the top of the global public health agenda by pledging $1 billion to supply birth control to 120 million women and prevent 110 million unwanted pregnancies, and in so doing, garnering a further $3.6 billion in investment from other organizations ranging from Planned Parenthood to the Hewlett and Bloomberg philanthropies.[102]

Gates' claim that it is advancing women's reproductive choice in the Global South, and hence working to eradicate poverty and disease, is not only contradicted by its failure to simply invest in the basic infrastructure and nutrition improvements that succeeded in improving living standards and ending infectious disease epidemics in the industrialized world. Its eugenicist affiliations are also revealed by Gates' long-standing partnership with EngenderHealth (formerly the Sterilization League for Human Betterment). EngenderHealth has received more than $36 million from Gates to fund "long-acting and permanent methods" of contraception such as injections, tubal ligations, and vasectomies. After fifteen women in India were killed during botched "cattle camp" tubal ligations in 2014, a high-profile meeting between Prime Minister Modi and Bill and Melinda Gates announced that the country would switch to emphasizing mass injectable contraceptive vaccines.[103] The Gates Foundation, of course, has been a major force behind the planning for the COVID-19 pandemic, as evidenced in its sponsorship of Event 201, the high-level pandemic preparedness exercise held October 18, 2019 (just prior to the official appearance of COVID-19 on the global scene), and through its funding of Operation Warp Speed.[104] Gates also has a long-standing partnership on vaccine research with the Wellcome Trust, an entity with its own deep-seated roots in eugenicist science.

The Wellcome Trust was established by the pharmaceutical magnate Henry Wellcome who founded the company that later became Glaxo-SmithKline. Today Wellcome has a $25.9 billion endowment and funds research and clinical trials. The Trust is heavily invested in eugenicist science, first through its long-standing association with the British Eugenics Society, and today through its promotion of race-based genetics research at the Wellcome Centre for Human Genetics. Among Wellcome's recent work is a mapping of the "genetic impacts of migration events," the role of genetics in disease susceptibility in Africa, and illegally exploiting and commercializing a gene chip developed using DNA collected from hundreds of southern Africans without their consent.[105] In 2011, Wellcome organized a seminar on the topic of "Selective Reproduction, Bioethics, and the Idea of Eugenics."[106] The meeting was framed around the question, "Is the fact that an action or policy is a case of eugenics necessarily a reason not to do it?" The seminar found that "once coercion is taken out of the equation, the answer to this is not obviously yes," and the gathering was thus largely concerned with exploring how choice and coercion could be construed in favor of eugenics. The British Eugenics Society, renamed the Galton Institute in 1989, houses its archives at Wellcome, and one of its leading officers asserts that eugenics in the twenty-first century "would cover methods of regulating population numbers as well as improving genome quality by selective artificial insemination by donor, gene therapy or gene manipulation of germ-line cells," and could be "made compulsory by the state, or left entirely to the personal choice of the individual."[107]

Not only is this racist science alive and well, but it is front and center in the COVID-19 pandemic through Wellcome's close involvement in the production of the Oxford-AstraZeneca shot. The lead research scientists on the Oxford-AstraZeneca shot are affiliated with both Wellcome and Galton, and in 2009 they conducted clinical trials in South Africa that resulted in the deaths of seven infants. In the South African trial, the researchers intentionally deceived parents by not informing them that the tuberculosis vaccine was experimental, and that results from previous animal studies had shown the vaccine to be ineffective.[108] This track record of manipulating data from animal studies, misrepresenting efficacy and safety, and working within a eugenics framework has reared its head again in the Oxford-AstraZeneca clinical trials. Oxford-AstraZeneca's manufacturing partners have their own track record of scandal, and the COVID-19 shot has been dogged by repeated adverse reactions throughout the trial period.[109] The trial had to be paused on two separate occasions due to the occurrence of conditions consistent with transverse myelitis, the syndrome discussed in Chapter 5 as a common side effect with a number of different vaccines over the years.[110] Transverse myelitis is a neurological disorder, for which there is no cure, that involves inflammation of the spinal cord leading to paralysis. A 2009 review of the medical science literature found transverse myelitis associated with vaccines for hepatitis B, measles-mumps-rubella, Diptheria, pertussis, tetanus, and others, leading the researchers to conclude that "the associations of different vaccines with a single autoimmune phenomenon allude to the idea that a common denominator of these vaccines, such as an adjuvant, might trigger this syndrome."[111] The repeated occurrence of additional problems like blood clotting led Canada, Denmark, Australia, Greece, Italy, and other nations to restrict or block access to the Oxford-AstraZeneca shot altogether.[112] Data released after Oxford-AstraZeneca had begun testing the shot in humans showed that their product was ineffective in stopping transmission or mitigating disease severity during animal studies on rhesus monkeys, suggesting that there was insufficient data to move into human trials in the first place.[113] It also has come to light that instead of the customary saline solution, the gold standard for control group design, trial administrators gave the placebo group Pfizer's Nimenrix, a meningitis vaccine.[114] Saline solution is the preferred placebo because researchers can be sure that it will not cause adverse reactions. The Oxford-AstraZeneca trial design, conversely, seems set up to ensure that the researchers can down play any adverse reactions to the COVID-19 shot by showing that the control group also had adverse reactions as well. As Mary Holland, general counsel at the Children's Health Defense, put it, "The meningitis vaccine in the AstraZeneca trial is what I would call a 'fauxcebo,' a fake control whose real purpose is to disguise or hide injury in the vaccine group. The trial sponsor can say, 'look, the vaccine group is as safe as the control group,' when in fact the trial proves that the control group was as dangerous as the vaccine group."[115]

These safety, efficacy, and ethicality problems with the Oxford-AstraZeneca shot come further into focus in terms of eugenics as this particular vaccine is the one being targeted to the Global South. The Oxford-AstraZeneca shot has less complicated storage requirements and it sells at a fraction of the cost of its competitors—running between 3 and 5 dollars per dose, compared with 25–37 dollars per dose for Moderna and Pfizer, respectively.[116] In December 2020, the editor of the leading medical journal *The Lancet*, Richard Horton, told *CNBC* that "the Oxford-AstraZeneca vaccine is the vaccine right now that is going to be able to immunize the planet more effectively, more rapidly than any other vaccine we have," in large part because it is a "vaccine that can get to lower-middle-income countries."[117] The *CNBC* story also quoted Andrew Baum, global head of health care for Citi Group, as saying that the Oxford-AstraZeneca vaccine "is really the only vaccine that is going to suppress or even eradicate SARS-CoV-2, the virus that causes COVID-19, in the many millions of individuals in the developing world." This marketing is wrapped up in a narrative of charitable largesse because the vaccine manufacturers are initially providing their biotechnology to the Global South on a not-for-profit basis, although Oxford, AstraZeneca, its manufacturing partners, and the various entities that have invested heavily in its production, including Wellcome, Gates, Google Ventures, and the lead scientists' own company Vaccitech, will reap windfall profits from royalties and "milestone" payments once the pandemic is officially declared over and COVID-19 vaccines become a seasonal event.[118]

In short, *Jacobson*'s suppression of the dissent intrinsic to the scientific method gives license to the eugenics movement's focus on vaccination as its preferred methodology for reproducing racial dominance in the twenty-first century. The imperative to vaccinate as a response to COVID-19 draws sustenance from the implicit racialism of the polluted body and a virus that supposedly originated in China, from the unstated white supremacy of global health practices, and from the racist constructs of population, poverty, and powerlessness among the "darker nations."[119] COVID-19 presents a panoply of racialized fears of contagion that are attached to immigration, foreignness, development, profitability, commodified bodies, the racial other within the national body, and class status within the national community, all of which gets hidden in the contemporary tropes of medical science.

The ramifications of the *Jacobson* Court's subordination of science—and the censorship of the open-ended debate intrinsic to the scientific method—to the "common belief" that people hold regardless of supporting evidence are rampant during the Pandemic Year. In late 2020, a trio of scientists proposed a "middle ground" approach to COVID-19. Their proposal, "Focused Protection: The Middle Ground Between Lockdowns and 'Let It Rip,'" aims "to minimize overall mortality" from COVID-19 and other diseases "by balancing the need to protect high-risk individuals from COVID-19 while reducing the harm that lockdowns have had on other aspects of medical care and public health. It recognizes that public health is concerned with the health and well-being of populations in a broader way than just infection control."[120] Their proposal led to the creation of the Great Barrington Declaration to collectively explore an alternative and less harmful approach to public health than the mass quarantine and lockdown protocols levied during the Pandemic Year.[121] Thousands of scientists have joined the Declaration as signatories (including the newly appointed Surgeon General of Florida, Dr. Joseph Ladapo). Sunetra Gupta, one of the authors of "Focused Protection," argues that lockdown "is a blunt, indiscriminate policy that forces the poorest and most vulnerable people to bear the brunt of the fight against coronavirus."[122] Gupta reports, however, that despite the reasoned and evidence-based argument presented in "Focused Protection," it has garnered mostly vitriolic hate in response. Rather than engage in serious rational (i.e., scientific) discussion, critics of "Focused Protection" have simply dismissed the proposal as "pixie dust," "wishful thinking," "not in the national interest," "fringe," and "dangerous." As Gupta explains,

> "[F]ringe" is a ridiculous word, implying that only mainstream science matters. If that were the case, science would stagnate. And dismissing us as "dangerous" is equally unhelpful, not least because it is an inflammatory, emotional term charged with implications of irresponsibility. When it is hurled around by people with influence, it becomes toxic. But this pandemic is an international crisis. To shut down the discussion with abuse and smears — that is truly dangerous.[123]

Or, in *Jacobsen*'s terminology, only the "common belief" about science matters. The *British Medical Journal* echoed Gupta's observations in an editorial published in November 2020 excoriating the corruption of science by the "medical-political complex."

> Science is being suppressed for political and financial gain. COVID-19 has unleashed state corruption on a grand scale, and it is harmful to public health. Politicians and industry are responsible for this opportunistic embezzlement. So too are scientists and health experts. The pandemic has revealed how the medical-political complex can be manipulated in an emergency—a time when it is even more important to safeguard science.[124]

The suppression of scientific inquiry by the "common belief" has also been confirmed by a recent study published by an international team of researchers. The experimental study shows that COVID-19 policies have become moralized, and as a result, "people are more likely to accept collateral damage from these efforts, such as social shaming, lost lives and illnesses, and police abuse of power. This moralization was so strong that people reacted negatively even when COVID-19 restrictions were merely questioned."[125] These findings are an alarming, but unsurprising, legacy for *Jacobson*. They remind us that the police power of "common belief" is punitive and repressive even when the law is not. As Susan Sontag wrote in *Illness as Metaphor* almost fifty years ago, "nothing is more punitive than to give a disease meaning—that meaning being invariably a moralistic one."[126] It is this dogmatic tyranny of the majority that has given rise to the set of rich COVID-19 colloquialisms meant to describe the silencing of dissent and the strait-jacket of group-think in the Pandemic

Year: "flu d'etat," "Branch Covidians," "medical totalitarianism," "coup d'flu," and "covidiots."

Although explicit eugenicist population control policies are no longer legitimate, they persist in the form of twenty-first-century medical racism. Moreover, *Buck* shows that *Jacobson* can be used in any way that the prevailing winds of the police power are blowing at a given point in time because it makes clear that what the law recognizes as "science" is itself subordinate to the police power of civil society, or what the Court termed "common belief." In the 2014 Ebola outbreak, racism led to the medical neglect of black patients, while public health hysteria produced a number of high-profile quarantines of people with connections to West Africa. In *Mayhew v. Hickox*, the Maine District Court overturned the forced quarantine of a Doctors Without Borders nurse, finding that "[t]he State has not met its burden...to prove by clear and convincing evidence that limiting [Hickox's] movements to the degree requested is 'necessary to protect other individuals from the dangers of infection.'"[127] Noting that Ms. Hickox did not show any symptoms of Ebola, the court declared that she was "not infectious."[128]

While the *Mayhew* court reasoned that Maine's quarantine orders in 2014 were scientifically unjustified, the nationwide mass lockdown orders implemented during the Pandemic Year have not yet been successfully challenged in court on medical science grounds. As with vaccination, if the strict scrutiny test were applied, the government must demonstrate that there is no other less restrictive means of protecting public health than quarantine and lockdown. There are such alternatives, however, and there would likely be many more were independent thinking not so severely punished in the Pandemic Year. In *Butler v. Wolf*, the federal district court in Western Pennsylvania held in late 2020 that certain COVID-19 mitigation policies implemented by Pennsylvania violated the First Amendment and the Due Process and Equal Protection clauses of the Fourteenth Amendment.[129] Since it found the state to be in violation of the U.S. Constitution, not merely the state constitution, the *Butler* decision has implications for public health protocols nationwide. In addition, *Butler* did not apply *Jacobson*'s extraordinary deference standard to the public health policies, instead applying normal deference because of the broad and extended implementation of the mitigation measures. The punitive effect of COVID-19 moralizing is to dissuade serious objections, legal as well as scientific, to the pandemic police power.

Additional law matters concern the legality of the pandemic itself. Following the argument against the PCR-based pandemic levied earlier in the previous chapter, we have a situation where the state is responsible for asserting false facts or misrepresentation. The PCR-based pandemic amounts to fraud: testing for a virus that has not been isolated with an instrument that cannot accurately find what it is looking for, and then calling healthy people "cases." Based on the rules of tort law, this translates into a duty to compensate for losses suffered as a result of lockdowns premised on the false information disseminated by entities like the CDC which acknowledges that PCR tests are inaccurate. An international legal group has proposed investigating the pandemic in terms of crimes against humanity as defined in international law.[130] The potential is there for a massive class action lawsuit. A current case in federal court in the Northern District of Ohio against that state's lockdown orders alleges fraud, house arrest without due process, future takings without just compensation, abuse of emergency declaration, violation of parental rights and of rights to privacy, free speech, assembly, and religion.[131] There is also the matter of HIPAA and ADA law. CDC guidelines state that people should not wear masks if it is medically inadvisable for them to do so, while HIPAA and ADA law protect an individual's medical or health privacy. This means that asking a person why they are not wearing a mask could be a violation of their privacy rights under HIPAA or ADA.[132] While some argue that these laws take a back seat to the pandemic Executive Orders for mask-wearing, these arguments collapse in light of the fraudulent claims driving the pandemic itself.[133]

Along the lines of mobilizing the law against the pandemic police power, there is the matter of contesting the legal scaffolding for the medical industrial complex. In the financial industry, we have the fateful repeal of Glass-Steagall in 1999 that deregulated Wall Street, eliminating the firewall between investment banks and commercial banks and creating the conditions for the mass fraudulence of the 2008 foreclosure crisis. In criminal justice, we have the 1994 Violent Crime Control and Law Enforcement Act that lowered the age at which youth can be tried as adults, provided incentives to prosecutors to charge youth in adult courts, enhanced sentencing, sent billions of dollars to states to hire thousands of new officers and build scores of new prisons, and established new anti-gang provisions, among other things, that facilitated the mass incarceration juggernaut and are currently being incrementally revised or thrown out. In medical science, two influential laws are the 1986 National Childhood Vaccine Injury Act (NCVIA) which, among other things, indemnified vaccine makers from liability when their products cause injury, and the Bayh-Dole Act, or the Patent and Trademark Laws Amendment Act of 1980, which changed the law to permit federal contractors to own patents on inventions made with federal funding.[134] Bayh-Dole fostered the biotech industry by allowing universities, private industry, and even public entities to commercialize and profit off of research—including vaccines—funded by taxpayers, while the NCVIA removes a major source of accountability for the vaccine makers. These laws are major impediments to producing safe and accountable medical science.

One of the major strikes against the prison industrial complex has long been the coupling of punishment and profits. Although private prisons have always been a fraction of the overall prison system, profit motives are realized at many different junctures in the criminal justice process.[135] NCVIA and Bayh-Dole are but the tip of a very large iceberg of profit in the medical science field that compromises healthcare, and the same analysis from the prison industrial complex applies. "The scientific-medical complex is a $2 trillion industry," says one former drug developer. "You can buy a tremendous amount of consensus for that kind of money." "Before the biotech boom," says another scientist, "we never had this incessant urging to produce something useful, meaning profitable. Everybody is caught up in it. Grants, millions of dollars flowing into laboratories, careers and stars being made. The only way to be a successful scientist today is to follow consensus."[136] To say the least, the conflicts of interest are mind-boggling: public health leaders set policies on medical practice that feature the use of biotech products for which they hold the patents.[137] Fauci directs a large portion of the overall medical science research conducted in the United States *and* holds a number of patents derived from this research.[138] Is it no wonder that they are pushing vaccines at the expense of actual healthy communities?

There are further legislative parallels between the state's pandemic response and the massive build-up of the prison industrial complex. Beginning with the Omnibus Crime Control and Safe Streets Act of 1968, each subsequent crime bill has devoted billions of dollars to law enforcement, directly creating mass incarceration. In particular, the 1994 crime bill featured financial incentives to encourage prosecutors to apply new federal drug statutes, send youth offenders to adult court, and seek life without parole and the death penalty in cases where they would not previously have sought such sentences. The 1994 crime bill also provided $12.5 billion in incentive grants to fund prison expansion, with nearly 50 percent earmarked to states that adopted tough "truth-in-sentencing" laws that scaled back parole.[139] The 2020 Coronavirus Aid, Relief, and Economic Security (CARES) Act, similarly, provides twenty percent more reimbursement to hospitals for COVID-19 treatment than the usual Medicare reimbursements. "Hospital administrators might well want to see COVID-19 attached to a discharge summary or a death certificate. Why? Because if it's a straightforward, garden-variety pneumonia that a person is admitted to the hospital for—if they're Medicare—typically, the diagnosis-related group lump sum payment would be $5,000," explained Minnesota lawmaker and family practitioner Dr. Scott Jensen. "But if it's COVID-19 pneumonia, then it's $13,000, and if that COVID-19 pneumonia patient ends up on a ventilator, it goes up to $39,000."[140] In a July 31, 2020 hearing before Congress, CDC Director Robert Redfield acknowledged this financial incentive to inflate COVID-19 caseloads, noting the same thing happens with other diseases as well. "In the HIV epidemic, somebody may have a heart attack but also have HIV," Redfield explained. "The hospital would prefer the DRG [death report] for HIV because there's greater reimbursement. So I do think there is some reality to that."[141]

The state also directly inflates the death rate through its official guidelines for determining a COVID-19 death. In an April 2020 news conference, Dr. Ngozi Ezike, Director of the Illinois Department of Health, explained that anyone who dies with a COVID-19 positive test on record is counted as a COVID-19 death—even if the actual cause of death is clearly something else:

> If you were in hospice and had already been given a few weeks to live, and then you also were found to have COVID, that would be counted as a COVID death. It means technically even if you died of a clear alternate cause, but you had COVID at the same time, it's still listed as a COVID death. So, everyone who's listed as a COVID death doesn't mean that that was the cause of the death, but they had COVID at the time of the death.[142]

This statement is remarkable in its naked admission of fraud and exposes the government's legal liability. Evidence for the legal case against the pandemic protocols is right there in the public record. What is even more incredible, however, is that so few people in the media and in society recognize such evidence of fraud for what it is. Just as the state has long been a dealer in crime by constructing new criminal categories and incentivizing jurisdictions to expand their carceral nets accordingly, so too the state is literally creating the pandemic through its construction of disease cases and morbidity.

Finally, the COVID-19 injections operate within a unique legal context. The government's declaration of a public health emergency, and subsequently, of the Public Readiness and Emergency Preparedness Act (PREP), creates a liability shield. PREP is a tort shield law that protects manufacturers, government, and healthcare providers from liability for "covered countermeasures" during a declared public emergency. Most of the COVID-19 shots still have not been approved by the FDA, which means they are experimental. While some advocates for these products dispute this designation on the grounds that the biologicals were studied for 3–6 months prior to their release onto the market, the "experimental" label is as much a legal status as a scientific one. As an unapproved product, the injections raise three matters of law that support the argument against their mandated use.

First, unapproved products can only enter the market under emergency use authorization (EUA). Section 564 of the Federal Food, Drug, and Cosmetic Act states that the FDA Commissioner "may allow unapproved medical products or unapproved uses of approved medical products to be used in an emergency to diagnose, treat, or prevent serious or life-threatening diseases *when there are no other adequate, approved, and available alternatives.*"[143] As extensively documented in *Pandemic Police Power*, there are numerous "adequate, approved, and available alternatives" to the mRNA products. EUA status should never have been granted to these products. Secondly, having conferred EUA status, however, the law clearly stipulates that any product with this designation must be voluntary and the risks must be clearly specified.[144] Federal law in this area trumps state law, so no state or local jurisdiction may mandate an EUA product.[145] Private employers, such as a school or hospital, cannot mandate an EUA product, and an employee cannot be denied healthcare coverage for declining an EUA vaccine.[146] In fact, the law preventing mandates of EUA products is so explicit that there has only been one precedent case regarding an attempt to mandate an EUA vaccine, and the court held that the vaccine could not be mandated. In *Doe #1 v. Rumsfeld*, six soldiers successfully challenged the Department of Defense mandated experimental anthrax vaccine. The court decided that since the anthrax vaccine was an EUA product, the soldiers had the right to refuse or accept vaccination.[147] Third, the right to decline medical experimentation is also a matter of international law. The Nuremberg Code stipulates that "the voluntary consent of the human subject is absolutely essential."[148] The Code is a set of research ethics principles for human experimentation stemming from *U.S.A. v. Karl Brandt* et al., the first of twelve trials for Nazi war crimes in Nuremberg, Germany at the end of World War II.

The international context of crimes against humanity has its more mundane iteration in domestic law in the form of so-called white-collar and state crime. The list of corporate fraud, faulty products, and coverups is long: Ford Pinto explosions, Ford Explorer roll-overs, Bridgestone tires, Volkswagen's fraudulent clean diesel, big tobacco, Enron and Arthur Andersen, WorldCom, Exxon Mobile, Chevron, Shell, British Petroleum, Apple, Microsoft, Boeing, Purdue Pharma and the Sacklers, Merck, Monsanto and Dow Chemical, Johnson & Johnson, AIG, Wells Fargo, JP Morgan Chase, Deutsch Bank, Lehman Brothers, savings and loan associations, and so on. So-called white-collar crime is merely a run-of-the-mill crime that is committed by persons or entities of high social status in the course of their occupations. Despite causing far more mayhem and destruction than so-called street crime, "white-collar criminals" routinely escape the criminal construct. One way that they are able to do this is by influencing legislation and law enforcement in their favor. NCVIA, Bayh-Dole, PREP, and emergency use authorizations are prime examples of this influence by the medical industrial complex. If a car company killed over 4000 people within the first six months of its new product rolling off the assembly line, as the new COVID-19 mRNA injections have done, the car would be immediately recalled and the company would be facing severe sanctions.

Lawsuits are beginning to emerge against public health policing. In New Mexico, *Legaretta, et al. v. Macias, et al.* challenges a Dona Ana County mandate requiring first responders to receive the COVID-19 shot as a condition of employment.[149] The lawsuit centers on the question of whether state and county agencies can bypass federal law that requires EUA biologicals to be voluntary, as noted above. A second lawsuit by New Mexico plaintiffs challenges the declaration of a public health emergency as invalid, arguing that the government's actions are based on unreliable data and have caused more harm than the disease itself.[150] Lawyers should continue to support people in standing up for their health rights, for students' right to an education without compromising their health status, and for workers' right to earn a living without being subjected to coercive public health policing.

Given the dubious and complex historical record for vaccination reviewed in this chapter, an unscientific method to defending the vaccination regime comes into view. When problems with vaccination become too significant to ignore, the first defense is to blame old vaccines as ineffective and less scientific. When the new ones produce more of the same problems, the response is that two or more courses of a vaccine are needed and that the previously vaccinated need to get revaccinated, with updates required more regularly. When periodic outbreaks continue, blame falls on the unvaccinated, faulty vaccine administration, a singular "bad batch," or new virus "variants" from abroad. And when it becomes clear that viral infection has become a disease of the vaccinated, the response is surprise and confusion, but *never* reevaluation of vaccination. This methodology has been historically consistent across the two centuries of the vaccine regime and is in full effect during COVID-19. It is a fundamental precept of scientific inquiry that comparative evaluation—in this case, between the reliance on vaccination versus an investment in other systemic methods to improving public health—is the best methodology for maximizing the efficacy of any one approach. What is happening during COVID-19, however, is the dogged refusal to second-guess vaccination, to subject it to the rigor of comparative scientific analysis, and to see what the evidence is showing us, rather than what we want to see.

Notes

1. Stuart Hall, "Race, Articulation and Societies Structured in Dominance," in UNESCO, ed., *Sociological Theories: Race and Colonialism* (Paris: UNESCO, 1980), 305–345.
2. *Jacobson v. Massachusetts*, 197 U.S. 11, 37 (1905).
3. Nicholas Mosvick, "On This Day, the Supreme Court Rules on Vaccines and Public Health," *National Constitution Center*, February 20, 2021, https://constitutioncenter.org/blog/on-this-day-the-supreme-court-rules-on-vaccines-and-public-health.
4. Mosvick, "On This Day."
5. Mosvick, "On This Day."
6. Robert M. Wolfe and Lisa K. Sharp, "Anti-Vaccinationists Past and Present," *British Medical Journal* 325 (2002): 430–431.
7. Kim Tolley, "School Vaccination Wars: The Rise of Anti-Science in the American Anti-Vaccination Societies, 1879–1929," *Historical Education Quarterly* 59(161) 2019: 161–163.
8. "Toward a Twenty-First-Century *Jacobsen v. Massachusetts*," *Harvard Law Review* 121 (2008): 1821.
9. Adeel Hassan, "Disneyland Visitor with Measles May Have Exposed Hundreds to Infection," *New York Times*, October 24, 2019, https://www.nytimes.com/2019/10/23/us/disneyland-measles.html.

10. S.B. 277, 2015–2016 Leg., Reg. Sess. (Cal. 2015) (approved by Governor Jerry Brown on June 30, 2015).
11. Dorit Reiss, "California Court of Appeal Rejects Challenge to Vaccine Law," *Bill of Health*, July 30, 2018, https://blog.petrie flom.law.harvard.edu/2018/07/30/california-court-of-appeal-rej ects-challenge-to-vaccine-law/.
12. Giovanni Rezza and Walter Ricciardi, "No Jab, No Pay, and Vaccine Mandates: Do Compulsory Policies Increase Vaccination Coverage? The Italian Experience," *Vaccine* 38(5089) 2020; Maxwell J. Mehlman and Michael M. Lederman, "Compulsory Immunization Protects Against Infection: What Law and Society Can Do," *Pathogens Immunity Journal* 5(1) 2020: 1–7; Marie Killmond, "Why Is Vaccination Different? A Comparative Analysis of Religious Exemptions," *Columbia Law Review* 117 (2017): 913.
13. Erwin Chemerinsky and Michele Goodwin, "Compulsory Vaccination Laws Are Constitutional," *Northwestern University Law Review* 110 (2016): 595.
14. Michele Goodwin and Erwin Chemerinsky, "No Immunity: Race, Class, and Civil Liberties in Times of Health Crisis," *Harvard Law Review* 129 (2016): 958.
15. Chemerinsky and Goodwin, 600.
16. In 2012, California voters passed Proposition 36, the Three Strikes Reform Act, to eliminate life sentences for non-violent offenses and provide parole opportunities for other inmates serving life under three strikes sentencing rules. See Three Strikes Basics, *Stanford Law School Three Strikes Project*, https://law.stanford.edu/three-str ikes-project/three-strikes-basics/ (last visited May 30, 2021).
17. Chemerinsky and Goodwin, 614.
18. Ethan Siegel, "What Does 'Scientific Consensus' Mean?" *Forbes*, June 24, 2016, https://www.forbes.com/sites/startswithabang/ 2016/06/24/what-does-scientific-consensus-mean/.
19. Michael Crichton, "Aliens Cause Global Warming," in *Three Speeches* 1, 6 (December 9, 2009), http://scienceandpublicpolicy. org/commentaries-essays/commentaries/crichton-three-speeches. This speech was delivered at California Institute of Technology, Pasadena, California and focuses on the "historical approach

detailing how over the last thirty years scientists have begun to intermingle scientific and political claims".
20. Michael Lederman et al., "Defeat COVID-19 by Requiring Vaccination for All: It's Not Un-American, It's Patriotic," *USA Today*, August 10, 2020, https://www.usatoday.com/story/opinion/2020/08/06/stop-coronavirus-compulsory-universal-vaccination-column/3289948001/.
21. "Could the Government Make a COVID-19 Vaccine Mandatory in Australia?" *ABC News*, September 15, 2020, https://www.abc.net.au/news/2020-09-16/fact-file-mandatory-vaccination-is-it-possible/12661804?nw=0.
22. Michal Ben-Gal, "New Law Lets Israeli Health Ministry Share Personal Info of Citizens Who Decline COVID Vaccine," *CBS News*, February 25, 2021, https://www.cbsnews.com/news/covid-vaccine-israel-law-personal-information-privacy/.
23. Shannon McMahon, "Everything Travelers Need to Know About Vaccine Passports," *The Washington Post*, February 25, 2021, https://www.washingtonpost.com/travel/2020/12/08/vaccine-passport-immunity-app-covid/.
24. Jillian Kramer, "COVID-19 Vaccines Could Become Mandatory: Here's How It Might Work," *National Geographic*, August 19, 2020, https://www.nationalgeographic.com/science/article/how-coronavirus-covid-vaccine-mandate-would-actually-work-cvd.
25. Amanda Holpuch, "'I'm Not an Anti-Vaxxer, But…' US Health Workers' Vaccine Hesitancy Raises Alarm," *The Guardian*, January 10, 2021, https://www.theguardian.com/world/2021/jan/10/coronavirus-covid-19-vaccine-hesitancy-us-health-workers.
26. Holpuch, "I'm Not an Anti-Vaxxer, But."
27. Sarah Al-Arshani, "Some Nurses Are Choosing to Get Fired Rather Than Get Vaccinated," *Business Insider*, September 4, 2021, https://www.businessinsider.com/some-nurses-choosing-to-get-fired-rather-than-get-vaccinated-2021-9.

28. Michael Rosenwald, "The Last Time the Government Sought A 'Warp Speed' Vaccine, It Was A Fiasco," *The Washington Post*, May 1, 2020, https://www.washingtonpost.com/history/2020/05/01/vaccine-swine-flu-coronavirus/.
29. *Zucht v. King*, 260 U.S. 174 (1922).
30. *Workman v. Mingo Cnty. Bd. of Ed.*, 419 F. App' × 348 (4th Cir. 2011).
31. *Prince v. Massachusetts*, 321 U.S. 158, 166–167 (1944).
32. *Meyer v. Nebraska*, 262 U.S. 390, 403 (1923). *Pierce v. Soc. of Sisters*, 268 U.S. 510 (1925); *Wisconsin v. Yoder*, 406 U.S. 205 (1972).
33. Perhaps the single most important text documenting the mythology of vaccine efficacy is Suzanne Humphries and Roman Bystrianyk, *Dissolving Illusions: Disease, Vaccines, and the Forgotten History* (https://www.dissolvingillusions.com, 2015).
34. Christine Hallett, "The Attempt to Understand Puerperal Fever in the Eighteenth and Early Nineteenth Centuries: The Influence of Inflammation Theory," *Medical History* 49(1) January 1, 2005: 1–28.
35. Frederick C. Irving, "Oliver Wendell Holmes and Puerperal Fever," *New England Journal of Medicine* 229(4) July 22, 1943: 133–137.
36. Richard W. Wertz and Dorothy C. Weritz, *Lying-in: A History of Childbirth in America* (New Haven: Yale, 1989), 122.
37. Walter R. Bett, ed., *The History and Conquest of Common Disease* (Norman: Oklahoma, 1954), 35.
38. M. Tanaka et al., "Effect of Antibiotics on Group A Streptococcus Exoprotein Production Analyzed by Two-Dimensional Gel Electrophoresis," *Antimicrobial Agents and Chemotherapy* 49(1) January 2005: 88–96.
39. D. L. Miller et al., "Whooping Cough and Whooping Cough Vaccine: The Risks and Benefits Debate," *Epidemiologic Reviews* 4 (1982): 2–3.
40. Clive E. West, "Vitamin A and Measles," *Nutrition Reviews* 58(2) February 2000: S46.

41. D. Mark Anderson et al., "Re-examining the Contribution of Public Health Efforts to the Decline in Urban Mortality," *American Economic Association* online appendix, https://www.aeaweb.org/content/file?id=10966.
42. Pavel Grigoriev et al., "The Recent Mortality Decline in Russia: Beginning of the Cardiovascular Revolution?" *Population and Development Review* 40(1) March 2014: 107–129; Asa G. Rakhmanova et al., "Diptheria Outbreak in St. Petersburg: Clinical Characteristics of 1,860 Adult Patients," *Scandinavian Journal of Infectious Diseases* 28(1) 1996: 37–40.
43. M. Gabr, "Undernutrition and Quality of Life," *World Review of Nutrition & Dietetics* 49 (1987): 1–21.
44. "Vaccination by Act of Parliament," *Westminster Review* 131 (1889): 96–97, 101.
45. "Vaccination by Act of Parliament," 101.
46. *The Lancet*, July 15, 1871, cited in "Vaccination by Act of Parliament," 102.
47. George Gregory, "Brief Notices of the Variolous Epidemic of 1844," *Royal Medical and Chirurgical Society*, January 28, 1845, 163.
48. "Small-Pox and Revaccination," *Boston Medical and Surgical Journal* CIV(6) February 10, 1881: 137; *Encyclopedia Britannica* 24 (1890): 29.
49. William Scott Tebb, *A Century of Vaccination and What It Teaches* (Swan Sonnenschein & Co.: London, 1898), 93–94.
50. J. T. Biggs, *Leicester: Sanitation Versus Vaccination, Its Vital Statistics Compared with Those of Other Towns, the Army, Navy, Japan, and England and Wales* (London: National Anti-Vaccination League, 1912), 459–460.
51. Centers for Disease Control and Prevention, "Measles Outbreak Among Vaccinated High School Students—Illinois," *MMWR* 33(24) June 22, 1984: 349–351.
52. Gregory A. Poland and Robert M. Jacobson, "Failure to Reach the Goal of Measles Elimination: Apparent Paradox of Measles Infections in Immunized Persons," *Archives of Internal Medicine*, August 22, 1994: 1816–1818.

53. *Encylopedia Britannica* 24 (1890): 26.
54. Alex R. Kemper et al., "Expected Adverse Events in a Mass Smallpox Vaccination Campaign," *Effective Clinical Practice* 5(2) March–April 2002: 84–90.
55. L. Qin et al., "Genomic Analysis of the Vaccinia Virus Strain Variants Found in Dryvax Vaccine," *Journal of Virology* 85(24) December 2011: 13049–13060.
56. Centers for Disease Control and Prevention, "Notice to Readers: Newly Licensed Smallpox Vaccine to Replace Old Smallpox Vaccine," *MMWR* 57(8) February 29, 2008: 207–208.
57. John R. Mohler and Milton J. Rosenau, "The Origin of the Recent Outbreak of Foot-and-Mouth Disease in the United States," U.S. Department of Agriculture, Bureau of Animal Industry, *Circular* 147 (1909): 11.
58. John T. Bowen, "Acute Infectious Pemphigus in a Butcher, During an Epizotic of Foot and Mouth Disease, with a Consideration of the Possible Relationship of the Two Affections," *Journal of Cutaneous Diseases Including Syphilis* 22(6) June 1904: 254.
59. *Jacobson v. Massachusetts*, 197 U.S. at 39.
60. "Measles as an Index of Immunological Function," *The Lancet*, September 14, 1968: 611; P. J. Lachmann, "Immunopathology of Measles," *Proceedings Royal Society of Medicine* 67 (November 1974): 1120.
61. A. Takada and Y. Kawaoka, "Antibody-Dependent Enhancement of Viral Infection: Molecular Mechanisms and in vivo Implications," *Reviews in Medical Virology* 13(6) November–December 2003: 387–398.
62. Sukathida Ubol and Scott B. Halstead, "How Innate Immune Mechanisms Contribute to Antibody-Enhanced Viral Infections," *Clinical and Vaccine Immunology* 17(12) December 2010: 1829–1835.
63. Arturo Casadevall and Liise-anne Pirofski, "A Reappraisal of Humoral Immunity Based on Mechanisms of Antibody Mediated Protection Against Intracellular Pathogens," *Advances in Immunology* 91(2006): 12–13.
64. Casadevall and Pirofski, 30.

65. Celia Farber, *Serious Adverse Events: An Uncensored History of AIDS* (Brooklyn: Melville House, 2006), 14.
66. D. Stephens et al., "Subclinical Vitamin A Deficiency: A Potentially Unrecognized Problem in the United States," *Pediatric Nursing Journal* 22(5) September–October 1996: 377–389; Wafaie W. Fawzi et al., "Vitamin A Supplementation and Child Mortality: A Meta-Analysis," *Journal of the American Medical Association* (February 17) 1993: 901; Prakash Shetty, *Nutrition, Immunity, and Infection* (Oxfordshire: CABI, 2010), 82.
67. Shetty, *Nutrition, Immunity, and Infection.*
68. S. Songül Yalçin and Kadriye Yurdakök, "Sex-Specific Differences in Serum Vitamin A Values After Measles Immunization," *The Pediatric Infectious Disease Journal* 18(8) August 1999: 747–748.
69. Antonio C. Arrieta et al., "Vitamin A Levels in Children with Measles in Long Beach, California," *The Journal of Pediatrics* 121(1) July 1992: 75–78.
70. A. J. Hall and F. T. Cutts, "Lessons from Measles Vaccination in Developing Countries," *British Medical Journal* 307 (November 1993): 1205.
71. J. V. Neel et al., "Studies of the Xavante Indians of the Brazilian Mato Grosso," *American Journal of Human Genetics* 16 (1964): 52–140.
72. F. Van Meer, "Poliomyelitis: The Role of Diet in the Development of Disease," *Medical Hypotheses* 3 (March 1992): 171–178.
73. M. Biskind, "DDT Poisoning and the Elusive 'Virus X': A New Cause for Gastroenteritis," *American Journal of Digestive Diseases* 16(3) 1949: 79–84; J. Gabliks, "Responses of Cell Cultures to Insecticides: Altered Susceptibility to Poliovirus and Diphtheria Toxin," *Proceedings of the Society for Experimental Biology and Medicine* 120 (October 1965): 172–175.
74. Mohammed Kunju et al., "Acute Flacid Paralysis Beyond Polio: A Case-Based Approach," *Indian Journal of Practical Pediatrics* 22(1) 2020: 36–45.
75. Rachana Dhiman et al., "Correlation Between Non-Polio Acute Flacid Paralysis Rates with Pulse Polio Frequency in India," *International Journal of Environmental Research and Public Health* 15(8) August 2018: 1755.

76. Dhiman et al., 1755.
77. See Victor Cohn, *Sister Kenny: The Woman Who Challenged the Doctors* (Minneapolis: Minnesota, 1975).
78. *Jacobson v. Massachusetts*, 197 U.S. at 30.
79. *Jacobson v. Massachusetts* at 35.
80. Lani Guinier, *Tyranny of the Majority: Fundamental Fairness in Representative Democracy* (New York: Free Press, 1995).
81. *Buck v. Bell*, 274 U.S. 200, 200 (1927).
82. *Buck v. Bell* at 207.
83. Goodwin and Chemerinsky, 959.
84. Harriet A. Washington, *Medical Apartheid: The Dark History of Medical Experimentation on Black Americans from Colonial Times to the Present* (New York: Doubleday, 2006), 202–203; Roberta Cepko, "Involuntary Sterilization of Mentally Disabled Women," *Berkeley Women's Law Journal* 8 (1993).
85. Washington, 199.
86. Washington, at 197.
87. Katherine Andrews, "The Dark History of Forced Sterilization of Latina Women," *Panoramas Scholarly Platform*, October 30, 2017, https://www.panoramas.pitt.edu/health-and-society/dark-history-forced-sterilization-latina-women; Jane Lawrence, "The Indian Health Service and the Sterilization of Native American Women," *American Indian Quarterly* 24(400) 2000.
88. Dorothy Roberts, *Killing the Black Body: Race, Reproduction, and the Meaning of Liberty* (New York: Basic, 1997), 104.
89. *Relf v. Weinberger* 565 F.2d 722 (D.C. Cir. 1977); Allan Chase, *The Legacy of Malthus: The Social Costs of the New Scientific Racism* (New York: Knopf, 1977), 16.
90. Erin McCormick, "Survivors of California's Forced Sterilizations: 'It's Like My Life Wasn't Worth Anything," *The Guardian*, July 19, 2021, https://www.theguardian.com/us-news/2021/jul/19/california-forced-sterilization-prison-survivors-reparations?CMP=Share_AndroidApp_Other.
91. Priscilla Alvarez, "Whistleblower Alleges High Rate of Hysterectomies and Medical Neglect at ICE Facility," *CNN*, September 16,

2020, https://www.cnn.com/2020/09/15/politics/immigration-customs-enforcement-medical-care-detainees/index.html.
92. http://www.cbc.ca/consumers/market/files/health/medical_devices/lawsuits.html.
93. Jeremy Loffredo and Whitney Webb, "Developers of Oxford-AstraZeneca Vaccine Tied to UK Eugenics Movement," *Unlimited Hangout*, December 26, 2020, https://unlimitedhangout.com/2020/12/investigative-series/developers-of-oxford-astrazeneca-vaccine-tied-to-uk-eugenics-movement/.
94. http://discover.lib.umn.edu/cgi/f/findaid/findaid-idx?c=umfa;cc=umfa;q1=Association%252520for%252520Voluntary%252520Sterilization%252520Records;rgn=main;view=text;didno=SW0015.
95. Roberts, *Killing the Black Body*, 146.
96. For a recent example of scientific commentary advocating injectable contraceptives in the name of women's empowerment, see https://www.nature.com/articles/d41586-020-03287-0.
97. Barbara Duden, "Population," in Wolfgang Sachs, ed., *The Development Dictionary: A Guide to Knowledge as Power* (London: Zed, 1992), 150.
98. Soutik Biswas, "India's Dark History of Sterilisation," *BBC News*, November 14, 2014, https://www.bbc.com/news/world-asia-india-30040790.
99. Mahmood Mamdani, *The Myth of Population Control: Family, Caste, and Class in an Indian Village* (New York: Monthly Review, 1972).
100. Jacob Levich, "Bill Gates and the Myth of Overpopulation," *Medium*, April 26, 2019, https://medium.com/@jacob.levich/bill-gates-and-the-myth-of-overpopulation-ca3b1d89680; Immanuel Ness and Zak Cope, eds., *The Palgrave Encyclopedia of Imperialism and Anti-Imperialism*, 2nd ed. (London: Palgrave, 2021), https://www.palgrave.com/gp/book/9783030299002#aboutAuthors; Asoka Bandarage, "Population and Development: Toward a Social Justice Agenda," *Monthly Review* 46(4) 1994: 43.
101. World Bank, "Population Growth," *World Bank Open Data*, 2017, https://data.worldbank.org/indicator/SP.POP.GROW.

102. Michelle Goldberg, "Melinda Gates' New Crusade: Investing Billions in Women's Health," *Newsweek*, May 7, 2012.
103. Ellen Barry and Celia Dugger, "India to Change Its Decades-Old Reliance on Female Sterilization," *NY Times*, February 20, 2016, http://www.nytimes.com/2016/02/21/world/asia/india-to-change-its-decades-old-reliance-on-female-sterilization.html.
104. https://centerforhealthsecurity.org/event201/.
105. https://www.well.ox.ac.uk/research/research-groups/myers; Erik Stokstad, "Major U.K. Genetics Lab Accused of Misusing African DNA," *Science*, October 30, 2019, https://www.science.org/news/2019/10/major-uk-genetics-lab-accused-misusing-african-dna.
106. https://www.bionews.org.uk/page_93056.
107. Loffredo and Webb, "Developers of Oxford-AstraZeneca Vaccine Tied to UK Eugenics Movement," *Unlimited Hangout*, December 26, 2020, https://unlimitedhangout.com/2020/12/investigative-series/developers-of-oxford-astrazeneca-vaccine-tied-to-uk-eugenics-movement. Also see David Galton, *Eugenics: The Future of Human Life in the Twenty-First Century* (New York: Time Warner, 2002).
108. Deborah Cohen, "Oxford TB Vaccine Study Calls into Question Selective Use of Animal Data," *British Medical Journal* 360 (2018), https://www.bmj.com/content/360/bmj.j5845.full.
109. Noah Manskar, "AstraZeneca's COVID-19 Vaccine Partner in China Plagued by Scandal," *New York Post*, December 7, 2020, https://nypost.com/2020/12/07/astrazeneca-vaccine-partner-in-china-has-history-of-scandal/.
110. Katherine Wu and Katie Thomas, "AstraZeneca Pauses Vaccine Trial for Safety Review," *New York Times*, September 9, 2020, https://www.nytimes.com/2020/09/08/health/coronavirus-astrazeneca-vaccine-safety.html.
111. N. Agmon-Levin et al., "Transverse Myelitis and Vaccines: A Multi-Analysis," *Lupus* 18(13) November 2009: 1198–1204.
112. Robert Hart, "Australia Restricts AstraZeneca COVID Shot," *Forbes*, June 17, 2021, https://www.forbes.com/sites/roberthart/2021/06/17/australia-restricts-astrazeneca-covid-shot-in-over-60s-

113. William A. Haseltine, "Did the Oxford COVID Vaccine Work in Monkeys? Not Really," *Forbes*, May 16, 2020, https://www.forbes.com/sites/williamhaseltine/2020/05/16/did-the-oxford-covid-vaccine-work-in-monkeys-not-really/?sh=134a03783c71; https://www.biorxiv.org/content/10.1101/2020.05.13.093195v1.full.pdf.
114. https://clinicaltrials.gov/ct2/show/NCT04536051.
115. Jeremy Loffredo, "AstraZeneca Under Scrutiny Again as Countries Spend Billions Purchasing Its Low-Cost Vaccine," *The Defender*, December 2, 2020, https://childrenshealthdefense.org/defender/astrazeneca-under-scrutiny-again-covid-vaccine/.
116. Sam Meredith, "Oxford-AstraZeneca COVID Vaccine to Immunize the Planet 'More Effectively,' Lancet Editor Says," *CNBC*, December 9, 2020, https://www.cnbc.com/2020/12/09/coronavirs-oxford-astrazeneca-vaccine-to-immunize-the-planet-more-effectively-lancet-editor-says.html.
117. Meredith, "Oxford-AstraZeneca COVID Vaccine to Immunize the Planet 'More Effectively,' Lancet Editor Says," *CNBC*, December 9, 2020, https://www.cnbc.com/2020/12/09/coronavirs-oxford-astrazeneca-vaccine-to-immunize-the-planet-more-effectively-lancet-editor-says.html.
118. Allan McLeod, "Successful Not-for-Profit Oxford COVID Vaccine Threatens Big Pharma Profit Logic," *MPN News*, November 23, 2020, https://www.mintpressnews.com/successful-not-for-profit-oxford-covid-vaccine-threatens-big-pharma/273242/; Loffredo and Webb, "Developers of Oxford-AstraZeneca Vaccine Tied to UK Eugenics Movement," *Unlimited Hangout*, December 26, 2020, https://unlimitedhangout.com/2020/12/investigative-series/developers-of-astrazeneca-vaccine-tied-to-uk-eugenics-movement.
119. See Vijay Prashad, *The Darker Nations: A People's History of the Third World* (New York: New Press, 2008).
120. Jay Bhattacharya et al., "Focused Protection: The Middle Ground Between Lockdowns and 'Let It Rip'," *Great Barrington Declaration*, November 25, 2020, https://gbdeclaration.org/wp-content/

(over-blood-clot-risks-joining-italy-greece-and-others/?sh=4e79d6f7a4e2.)

uploads/2020/12/Focused-Protection-is-the-Middle-Ground-v7-clean.pdf.
121. *Great Barrington Declaration*, https://gbdeclaration.org/.
122. Sunetra Gupta, "A Contagion of Hatred and Hysteria," *American Institute for Economic Research*, November 1, 2020, https://www.aier.org/article/a-contagion-of-hatred-and-hysteria/.
123. *Id.*
124. Kamran Abbasi, "COVID-19: Politicization, 'Corruption,' Suppression of Science," *The British Medical Journal* 371, November 13, 2020, https://www.bmj.com/content/371/bmj.m4425.full.
125. "Study Highlights 'Moralisation' of COVID Response and Restrictions," *University of Otago News*, December 9, 2020, https://www.otago.ac.nz/news/news/releases/otago758988.html; Maja Graso et al., "Moralization of COVID-19 Health Response: Asymmetry in Tolerance for Human Costs," *Journal of Experimental Social Psychology* 93(1) 2021, https://www.sciencedirect.com/science/article/pii/S0022103120304248.
126. Susan Sontag, *Illness as Metaphor/AIDS and Its Metaphors* (New York: Anchor, 1989), 58.
127. *Mayhew v. Hickox*, No. CV-2014-36 (Me. Dist. Ct. October 31, 2014).
128. *Mayhew v. Hickox*.
129. *Cnty. of Butler v. Wolf*, 486 F. Supp. 3d 883, 891 (W.D. Pa. 2020).
130. "'Covid19 Crisis' Is a Crime Against Humanity," German Corona Investigative Committee, *Covert Geopolitics*, October 26, 2020, https://geopolitics.co/2020/10/26/covid19-crisis-is-a-crime-against-humanity-german-corona-investigative-committee/.
131. Complaint at 46–51, *Renz v. Ohio*, No. 3:20CV1948, 2021 WL 485534, *1 (N.D. Ohio February 9, 2021) (No. 3:20 Civ. 1945), https://storage.courtlistener.com/recap/gov.uscourts.ohnd.269202/gov.uscourts.ohnd.269202.1.0.pdf.
132. "Mask Mandate," *HIPAA Secure Now!* July 20, 2020, https://www.hipaasecurenow.com/index.php/mask-mandate/; "The ADA and Face Mask Policies," *Southeast ADA Center* 7–8 (July 2,

2020), https://www.nationaldisabilityinstitute.org/wp-content/uploads/2020/06/ada-and-face-mask-policies.pdf.
133. "HIPAA and Mask Inquires: Is It a HIPAA Violation?" *Compliancy Group*, August 3, 2020, https://compliancy-group.com/hipaa-and-mask-inquires-is-it-a-hipaa-violation/.
134. National Childhood Vaccine Injury Act of 1986, H.R. 5546, 99th Cong. (1985–1986), https://www.congress.gov/bill/99th-congress/house-bill/5546; An Act to Amend the Patent and Trademark Laws, H.R. 6933, 96th Cong. (1979–1980), https://www.congress.gov/bill/96th-congress/house-bill/6933.
135. Eric Schlosser, "The Prison-Industrial Complex," *The Atlantic*, December 1998, https://www.theatlantic.com/magazine/archive/1998/12/the-prison-industrial-complex/304669/.
136. Celia Farber, "Out of Control: AIDS and the Corruption of Medical Science," *Harper's*, March 2006, 48–49, https://www.immunity.org.uk/wp-content/uploads/2013/07/Harpers_Celia.pdf.
137. The National Institutes of Health owns part of the patent for Moderna's COVID-19 vaccine. Bob Herman, "The NIH Claims Joint Ownership of Moderna's Coronavirus Vaccine," *Axios*, June 25, 2020, https://www.axios.com/moderna-nih-coronavirus-vaccine-ownership-agreements-22051c42-2dee-4b19-938d-099afd71f6a0.html. When *Axios* inquired about the Moderna vaccine patent, NIH confirmed that it is seeking a stake in the patent for the vaccine. Bob Herman, "Statement from National Institutes of Health to Axios," https://www.documentcloud.org/documents/6956323-NIH-Statement-to-Axios.html.
138. For a partial list of Fauci's patents see "Patents by Inventor Anthony S. Fauci," *Justia Patents*, https://patents.justia.com/inventor/anthony-s-fauci; *Anthony S. Fauci, M.D.*, NIH, https://www.niaid.nih.gov/research/anthony-s-fauci-md.
139. Lauren-Brooke Eisen, "The 1994 Crime Bill and Beyond: How Federal Funding Shapes the Criminal Justice System," *Brennan Center for Justice*, September 9, 2019, https://www.brennancenter.org/our-work/analysis-opinion/1994-crime-bill-and-beyond-how-federal-funding-shapes-criminal-justice.

140. Michelle Rogers, "Fact Check: Hospitals Get Paid More if Patients Listed as COVID-19, on Ventilators," *USA Today*, April 27, 2020, https://www.usatoday.com/story/news/factcheck/2020/04/24/fact-check-medicare-hospitals-paid-more-covid-19-patients-coronavirus/3000638001/.
141. Oversight Committee, "Select Subcommittee Hearing 'The Urgent Need for a National Plan to Contain the Coronavirus'," *YouTube*, July 31, 2020, https://www.youtube.com/watch?v=YkP1t_2u5B0.
142. Lauren Melendez, "IDPH Director Explains How Covid Deaths Are Classified," *Week.com*, April 20, 2020, https://week.com/2020/04/20/idph-director-explains-how-covid-deaths-are-classified/.
143. U.S. Food and Drug Administration, "Emergency Use Authorization," May 21, 2021, https://www.fda.gov/emergency-preparedness-and-response/mcm-legal-regulatory-and-policy-framework/emergency-use-authorization.
144. 21 U.S.C. § 360bbb–3.
145. U.S. Food and Drug Administration, "Emergency Use Authorization of Medical Products and Related Authorities," January 2017, https://www.fda.gov/regulatory-information/search-fda-guidance-documents/emergency-use-authorization-medical-products-and-related-authorities.
146. Greg Glaser, "Under Federal Law, Can Your Employer Make You Get the COVID Vaccine," *The Defender*, January 29, 2021, https://childrenshealthdefense.org/defender/under-federal-law-can-your-employer-make-you-get-covid-vaccine/.
147. *Doe # 1 v. Rumsfeld*, 297 F. Supp. 2d 119, 122 (D.D.C. 2003).
148. Alexander Mitscherlich and Fred Mielke, *Doctors of Infamy: The Story of the Nazi Medical Crimes* (Heidelberg: Lambert Schneider, 1947), xxiii–xxv.
149. *Legaretta v. Macias*, No. 21-cv-179 MV/GBW, 2021 U.S. Dist. LEXIS 44474 (D.N.M. March 4, 2021).
150. Complaint at 7, *McKinley et al. v. Grisham et al.*, No. 1:30-CV-01331, 2020 WL 7624169 (D.N.M. December 21, 2020), https://d697c6dd-b94d-4c338cefd36ec2a5eb54.filesusr.com/ugd/218232_58ca36485fac43d5aa3a457c5bab87b7.pdf.

7

Black Life-Matters, Medical Racism, and Health Self-Determination

In the midst of the tumultuous Pandemic Year, on October 30, 2020, as many Philadelphians were protesting the police killing of Walter Wallace, Jr. two days prior, a young black mother, Rickia Young, was attempting to navigate the city streets blockaded for the protests.[1] Young was driving her sixteen-year-old nephew and her two-year old son when police attacked her vehicle, smashed the windows, yanked her and her nephew out of the vehicle, and beat them on the pavement. Meanwhile, another officer took the two-year-old from the backseat and walked away.[2] When Young asked the police where they took her child, they replied "he's gonna go to a better place, we're gonna report it to [the Department of Human Services]."[3] Assaults such as these are familial and are meant at disrupting black social reproduction, the essence of health.

The long civil rights era was in large measure driven by black people's commitment to regaining control over bodily and communal health by confronting those forces that historically threatened it: lynching, Jim Crow segregation, unequal laws, inequitable healthcare, education, and employment, poverty, and state violence. When the Black Panther Party emerged during this period, it famously sought to protect the black community from police violence, taking up a longstanding tradition of black self-defense central to the civil rights era—but it also aimed to provide the services that black people needed but were largely displaced from due to race or poverty or both.[4] The Panthers established no-cost community-based medical clinics that provided all manner of health treatment, patient advocacy, and preventive education.[5] Defining health as "a state of physical, social, and mental well-being" and "one of the most basic human rights of all human beings," the Panthers pursued an expansive conception of "social health" that departed from the narrow civil rights gains at the time.[6] This remains one of the Panthers more radical contributions: to conceptualize health holistically, with repelling state violence but one facet of a much larger and dynamic struggle. Pursuing the Panthers' "social health" digs deep into the way the police power of state and civil society is organized.

The exhortation *black life matters* risks turning in on itself, serving as confirmation that black life does *not* matter under the present social order, for who alone in the human family has to proclaim what everyone else takes for themselves as self-evident? Indeed, the modern world is oriented to its very core to negate black humanity. Protests and appeals to the state and to civil society to stop devaluing black life fall into this trap of extending, or confirming, the structure of antiblackness. The police power as explored in this study is the methodology by which the antiblack world is organized and reproduced as such. In other words, gratuitous violence against black people—not simply at the hands of police officers, but from all quarters—is one of the primary vectors of social cohesion for civil society. For this reason, rooting out this fundamental principle and its institutional life throughout society requires radical transformation, along the lines of Ella Baker's definition noted in Chapter 5 of radical in terms of excavating root causes of current conditions. Baker was part of a critical tradition of black thought that sought to remake the very edifice of our social world, rather than simply appeal for inclusion within its antiblack structure. The metaphor of the burning house reverberates within this tradition. Martin Luther King, Jr. once lamented, just before his assassination, "I have come to believe that we are integrating into a burning house."[7] James Baldwin echoed the sentiment thusly, "Do I really want to be integrated into a burning house?"[8] And in his speech "Message to the Grass Roots," Malcolm X famously contrasted the house Negro with the field Negro. When the master's house caught fire, the house Negro would rush to put it out, explained Malcolm, while the field Negro "didn't try to put it out…[but instead] prayed for a wind, for a breeze."[9]

Sylvia Wynter's term for this effort to hold slaveholding culture at a critical distance while redefining the way we conceive of and live in the world is "ontological sovereignty." Wynter explains that this alternative form of sovereignty could only arise from the collective experience of systemic marginalization, in which that group is compelled to confront their own existence in the form of their "*imposed* liminal status with respect both to the normative order, and to what it is to be human in the terms of that order."[10] For example, it is well known that Malcolm chose to replace his last name with 'X' to signify his refusal of the world-rupturing and world-making violence of slavery, its imposition of marginality and disposability, all in one name. In a 1962 speech, Malcolm would famously challenge his audience: "Who are you? You don't know!…What was your name? And why don't you now know what your name was then?!"[11] Malcolm here evinces the very quandary that Wynter elaborates when she states, "I'm being so bold as to say that in order to *speak* the conception of ontological sovereignty, we would have to move completely outside our present conception of what it is to be human, and therefore outside the ground of the orthodox body of knowledge which institutes and reproduces such a conception." Baldwin put it differently: "The only thing white people have that black people need, or should want, is power—and no one holds power forever. White people cannot in the generality, be taken as models of how to live. Rather, the white man is himself in sore need of new standards, which will release him from his confusion and place him once again in fruitful communion with the depths of his own being."[12] Taken together, the black movement's varied expressions of ontological sovereignty apply rigorous critique as the tropology for moving outside the "orthodox body of knowledge," as Wynter puts it, that props up Western society. It is time to apply ontological sovereignty to our analysis of medical science and public health.

Given the litany of injury experienced by black people at the hands of the Western world's medical science, it is a testament to the ubiquitous and disarming reach of antiblackness that black people still look to Western medicine and state-defined public health at all. This needs to change in the same manner that people need to stop looking to the criminal law for "justice" and "security." The history and present reality of medical racism is very much informing many black people's feelings on the current COVID-19 vaccine.[13] It is antiblack racism's own ignorance, pure and simple, which suggests that black people who decline the shots are "uninformed." Ignorant of how the 1918–1919 Spanish Flu pandemic disproportionately impacted black families confined by segregation, lynching, and policing into cramped kitchenettes.[14] This geography of disease is replicated today in that the states with the highest rates of black COVID-19 cases are also the worst places for black people to live in terms of environmental toxins.[15]

The claim that black people are "uninformed" as to the risks to black health posed by the public health establishment is ignorant, as well, of Ft. Detrick's history conducting bioweapons studies on black communities. In the 1960s, a joint Army-CIA program bred more than four million mosquitoes per day and released them in hordes in black communities in Florida to see if they could be used as first-strike biological weapons to spread yellow fever and other infectious diseases. Black residents were soon plagued by a rash of mysterious illnesses, including the symptoms of dengue and yellow fever, and deaths.[16] It is also ignorant of how between 1954 and 1962 the Memorial Sloan-Kettering Cancer Center, which receives hundreds of millions of dollars in National Institutes of Health funding annually, injected over four hundred black inmates at the Ohio State Prison with live cancer cells in order to observe how the body might react.[17] Medical experimentation on black inmates in U.S. prisons and jails routinely went on throughout most of the twentieth century, right up through the 1980s.[18] When Nazi physicians and scientists were prosecuted for their crimes against humanity during the Holocaust, their vigorous defense pointed to the longstanding practice by their American counterparts. In no small historic irony, the American-led Nuremburg war crimes tribunal produced as one of its lasting contradictions the Nuremburg Code prohibiting medical experimentation on human subjects without their consent. Since prisoners, by definition, are unable to freely give or withhold their consent due to their confinement, the use of inmate "volunteers" violates the principles of the Code enshrined as a result of Nazis adopting American medical science practices.

The claim that black people today are "uninformed" about the danger Western medical science poses to black health also ignores how U.S. researchers administered as much as five hundred times the approved dosage of an experimental measles vaccine to black and Latino babies in low-income Los Angeles neighborhoods from 1987 through 1991. Consent forms did not inform parents about the high dosage, that the vaccine was experimental, nor that it had been given to two thousand children in Haiti and West Africa with disastrous results.[19] Children in Senegal who received the experimental vaccine died at a rate 80 percent higher than children who did not receive it.[20] Also in West Africa, there was the case of Pfizer's poisoning of Nigerian children in 1996. During the height of a meningococcal meningitis epidemic, scientists offered parents in Kano, Nigeria Pfizer's experimental drug Trovan (floxacin). By the end of the experiment, over two hundred kids were disabled and eleven were dead.[21]

The notion that black people are "uninformed" is also ignorant of how the Department of Health and Human Services passed 21CFR50.24 in October 1996, a regulation that permitted researchers to legally enroll seriously ill emergency room patients in medical research studies and test experimental therapies on them without their consent. Emergency room deaths followed shortly thereafter and did not stop until the Occupational Health and Hygiene Plan suspended a clinical trial in which many more had died from the experimental treatment than those receiving standard care. None of the deceased gave their consent to the treatments that killed them.[22] Ignorant, as well, of the waiver from the FDA successfully sought by the Department of Defense in 1990 to allow medical experimentation on its soldiers without their consent. Almost a million soldiers were forced to take the experimental anthrax vaccine, until hundreds of soldiers began refusing to comply, citing the devastating side effects and deaths associated with it. Black soldiers are twice as common among ground troops as in the overall American society.[23] Ignorant of how the lead poisoning of Washington, DC's water supply in 2004 was 20–30 times more extensive than the well-known crisis in Flint, MI a decade later, and of how at the height of the District's crisis, the CDC produced a falsified report claiming there was no toxic levels of lead in the water.[24] Ignorant of how GlaxoSmithKline and the New York City Administration for Children's Services used black foster children to test experimental AIDS drugs in 2003–2005. When children resisted, the powerful drugs were administered through gastronomy tubes inserted directly into their abdomens. Some children died but no autopsies were performed and state and city agencies claimed that there was no evidence that any deaths were directly caused by the experimental treatments.[25] And ignorant of how the entire vaccine-autism controversy stems from a censored study of black boys in Atlanta. The 2004 study by the CDC of the measles-mumps-rubella vaccine found three times as many autism diagnoses in children who received the MMR vaccine on time, but the damning data was omitted and the research plan was deviated to obscure the findings.[26]

Black life-matters in the late twentieth and early twenty-first centuries are indelibly bound up with HIV/AIDS. The history of discriminatory medical treatment against black people, as the preceding paragraphs attest, is lengthy and suggests the racist orientation of the medical industrial complex, but it does not exhaust the problem presented by today's pandemic police power. In order to better understand how the pandemic police power relies on a particularly ingrained antiblack racism, it is necessary to revisit AIDS through the lens of the medical industrial complex. This history reveals the error in seeking inclusion into the state's public health protocols and the medical establishment's treatment complex. The sacred cow of vaccination is mirrored in the equally sacrosanct dogma regarding HIV/AIDS and its drug therapies. As explored in the preceding two chapters with respect to vaccination, and with the prison industrial complex before that, the received knowledge about AIDS cannot be taken at face value if the goal is self-determination in health matters. This reevaluation has critical implications for overhauling the leading discourse today on COVID-19 and race, which simply asserts that black people and other people of color have been disproportionately impacted by the pandemic. As a remedy for this problem, the discourse doubles-down on the call for equal access to healthcare provision for all people. Given the historical and present formation of the medical industrial complex, however, greater "access" for black people and historically marginalized groups will not produce healthy outcomes, only more subjection to the disempowerment on which the system spins. Disempowerment in a system stratified by race and class is a path toward unhealthy outcomes, not healthy communities. Rethinking AIDS will facilitate the crucial shift away from "access" and toward self-determination regarding the pandemic police power.

In 2017, black people accounted for approximately 13 percent of the U.S. population, but 43 percent of new HIV diagnoses.[27] The twin poisons of racialized disease stigma and institutional discrimination in healthcare have been consequential for blacks living with HIV/AIDS not named Magic Johnson.[28] Black people were systematically excluded from early AZT therapy, and have had unequal access to the latest treatments ever since.[29] This exclusion turned out to be fortuitous, however, as the AZT trials were repeatedly aborted due to deaths from the treatment, or from major methodological errors, with these facts covered up in order to bring AZT to market.[30] If ever there was a slam-dunk argument for disabusing people of the concept of "access" in healthcare, it would be AIDS drugs. A cozy relationship developed between pharmaceutical companies and AIDS service organizations (ostensibly "community-based") in which the corporations funded the AIDS activists, who in turn trumpeted the industry byline that AIDS drugs save lives.[31] Indeed, "patient activism" in AIDS was built on a philosophy of "Drugs Into Bodies." As Celia Farber explains, this approach was based on the belief that people with HIV did not have time to wait and see whether drugs worked or not, but had to gamble—"and in the first round of gambling—with AZT—they undeniably lost."[32] AZT was an old cancer chemotherapeutic agent discarded into the pharmaceutical dustbin for being too toxic when the drug company Burroughs Wellcome (the same Wellcome of the eugenics science tradition examined in the previous chapter) brought it back repackaged as a life-saving anti-retroviral. A proven immune suppressant was thus now being prescribed for the treatment of an immune suppressing virus. The severe toxicity of AIDS drug "cocktails" rivals that of cancer treatments and has led many scientists to argue that untold scores of AIDS patients died of their treatments, not from the disease.[33]

The AIDS activist establishment functions within the police power of medical science which holds out "access" to its drug treatments as the panacea. Pressure on the state from AIDS organizations to get new drug therapies onto the market quickly works for the pharmaceutical companies by short-circuiting questions about whether their drugs actually work, let alone whether they are safe. Activists sought primarily one kind of treatment, pharmacological, which meant integration into the state-corporate nexus of industry and power. An AIDS "activist" is therefore more properly understood as an AIDS *agent*. Much like philanthropic foundations, an AIDS agent does the work of the state by integrating people into its client structure and shoring up existing gaps in service. Subsequent generations of agents continue this deep integration with the state-corporate nexus today. For instance, in the midst of the Pandemic Year, Kenyon Farrow dismissed non-pharmacological-based responses to illness as "conspiracy" theories that disempower people who should be demanding care from the state.[34] Farrow works with the Treatment Action Group, which splintered off of ACT UP in order to create an organization focused exclusively on accelerating AIDS treatment research, and with Data & Society, which researches the development of and access to technology, and receives a majority of its funding from Microsoft and the Gates Foundation.[35] In its demand for drug treatment, ACT UP succeeded in fast-tracking the FDA approval process for new drugs, blaming the government's scientific safety and efficacy studies for the deaths of their friends. As Farber puts it, "[t]o the pharmaceutical industry, it was a dream come true."[36]

The ensuing relationship between the drug companies and their AIDS agents reflects the ties between Wall Street and its state regulators, between philanthropies and capitalist accumulation, and between abolitionists and the academy: the alliance looks like discord but is actually "a conjoined will and agenda, one that persists to this day," to deregulate the FDA and get drugs onto the market as quickly as possible.[37] The lethality of AZT has not diminished the zeal for hastily approved toxic HIV drugs, of which there are now twenty-six. One of them was approved in less than six weeks; the longest approval time for any of them was eleven months. Prior to AIDS, the FDA approval process typically ran eight years or more. One observer concludes that the AIDS agents' mission was literally a suicidal one:

> I don't think they intended it, but the AIDS activists went on a kind of kamikaze assault. I would be fascinated to see the documents and internal memos from the pharmaceutical companies when they realized…hey, look what we've got here. These guys opened the floodgates; they did for the industry what it couldn't do itself…It's tragic how the drug industry exploited them, really. The industry got everything out of it. Everything.[38]

AIDS changed the approval process for all kinds of drugs and vaccines. The industry, in turn, handsomely rewards the AIDS organizations with millions of dollars in funding. Echoing the SEC regulators who assure us that they can objectively perform their oversight function on the very banks for whom the regulators used to work and from whom they now earn thousands of dollars in speaking fees, or the physicians who claim that their medical practice is uninfluenced by their close relationship with pharmaceutical representatives, the AIDS organizations believe that they are able to retain their independence from the pharmaceutical industry, despite the drug company money that sustains them. "In no case do any of these groups report to Burroughs Wellcome," states one AIDS agency director about the manufacturer of AZT. "It is entirely appropriate that we seek funding from the companies that have profited from this epidemic."[39] The notion that drug company sponsorship of AIDS agencies is some kind of restitution is preposterous and deeply mystifies these agents' own complicity in the reproduction of the medical industrial complex.

AIDS agents are in fact major players in setting medical science and health policy. Despite killing relatively small numbers of people,

AIDS consumes an "inexplicably colossal" portion of the federal research budget: the CDC estimates that 15,798 people died of AIDS in 2004, which is 7 percent of the total annual iatrogenic deaths (death by medical treatment).[40] The NIH research budget allocation by patient for AIDS was $3084 in 2005; by comparison, the corresponding research allocation per patient for diabetes, which kills more people than AIDS and breast cancer combined, was all of eighty dollars.[41] In this light, Farrow's response to a question about "medical misinformation campaigns" predictably focuses on "access to care and treatment, and even access to clinical trials, [as] a racial justice issue."[42] Farrow continues:

> If you are believing that somebody out here used alkaline water and, you know, a diet to cure people of HIV and other kinds of infectious diseases, that actually doesn't benefit us. And secondly with some of the conspiracy theories...part of what they do is, formulated from some level of white supremacy because they suggest that the white man or woman, through the state, is omniscient and knows everything, so any infectious disease or pandemic that happens must be man-made, which gives power away from us to actively respond and demand that we have access to care...[43]

It is unsurprising for AIDS agents like Farrow to dismiss the successes of natural therapies with a whole range of diseases, including HIV and AIDS, since he is well embedded within the medical industrial complex, and as such, it is his job to draw our focus to pharmacological therapies at the exclusion of almost all alternative avenues to health. As Thomas Kuhn wrote over sixty years ago, "[w]hat a man sees depends on what he looks at and also upon what his previous visual-conceptual experience has taught him to see."[44]

The reality is far different than that portrayed by AIDS agents like Farrow. From 1988 to 1999, the Tri-State Healing Center in Manhattan successfully treated 1200 advanced AIDS patients—*without* AIDS drugs. None of the patients died, and eighteen reversed all of their AIDS-related conditions, regained full health, and converted to HIV-negative. This period coincides with the most acute mortality rates in the history of AIDS treatment, due largely to the arrival of AZT and other retroviral drug therapies. Luanne Pennesi was a senior nurse administrator who worked with the Center.

> After several months I saw people completely seroconverting and reversing AIDS. In conventional medicine when a person is diagnosed with AIDS or cancer, we want you to be afraid so you will do whatever we say. But these people [at the Center] were all managing their diets, all were on plant-based diets. They were taking herbs to detox their liver, taking immune enhancing herbs, and supplements. And they were all very excited and very optimistic and hopeful. It was a completely different picture for me of people with AIDS. I watched these people's lab counts improve significantly over time. Then I saw them do bio-oxidative therapy. Viruses cannot live in a high oxygen environment. So when you flood the body with oxygen like bio-oxidative therapy, you are killing off viruses in large proportions. It was a completely new ball game for me. If I had not seen the lab results with my own eyes, I probably would never have believed something like this was possible. And during my time there I saw no less than 8 people completely reverse AIDS. I had never seen this in the medical community in the hospital. Not only did I see people with AIDS seroconvert, but I also saw people with many viruses — hepatitis, herpes, Epstein Barr, coxsackie virus, mycoplasma. I saw all these people seroconverting and getting happier and healthier. It was an empowerment model.[45]

The Center's protocols included botanicals and medicinal herbs, naturopathic remedies, intravenous drips and oral supplementation of the antioxidants glutathione and Vitamin C, oxygen and ozone therapies, detoxification regimens, stress reduction and behavior modification techniques, and plant-based diets. Unlike the conventional treatments, the multi-disciplinary practitioners at the Center were not trying to stage a war against a virus with drugs alone. Instead, their approach was to restore and increase patients' natural immunity in order to strengthen the body's own defense mechanisms to handle infection. In so doing, they avoided the adverse effects of the antiretroviral drugs, including severe anemia, acute liver toxicity, dementia, renal failure, and death.

Approximately half of the Center's patients were black, partly due to the investigative reporting on the Center's work by the black news media.

The prominent black journalists who investigated the Center included Tony Brown of *Tony Brown's Journal*, a long-running syndicated program on PBS; Bill Tatum, publisher of *The Amsterdam News*; Bill McCreary of *McCreary Report*; and Earl Caldwell, who as a *New York Times* journalist reported from within the Black Panther Party in the early 1970s. Another black journalist, Doug Henderson, recalls his experience with the Center.

> AIDS back then meant death but not today. Since 1977 I had been listening to Gary Null and he started talking about AIDS in the mid-1980s... He had on his program people whom he said had seroconverted, meaning they were HIV positive and went negative, or they had full blown AIDS and subsequent blood tests revealed there was no trace of HIV or any of the other 29 co-factors that at that time compromised AIDS. I found that hard to believe... I went to his Center really on a reconnaissance mission. I wanted to find out if what Gary said was really true because there are a lot of hustlers out there. I needed hard proof. Then one man said he had had the HIV virus but didn't have it any more. I found that a little hard to believe. As time went by 5 or 6 people told me the same thing.... [Later] Gary took me into his office and showed me 5 or 6 medical records and I could see that according to the records they had no trace of HIV in their system... It was remarkable the work they were doing at the Tri State Healing Center.[46]

Black celebrities like Arthur Ashe, Dick Gregory, Isaac Hayes, and Kwame Ture lent their support. Henderson believes that if his friend Ashe had adopted the Center's protocols for himself, he might still be alive today. In the least, Henderson says, Ashe would certainly not have died of AIDS-related pneumocystis carinii pneumonia in 1993. The Center, and other physicians such as Dr. Robert Cathcart of Stanford who adopted its protocols, never lost a single AIDS patient to PCP.

Part of the reason why AIDS retroviral therapies do not work very well—obvious toxicities aside—has to do with the likelihood that AIDS is not caused by HIV in the first place. It is the gospel in medical science and public health that HIV is the AIDS virus—*despite* significant scientific evidence to the contrary. The problem with the HIV/AIDS hypothesis is that HIV does not fulfill the traditional scientific rules of evidence, known as "Koch's postulates," for identifying the causative agent of a particular disease. The four criteria are:

1. the microorganism or other pathogen must be **present in all cases of the disease**;
2. the pathogen can be isolated from the diseased host and **grown in pure culture**;
3. the pathogen from the pure culture must **cause the disease when inoculated into a healthy, susceptible laboratory animal**; and
4. the pathogen must be **reisolated** from the new host and **shown to be the same** as the originally inoculated pathogen.[47]

HIV meets the second criteria tenuously, but does not meet the first, third, and fourth criteria. As early as the late 1980s, physicians and scientists were reporting numerous cases of AIDS in which there was no HIV present. As one scientist pointed out at a 1988 forum sponsored by the American Foundation for AIDS Research (amfAR), "sometimes even a single exception is sufficient to disprove a theory…This is the crux of the matter. The virus cannot be found in all cases of AIDS."[48] Peter Duesberg has shown over 4000 cases documented in the scientific literature of HIV-negative AIDS.[49] AIDS is a syndrome comprising twenty-five different diseases, all of which exist independent of HIV—and yet the mere presence of HIV makes it AIDS, despite no proof of how HIV supposedly causes all of these different diseases. At the 1992 international AIDS conference in Amsterdam, numerous reports of HIV-negative AIDS raised the possibility of *two* immune depleting retroviruses, but the medical science establishment led by Anthony Fauci covered up these anomalies by simply giving HIV-negative AIDS a new name and declaring by fiat that they were not really AIDS cases because they did not fit the epidemiological criteria.[50] HIV-negative AIDS would turn out to be myalgic encephalomyelitis (ME), or "chronic fatigue syndrome," caused by XMRV, the xenotropic murine retrovirus. Fauci, however, would tell the one million ME sufferers in the United States that their problem was merely psychiatric, while at the same time broadcasting all manner of salacious falsehoods about AIDS meant to generate fear and dependency on the medical industrial complex.[51]

Another curious aspect of the HIV/AIDS hypothesis is that most AIDS patients do not have active HIV in their systems because the virus has been neutralized by antibodies. Just like its use with COVID-19, when PCR is used to reveal "viral load" in AIDS patients, one of the customary clinical markers for HIV, the test is actually measuring amplified fragments of DNA left over from an infection suppressed by antibodies, not the presence of actual live virus in the body. Nonetheless, the presence of HIV antibodies is used to designate a person HIV-positive. This designation completely contravenes the established medical practice for all other diseases (except COVID-19) wherein antibodies are an indication that the body has produced a successful immune response to the virus, and thus cleared the infection. Meanwhile, scientists have found that an altogether different virus, Human Herpes Virus 6 (HHV-6), directly causes *all* of the complications associated with AIDS, *but without the presence of HIV*.[52]

Kuhn explained that the decision to reject one paradigm is always at once the acceptance of another, and the judgment leading to that decision involves the comparison of both paradigms with nature and with each other.[53] Unfortunately, Kuhn's model of scientific development depicts an ideal type removed from the political reality in which science is actually practiced. The problem with AIDS science has been that the censure of fertile intellectual process robbed the world of an adequate comparative evaluation. Or, as Kuhn would have it: "To reject one paradigm without simultaneously substituting another is to reject science itself."[54] Whether HIV causes AIDS or is merely a passenger virus, as Duesberg claims; whether or not AIDS and ME are twin sides of the same immune compromising coin; or whether or not the multi-systemic problems connected to HHV-6 (like multiple sclerosis, fibromyalgia, autism, and even the skin disorder Morgellons disease) are intertwined somehow with the HIV and XMRV retroviruses—the science remains incomplete and stunted.

What is crystal clear, however, is that the politics of AIDS research leaves us with three conclusions for black life-matters in the COVID-19 era. First, AIDS is epidemiological and not etiological. It has been shaped by its political construction as a gay disease, and then as a black and African disease, rather than by the science of causality. To put it differently, AIDS is foremost a cultural and political phenomenon, not a scientific or natural one, which is why it is a central exposition of the police power of the medical industrial complex. This recognition is not novel, but I am arguing here for it to translate into a new kind of medical science abolition, rather than the customary appeal for better "access" to treatment that we see predominating discourse on race and COVID-19. Understanding the history of AIDS politics can be helpful in cutting through the mystification swirling around today's pandemic. AIDS testing foreshadowed the fraudulent nature of COVID-19 testing. HIV tests, like the COVID-19 tests today, detect impressions of viral presence, but never the virus itself. HIV tests do this by means of molecular protein weights, quantified in terms of "band density," and there are as many as eleven different criteria for how many and which proteins signal "positive." The most stringent criteria (four bands) are employed in Australia and France; a middle-of-the-road three bands are used in the United States; while in Africa, the least stringent (two bands) is upheld. This means that you could start your day HIV-positive in Tanzania, get on an airplane and disembark in Australia having seroconverted back to HIV-negative simply by crossing a geo-political border.

This decidedly unscientific phenomenon will be familiar to black Americans in particular, who know all too well the fallacious science of the rule of hypodescent, or the "one-drop rule," used to determine racial classification in the United States. Beginning with a 1662 Virginia law, each state or jurisdiction subsequently defined the meaning of race differently, such that a person could be designated black in one state, but turn white simply by crossing state lines, or vice versa. Likewise, the definition of AIDS in Africa turns out to be heavily weighted by racial fictions. By reserving a hyper-sensitive protein weight criteria for Africa alone, the incidence of HIV infection on the continent appears to be of "epidemic" proportions. Estimates of HIV-positives are then doubled, tripled, and even quadrupled to project continent-wide infection rates. Farber quotes a UNAIDS official who acknowledged that the figures put out by WHO and the UN are "pure fiction."[55] Much like COVID-19, a purified isolate of HIV that could be used to definitively test for its presence or absence has never been identified. The series of proteins tested for are not unique constituents of HIV, but rather can appear wherever certain immune stressors, microbes, and antigens congregate in high volume. The clinical definition of AIDS on the continent gets even murkier from there, being so broad and generic as to encompass most non-AIDS diseases, as well as the common ailments of malnutrition, malaria, and parasitic infections.[56] Established at a 1985 conference in the Central African Republic, the definition requires neither a positive HIV test nor a T-cell count, but only the presence of chronic diarrhea, fever, significant weight loss, and asthenia (weakness).[57] And when WHO, the United States, and the massive international aid NGO sector spends billions of dollars on AIDS in Africa, while allotting only a small fraction of this amount for all other health matters combined, there is extraordinary pressure to "call everything AIDS."[58] As noted in the previous chapter, financially incentivizing the fraudulent inflation of caseloads and deaths is also occurring with COVID-19.

The point is not that HIV/AIDS and COVID-19 do not exist, notwithstanding the many mysteries, contradictions, and medical failures that have yet to be adequately and accurately explained by science. Any time someone critiques the epidemiology or questions the case load and mortality figures, they are labeled a "denialist," which invokes the notion of the evil Jewish Holocaust denier. As Farber puts it regarding the apocalyptic AIDS predictions for Africa, "It is as though a message of imminent mass death, from sex no less, is a kind of humanitarian courtesy to the continent of Africa."[59] The point, rather, is to understand the purpose and manner in which these specious claims of death and destruction are promulgated. Regarding AIDS, the specter of mass *black* death is based on racialized fears of black sex. One researcher put it thusly: "Under such diagnostic rigor, the example of thousands of African men and women who are essentially suffering from symptoms and diseases all called other names before 1981 [when AIDS arrived on the scene], is held up as proof that the West is menaced by the threat of heterosexually transmitted AIDS."[60] The portrait of an African AIDS crisis spreading like wildfire is fueled by racist notions of the extent and manner of black sex. This sexualized racial paranoia extends the basic features of the AIDS origin myths which included claims that AIDS jumped from chimpanzees to humans because Africans have sex with monkeys, are extremely sexually promiscuous, engage in blood rituals, and allow children to play with dead monkeys. Given that fears of an explosion in AIDS cases in the West as a result of heterosexual sex have not borne out, the sum total of the discourse on AIDS in Africa amounts to the fantasy that African sexuality is fundamentally different from Western sexuality.

The racial-sexual discourse on AIDS in Africa accomplishes two tasks: to cover up the systematic underdevelopment of Africa by the West across the eras, from the slave trade, to colonization, to the present neo-colonial period; and to create a massive market for Western drugs and vaccines—some of which may be helpful under certain conditions, but most of which are counterproductive or outright harmful, and all of which distract resources and political accountability from the social production of disease and ill-health in the first place.[61] If most of what is now called AIDS in Africa are in fact the symptoms of poverty, malnutrition, and poor sanitation and infrastructure, then "AIDS" is a direct outgrowth of the relations of dominance between Africa and the West across the past five centuries. As with the rapid decline in infectious disease outbreaks in the West by the early twentieth century with the dawn of improved sanitation, drinking water, and nutrition, similar outcomes could easily be attained in Africa through the same basic measures. The problem of AIDS, therefore, is historical and political in a way that is obscured when it is construed in terms of interpersonal behaviors, pathological sex, and tropes of black people as sub-human or a qualitatively different species of human being.

Antiblack societies like the United States treat its black residents and their health status similarly. This is a racist bait-and-switch that sustains the medical industrial complex: systematically destabilize black communities and societies to the tune of every poor health indicator and manner of premature death, and then rush to fill the void with costly and suspect pharmacological and biotechnological antidotes. As explored in previous chapters, not only are drug interventions and vaccines ineffective in counteracting or remedying the fundamental social conditions that create poor health outcomes, they can also augment these pathogenic environments. Former South African president Thabo Mbeki was pilloried by the West for raising these very same questions about the toxicity of unproven AIDS drugs, but his wisdom has proven prophetic as those same drugs have been removed from the U.S. market. The same lessons apply to COVID-19. When compared with the longstanding structural violence that black people face at every turn, the pandemic is largely a red herring, at worst, and a symptom of an unhealthy society, at best.

The second lesson for COVID-19 from the AIDS debacle is the danger of treating health problems as distinct from one another, rather than as features of a complex whole. None of the problems associated with the retroviruses HIV and XMRV will be solved by treating them as distinct from each other. Until the medical industrial complex's denial that they are related is overcome, it is hard to imagine how any of the sufferings can be ended. Regarding COVID-19, this points to the basic lesson that effective immune responses to illness are a function of *lifestyle*, not vaccination. The ability to live a certain kind of life, with access to clean water, safe housing, and healthy food options, is itself a function of a political and historical process from which far too many people are excluded. AIDS agents are also partly responsible for sidestepping this basic fact by militantly resisting evidence that the immune suppressive effects of heavy drug use in the gay community played a major role in early susceptibility to AIDS. The fact that this finding was frequently subsumed in homophobic messages about "gay sex" should not prevent reckoning with the realities of lifestyle for preventing illness. Racial justice advocates today are reproducing with COVID-19 this same failure from the AIDS era. They use the fact that black people disproportionately suffer from a variety of chronic and debilitating health conditions to justify prioritized vaccination and greater access to the medical industrial complex rather than agitating for improved social conditions and advocating healthy lifestyle choices that would actually foster enhanced immune system function. It is the same insidious trap from the AIDS era: the tragedy here is that people who mean well are promoting solutions that only deepen the problem of racial inequities in health status. That said, we work with the hands we are dealt and until people from all walks of life recognize that their health is their hands, and their hands alone, the medical industrial complex will continue to sustain itself by convincing people to give up their own personal health sovereignty.

Which brings us to the third implication, which is that the politics of AIDS has dire consequences for its prescribed pharmacological therapies, but less so for natural or alternative approaches. Alternative medicines are less negatively impacted by AIDS politics because they are not dependent upon the agendas set by the medical industrial complex, and they are centered on the science of immunology and the treatment of the body as an integrated system, neither of which change as the debates on causality unfold. The glaring caveat here is that mainstream medical science robs alternative medicine of resources and the attention it needs to make a broader impact on society. It is no accident that the success of the Tri-State Healing Center in treating AIDS has been largely obscured. The Center's methods are a major indictment of medical science not simply because of its non-pharmacological approach. The real indictment comes from the fact that every protocol followed by the Center was borne from extensively documented scientific evidence. It is not that alternative therapies are unproven or unscientific; there is ample science behind it all. The problem is a paradigmatic one because the medical science model requires suppressing any possibility of alternative science-based healing.

The suppression of alternative healing, and the failure to reject the medical industrial complex in order to take control over personal and communal health matters is especially consequential for black people, given the endemic racism of medical science. The eugenicist history of the vaccine regime reviewed in the previous chapter has taken on newly insidious forms during the COVID-19 situation, and racial justice advocates are proving incapable of identifying and resisting this racist medical violence. Police and prison abolitionists are in fact causing more harm than good by pushing people further into the medical industrial complex. The COVID-19 Policing Project at the Community Hub for Safety and Accountability has produced several media-savvy reports on policing during the pandemic that advances their abolitionist agenda of defunding the police. The reports provide useful information on funding streams created by the CARES Act and the American Rescue Plan Act (ARPA), President Biden's March 2021 pandemic economic relief package, but they join all other messaging today by abolitionists in promoting the medical industrial complex narrative on the pandemic and advocating for equitable distribution of vaccines. More tellingly, the reports point to low vaccination rates among law enforcement and prison system personnel as another way in which policing puts black and brown communities at greater risk for infection.[62] This take on pandemic policing plays right into the planners' playbook, something the abolitionists might have uncovered if their research were not blinded by the medical science paradigm.

The government's own planning documents show that the vaccine allocation plan, known as Operation Warp Speed, diverges dramatically from all previous such vaccination programs, and that it has already incorporated the expected criticisms from racial justice advocates. First, Operation Warp Speed is being managed almost entirely by the U.S. military, along with the Department of Homeland Security (DHS) and the National Security Agency (NSA), rather than by civilian health agencies.[63] Second, for the first time since 2001, law enforcement officers and DHS officials are *not* being prioritized for early vaccination.[64] Third, amidst the escalation in mandatory vaccination across the United States and the globe throughout 2021, these U.S. officers and officials are *not* being subjected to compulsory participation. As the COVID-19 Policing Project notes,

> [a]n estimated three-quarters of the Chicago police department has refused city-administered vaccines, causing concern among public health experts. Similarly low rates of vaccination are reported among New York, Washington, D.C., Las Vegas, Columbus, OH, Atlanta, and Phoenix police departments, with Phoenix offering cops $75 to get vaccinated as organizers call to defund the department and invest in community safety strategies…"I hate to sound like I don't care, but I really don't," Vince Champion, the Atlanta-based southeast regional director of the International Brotherhood of Police Officers, said of low vaccination rates. Widespread refusal of vaccination by police and jail and prison staff while simultaneously refusing to prioritize incarcerated people and criminalized populations for informed and consensual vaccination is increasing risk of transmission, illness, and death.[65]

Fourth, the vaccine allocation strategy emphasizes the need to prioritize racial minorities, but in such a way that these groups feel comfortable and not like "guinea pigs" when receiving an experimental biological product.[66] The CDC took guidance from the Center on Health Security (CHS) at Johns Hopkins University, citing the August 2020 CHS publication *Interim Framework for COVID-19 Vaccine Allocation and Distribution* in its nationwide allocation recommendations for Operation Warp Speed.[67] CHS has been at the center of COVID-19 pandemic planning and response since it sponsored the Event 201 preparedness summit with WHO and Gates in October 2019; it has also been an active framer of earlier epidemic response planning, going back to 2001.[68] Johns Hopkins also maintains the "coronavirus tracker" database used by virtually every mainstream news source since the beginning of the pandemic.

In a remarkable distillation of all of the primary concerns regularly voiced by racial justice advocates and abolitionists alike, CHS frames vaccine distribution in terms of the national protests against police violence, arguing that allocation needs to reflect "fairness and justice."

> It is important to acknowledge that a critical difference between the current pandemic and the context envisioned in the 2018 guidance for pandemic influenza vaccine allocation is not only the epidemiological differences between COVID-19 and influenza, such as the higher rates of asymptomatic transmission and fatality risk, but also that we are currently in the midst of a national reckoning on racial injustice, prompted by cases of police brutality and murder. The structural racism that is the root cause of police brutality is also the root cause of the disproportionate impact of the current pandemic on people of color and people living in poverty. Although structural racism was as present in the 2018 and previous influenza epidemics as it is today, the general public acknowledgment of racial injustice was not. Longstanding societal and economic inequities and structural racism in health systems have been barriers to disadvantaged populations gaining access to healthcare, contributing to their lack of trust in governments and public health authorities to meet their needs. Furthermore, communities of color, particularly Black populations, may be more wary of officials responsible for vaccine-related decisions due to past medical injustices committed by authorities on Black communities.[69]

The CHS report goes on to state that racial health disparities such as "higher rates of COVID-19-related severe illness and mortality among systematically disadvantaged or marginalized groups" should be factored into the overall COVID-19 response.[70] CHS contradicts this concern with racial justice by noting that

> The ultimate safety of an approved vaccine is not completely knowable until it has been administered to millions of people. During clinical trials, tens of thousands of individuals will receive the vaccine but that may fail to show safety concerns that occur with less frequency, such as 1 in a million. This can be a concern for particularly severe adverse effects. It is also possible that certain adverse effects may occur more frequently in certain population subgroups, which may not be apparent until millions are vaccinated.[71]

Indeed, studies show that black people are generally at greater risk for adverse reactions to vaccines, partly because of higher immune responses which can cause inflammatory scenarios like transverse myelitis, the debilitating neurological condition that has come up repeatedly throughout *Pandemic Police Power* in relation to vaccines.[72]

The decision to prioritize black people for a poorly tested vaccine for which they may be particularly vulnerable to serious adverse reactions is telling, and leads to CHS's recommendations on messaging, taken up by the CDC. Instead of targeting black and Latino communities directly, CHS recommends "prioritizing other cohorts of the population, such as essential workers or those with underlying health conditions associated with poorer COVID-19 outcomes" due to the high representation of people of color in the "essential" workforce, utilizing culturally competent approaches with the targeted populations such as vaccinating at "churches, schools, culturally specific community centers and senior homes," "using outside groups who have relationships with the community, instead of direct government involvement," and making sure that there is not a police presence at vaccination sites which may signal "that the site may be unsafe for Black or other minority communities."[73] CHS also recommends targeting black and Latino communities by prioritizing the very comorbidities that disproportionately affect these populations (hypertension, diabetes, cardiovascular disease, chronic kidney disease, immunosuppression, obesity, chronic obstructive pulmonary disease), and by recognizing that "incarcerated populations are highly vulnerable" to infection.[74]

We have reviewed above and in the previous chapter the health dangers posed by vaccination and the COVID-19 shots in particular. Again, as discussed in the previous chapter, the nature of the COVID-19 shots means that people with comorbidities are acutely vulnerable not only to serious adverse events, but also to long-term immune dysfunction brought on by how the vaccines interfere with immune system response. These immune system problems will likely be blamed on the prior existence of comorbidities instead of the precipitating role played by the COVID-19 biologicals. In other words, black and brown people will be blamed for their further health degradation, while the vaccine regime will remain unaccountable. Furthermore, one of the most outrageous contradictions about the COVID-19 vaccination program that is hiding in plain sight is that the most vulnerable populations are being targeted for the vaccine despite the fact that it was precisely those groups that were excluded from the vaccine trials in the first place.

Abolitionists are not heeding this dire situation, but instead are ushering their communities further into harm's way. The Operation Warp Speed planning document, along with the CDC's and CHS's recommendations, further illuminate the failure of abolitionists and other racial justice advocates to accurately pinpoint the source of danger. The planners' recommendations to target racial minorities echoes the early twentieth-century eugenicists in three ways. First, black and brown people are being targeted for medical experimentation. Second, just like Margaret Sanger utilizing black community leaders to implement her Negro Project, the state is finding indirect and "culturally competent" methods to circumvent historically informed objections to state medicine. Third, the fact that law enforcement and Homeland Security are not prioritized for COVID-19 shots, and have not been subject to compulsory participation, only seems to confirm the analysis that they are merely the backups to the pandemic police power enforcing the terms of racial sacrifice.

It seems especially troubling that the state and its corporate elite planning partners can count on abolitionists to reliably perform the pandemic police power. When the state-corporate planners preempt the abolitionists' analysis, then we are not witnessing confrontation or contestation, but merely two conjoined sides of the paradigm's unity. The abolitionist reports published at the Community Resource Hub are supported by funding and technical assistance from elite corporate universities, philanthropies, and liberal legal reform and civil liberties organizations like the American Civil Liberties Union (ACLU) and the Center for Constitutional Rights (CCR). Prior to COVID-19, the ACLU had denounced vaccine mandates and coercive measures to fight previous pandemics.[75] The organization has now reversed its long-standing position, abandoning its own mandate to protect civil liberties, and the abolitionists, in turn, are not offering any push back on mandates and coercion. These are the contorted racial politics of COVID-19's new Negro Project: abolitionists assume that law enforcement's lack of participation in the vaccine regime is due to its racist antipathies toward the communities of color that it polices, when in fact this assumption itself is recruited toward serving the pandemic police power because it promotes basic racial reasoning that obscures how power is actually operating in the extant circumstance.

The abolitionists' concern with the spread of surveillance technologies throughout the prison industrial complex is also waylaid by their silence on COVID-19 surveillance. The abolitionist's focus on new technologies is well-founded, but all too frequently neglects the primary mode of surveillance, the body.[76] As P. Khalil Saucier writes, "In the era of big data, electronic surveillance, biometric observation, and high-tech racial profiling, rudimentary technologies go unacknowledged."[77] In this case, the body remains the primary site of an expansive surveillance state apparatus through mask wearing, contact tracing, PCR test reporting, and vaccination. Operation Warp Speed includes contracts with Google and Oracle to monitor vaccine recipients for years to come, "with incredibly precise...tracking systems" that will "ensure that patients each get two doses of the same vaccine and to monitor them for adverse health effects."[78] As noted in Chapter 4, the data collected by technology companies inevitably finds other uses than those explicitly stated. If abolitionists and racial justice advocates were not beholden to the medical industrial complex, they would be able to connect COVID-19 surveillance to the 13th Amendment. In 1968, the U.S. Supreme

Court handed down one of the first interpretations of the Amendment in almost a century. In *Jones v. Alfred H. Mayer Co.*, the Court construed the Amendment as not only abolishing slavery, but also empowering Congress to "pass all laws necessary and proper for abolishing all badges and incidents of slavery in the United States."[79] The Court's holding in *Jones* was a momentary return to the 1883 decision in the *Civil Rights Cases*, where it first declared that the Amendment prohibits all of the "badges and incidents" of slavery.[80] The *Jones* decision struck down racial discrimination in the private housing market as one such "badge of slavery," and reminds us that the Amendment is not a dead letter that only served to oversee the formal removal of the ex-slave's bonds. *Jones* has been largely ignored by the courts, legal scholars, and racial justice advocates alike, but it remains available for strategic agitation on the endless array of "badges and incidents of slavery" in contemporary life, such as the twenty-first-century branding of the body by COVID-19 surveillance technologies.

Abolitionists and racial justice advocates during COVID-19 seem especially ill-equipped to contest how the medical industrial complex relies more than ever on the biologizing of race—or eugenics by other names. With the completion in 2003 of the Human Genome Project's comprehensive mapping of the entire genetic makeup of *Homo sapiens*, the racial basis of genetics was definitively disproved on its own scientific terms. In the wake of the sequencing of the human genome, however, the use of race as a biological category has only increased.[81] Explicitly eugenicist scientists have embraced the new technologies as powerful tools for manipulating DNA. At the same time, the study of health disparities has become a major research and funding stream for the medical industrial complex as a whole. As Dorothy Roberts explains, race continues to be treated as an immutable biological category in these studies, rather than as an effect of political, economic, and social arrangements.[82] "Race-neutral economic differences" are treated as mere "correlates" for health status, instead of the very processes by which race is constructed as unequal health outcomes. While on the one hand, the political economic explanation for health disparities discounts the central role of race, on the other hand, countless research projects at elite universities and biotech firms search for the genetic basis for disease susceptibility and the overall genetic cause of health disparities. To be clear, treating race as a fixed biological factor is itself a feature of racist culture in that it naturalizes the effects of power. Racism is an act of violence in that it seeks to enact subjection to a hierarchy of human groupings, and then attempts to construe the outcome of this violence—racial inequality—as evidence of the innate meaning of "race." That much of the scientific community continues to elide or even debate this fact is testament to slaveholding culture's centrality to the medical industrial complex.

That racial justice advocates and abolitionists alike have failed to adequately contest this key pillar of modern medicine is also the means by which the pandemic police power performs its work. The continued biologizing of race has led in the past decade to the appearance of race-specific medicines. Prominent black scientists, doctors, and advocates have heralded the development of racial medicines as critical for redressing the medical wrongs against black people across the centuries.[83] Normalizing biological race through race-specific medicine is simply the latest iteration by which slaveholding culture constructs black people as a fundamentally distinct kind of human being; cloaking this racism in the supposed physiological differences in disease mortality and drug response diverts attention from the antiblack structure of modern society and onto purported biological flaws within black people's bodies. Nothing could be more simplistic and timeless than this medical racism—and yet it is precisely what connects the medical industrial complex to the early medical scientists of the slavocracy who experimented on enslaved people without anesthesia because they claimed black people have fundamentally different pain thresholds. Perhaps most dangerously, it paves the way deeper into the dead zone of pharmacological therapies at the expense of wholistic health approaches that are always stronger and more enduring because they require people to take control over their whole lives. The next step will be race-specific vaccines. The lack of resistance to the medical science of the pandemic police power suggests that this coming development, unfortunately, will be welcomed by many people concerned about black health matters.

The censorship against alternative medicine, despite the scientific validity of natural approaches, and against a full and proper investigation of immune compromising retroviruses, is a function of the forces analyzed in *Pandemic Police Power*—private philanthropy's delegitimation of natural medicine through its Flexner Report, the medical industrial complex, the widespread fear of contagion, and the ignorance of nature's healing powers that is the byproduct of medical science's disempowerment model. This formula is especially disastrous for black people who must also endure the toxicities of an antiblack world in its almost infinite forms, including being construed by white supremacist global culture as walking-stalking pathological contagions personified. The problems with pharmacological solutions are well documented: drug companies suppressed data showing that anti-depressants caused suicide in teenagers, as well as other violent behaviors in both teens and adults, including homicide; ADHD drugs have killed scores of children; a common heartburn drug had caused at least eighty deaths and hundreds of heart attacks before it was withdrawn from the market; and so on.[84] Diabetes is 60 percent more prevalent in black Americans than in whites, and the most commonly prescribed diabetes medications produce their own set of problems for which black people are also overrepresented, such as weight gain, bowel dysfunction, and organ failure.[85] By all rights, therefore, there should be a mass black public health campaign against sugar. Sugar serves no nutritional purpose; cancers love glucose; and sugar is a proven overall immune suppressant.[86] As an eighteenth-century observer of the New World plantations commented: "I do not know if coffee and sugar are essential to the happiness of Europe, but I know well that these two products have accounted for the unhappiness of two great regions of the world: America has been depopulated so as to have land on which to plant them; Africa has been depopulated so as to have the people to cultivate them."[87] Since sugar was part of the impetus for much of the Atlantic slave economy that built this antiblack world we strive to deconstruct, nutritional health constitutes a far more radical healing agenda for black people than anything drug monies can buy. For this reason, it is particularly shameful for AIDS agents and COVID-19 racial justice activists alike to *not* advocate natural medicine. Whether it is the poison of treatment or the toxicity of neglect or the violence of experimentation, the lessons of the Panthers to take care of your own and not look to the state for care have been lost.

Many of the same activist organizations and abolitionist academics calling for the abolition of the prison industrial complex have been either at the forefront of calling for equitable access to the COVID-19 shots or silent on the whole pandemic police power. Ironically, one of the few black voices to call into question this madness during the Pandemic Year has been Dr. Joseph Ladapo. When he was appointed Surgeon General of Florida on September 21, 2021, Dr. Ladapo proclaimed, "We're done with fear. That's been something that unfortunately has been a centerpiece of health policy in the United States ever since the beginning of the pandemic, and it's over here. Expiration date. It's done."[88] Dr. Ladapo also suggested that vaccination is but one of a number of options on the path toward healthy publics, and proceeded to note the ill effects of lockdowns, the crucial role of nutrition and exercise, every person's essential health autonomy, and the adverse agendas of medical science. Not even the abolitionists—who should know better than most how central paranoia has been to the ramp up of law and order over the generations—have critiqued the fear-driven pandemic. While some people may reject Dr. Ladapo's approach simply based on the fact that it comes from a Republican administration in the Florida state capitol, black people especially can ill afford to ignore historic opportunities when they present themselves. As noted in the first chapter, enslaved people liberated themselves in the United States by forcing emancipation on the conflict between the slaveholding class (North vs. South). Abolition was never the intended outcome of the Civil War, as the aftermath has verified. Neither North nor South was a friend of black people. Today, it would be foolish to uncritically follow any leader in the state-corporate nexus, and by the same token the black freedom struggle can ill afford to tarry over the messengers, while failing to critically interrogate all messages. With respect to the pandemic police power, it does not matter who Dr. Ladapo is or who he works for, or what Governor Ron DeSantis' policies in other areas are. What matters is how we might take advantage of this opening to strengthen health self-determination against both illness and the police power where ever they may appear.

The eugenicist imperative to vaccinate, in the least, should remind us to beware of the razor's edge connecting racial domination and state-corporate control over health. The AIDS debacle, followed closely behind by the COVID-19 pandemic, replays this dual process of exploitation. Black people do not need reminding of this history—and yet, the ongoing demands for "access" testifies to a profound lack of clarity as to how to confront this past in the present. The reasons for this failure of analysis and action today are bound up with an indelible historical trauma that the ongoing realities of state violence show is not yet over. The Panthers were the last of a long line of black freedom fighters to be drummed out of existence through COINTELPRO violence or by assimilation into the white nation's various institutions of control against which black liberation has historically staked its claims. As I explain elsewhere, the signature feature of the post-civil rights era is not that it is "post-racial."[89] That fig leaf is a diversion. The real problem of the post-COINTELPRO period is that the ethos of self-determination has been buried beneath the rubble of generation upon generation of state violence and corporate power. Empowering sentiments on social media are *not* the same thing as communal self-efficacy, nor is it the same thing as actually controlling your own health by deciding for yourself what goes into your body, what kind of air and water you consume, and on which piece of unpolluted land you call home. It is not altogether exterminated, but COVID-19 and the pandemic police power are severe tests of collective analysis, will, and self-determination.

Notes

1. https://www.cnn.com/2020/10/28/us/philadelphia-walter-wallace-jr-shooting/index.html.
2. https://www.npr.org/2020/10/30/929752605/mom-dragged-from-suv-beaten-by-officers-with-toddler-in-back-seat-filing-suit.
3. https://www.cnn.com/2020/10/28/us/philadelphia-walter-wallace-jr-shooting/index.html.

4. See Charles E. Cobb, Jr., *This Non-Violent Stuff'll Get You Killed: How Guns Made the Civil Rights Movement Possible* (Durham: Duke, 2015); Lance Hill, *The Deacons for Defense: Armed Resistance and the Civil Rights Movement* (Chapel Hill: North Carolina, 2006); Akinyele Omowale Umoja, *We Will Shoot Back: Armed Resistance in the Mississippi Freedom Movement* (New York: NYU, 2014); Robert F. Williams, *Negroes With Guns* (New York: Marzani & Munsell, 1962).
5. See Alondra Nelson, *Body and Soul: The Black Panther Party and the Fight Against Medical Discrimination* (Minneapolis: Minnesota, 2011).
6. Nelson, 11.
7. Cited in http://amsterdamnews.com/news/2017/jan/12/dr-martin-luther-king-jr-i-fear-i-am-integrating-m/.
8. Cited in J. Noel Heermance, "The Modern Negro Novel," *Negro Digest*, May 1964, 75.
9. *Malcolm X Speaks*, George Breitman, ed. (New York: Grove, 1965), 10–11.
10. Sylvia Wynter, "The Re-Enchantment of Humanism: An Interview with Sylvia Wynter," by David Scott, *Small Axe: A Journal of Caribbean Criticism* 8 (September 2000): 135.
11. *Malcolm X: Make It Plain*, Orlando Bagwell, dir. (PBS, 1994).
12. James Baldwin, "Down at the Cross: Letter from a Region of My Mind," in *The Price of the Ticket, Collected Nonfiction 1948–1985* (New York: St. Martin's, 1985), 375.
13. See https://www.webmd.com/vaccines/covid-19-vaccine/news/20210202/black-vaccine-hesitancy-rooted-in-mistrust-doubts.
14. St. Clair Drake and Horace R. Clayton, *Black Metropolis: A Study of Negro Life in a Northern City* (Chicago: Chicago, [1945] 2015); Rashad Shabazz, *Spatializing Blackness: Architectures of Confinement and Masculinity in Chicago* (Urbana: Illinois, 2017).
15. See https://www.youtube.com/watch?v=kUgaeZilGus.
16. Harriet A. Washington, *Medical Apartheid: The Dark History of Medical Experimentation on Black Americans from Colonial Times to the Present* (New York: Anchor, 2006), 360–362.

17. Allen M. Hornblum, "They Were Cheap and Available: Prisoners as Research Subjects in Twentieth Century America," *British Medical Journal* 315 (1997): 1437, https://doi.org/10/1136/bmj.315.7120.1437; https://report.nih.gov/award/index.cfm?ot=&fy=2020&state=&ic=&fm=&orgid=5079201&distr=&rfa=&om=y&pid=&view=state.
18. Hornblum, *Acres of Skin: Human Experiments at Holmesburg Prison* (New York: Routledge, 1999).
19. Barbara Joe Fisher, "Measles Vaccine Experiments on Minority Children Turn Deadly," *National Vaccine Information Center*, June 1996, https://www.nvic.org/nvic-archives/newsletter/vaccinereactionjune1996.aspx.
20. M. Garenne, et al., "Child Mortality After High-Titre Measles Vaccines: Prospective Study in Senegal," *Lancet* 339 (8772) 1991: 903–907, https://doi.org/10.1016/0140-6736(91)91771-l.
21. Washington, 392.
22. Washington, 396–397.
23. Washington, 398–399.
24. https://wtop.com/dc/2016/04/flint-d-c-s-drinking-water-crisis-even-worse/.
25. Celia Farber, *Serious Adverse Events: An Uncensored History of AIDS* (Hoboken, NJ: Melville House, 2006), 266–273.
26. The original CDC documents related to this case are available for download here https://www.vaxxed.com/thompson-file-releases/. The study as it was initially published, https://pediatrics.aappublications.org/content/113/2/259. The CDC whistleblower William Thompson, before making his allegations about the censored study public, also published another paper that claims to have not found a causal relationship between thimerosal (the aluminum adjuvant used as a preservative in many vaccines) and autism, but nevertheless documents the many negative effects of the toxin on vaccinated children—see https://www.nejm.org/doi/full/10.1056/NEJMoa071434.
27. https://www.hiv.gov/blog/new-factsheets-hiv-s-impact-african-american-community.

28. See Cathy J. Cohen, *The Boundaries of Blackness: AIDS and the Breakdown of Black Politics* (Chicago: University of Chicago Press, 1999).
29. Washington, 400.
30. Farber, "Out of Control: AIDS and the Corruption of Medical Science," *Harper's Magazine* (March 2006): 37–40, 47.
31. Farber, "Out of Control," 40.
32. Farber, *Serious Adverse Events*, 224.
33. Farber, "Out of Control," 47.
34. See https://www.youtube.com/watch?v=EmrY_r6v7Dc.
35. https://www.treatmentactiongroup.org/about-us/history/; https://datasociety.net/about/; https://datasociety.net/wp-content/uploads/2021/01/Funders-List-2021.pdf.
36. Farber, *Serious Adverse Events*, 259.
37. Farber, *Serious Adverse Events*, 259.
38. Cited in Farber, *Serious Adverse Events*, 259.
39. Cited in Farber, *Serious Adverse Events*, 261.
40. Farber, *Serious Adverse Events*, 264.
41. Farber, *Serious Adverse Events*, 264.
42. See, beginning at 56:30, https://www.youtube.com/watch?v=EmrY_r6v7Dc.
43. See, beginning at 56:30, https://www.youtube.com/watch?v=EmrY_r6v7Dc.
44. Thomas S. Kuhn, *The Structure of Scientific Revolutions* (Chicago: University of Chicago Press, [1962] 2012), 113.
45. See the documentary by the Society for Independent Investigative Journalists, *The Cost of Denial*, https://prn.fm/.
46. *The Cost of Denial*.
47. See https://www.sciencedirect.com/topics/medicine-and-dentistry/kochs-postulates.
48. Cited in John Lauritsen, *Poison by Prescription: The AZT Story* (New York: Pagan, 1990), 151.
49. See Peter H. Duesberg, "Retroviruses as Carcinogens and Pathogens: Expectations and Reality," *Cancer Research* 47 (March 1, 1987): 1199–1220; Duesberg, *Inventing the AIDS Virus* (Washington, DC: Regenery, 1996).

50. Charles Ortleb, *The Chronic Fatigue Syndrome Epidemic Cover-Up, Volume Two: The Origins of Totalitarianism in Science and Medicine* (Salem: Rubicon, 2018), 32.
51. Hillary Johnson, *Osler's Web: Inside the Labyrinth of the Chronic Fatigue Syndrome* (New York: Crown, 1996), 334; on Fauci's scandalous role in the AIDS era, see https://www.youtube.com/watch?v=ezKb_AFvU4g.
52. See Nicholas Regush, *The Virus Within: A Coming Epidemic* (New York: Plume, 2001).
53. Kuhn, 77.
54. Kuhn, 79.
55. Farber, *Serious Adverse Events*, 164.
56. For an example of a disease that long predates the arrival of AIDS, but which comes to be bound up with AIDS diagnoses in the post-1980s period, see Pawan Singh, et al., "African Kaposi's Sarcoma in the Light of Global AIDS: Antiblackness and Viral Visibility," *Journal of Bioethical Inquiry* 11(4) December 2014: 467–478, https://pubmed.ncbi.nlm.nih.gov/25304011/. Although the authors are uncritical of the medical industrial complex construction of AIDS on the continent, seeking instead to belabor the racist exclusion of black people from AIDS treatment, the historical evidence they produce supports the argument advanced in *Pandemic Police Power* that the epidemiology and etiology of the disease is fundamentally flawed.
57. Farber, *Serious Adverse Events*, 167–168.
58. Farber, *Serious Adverse Events*, 167.
59. Farber, *Serious Adverse Events*, 166.
60. Cited in Farber, *Serious Adverse Events*, 172.
61. Walter Rodney, *How Europe Underdeveloped Africa* (Washington, DC: Howard, 1981).
62. Timothy Colman, et al., *Divesting from Pandemic Policing and Investing in a Just Recovery*, May 19, 2021, https://communityresourcehub.org/wp-content/uploads/2021/05/Unmasked_Update.pdf.
63. U.S. Department of Health and Human Services and Department of Defense, *From the Factory to the Frontlines: The Operation Warp Speed Strategy for Distributing COVID-19 Vaccines*, September

23, 2020, https://www.hhs.gov/sites/default/files/strategy-for-distributing-covid-19-vaccine.pdf.
64. Jeremy Loffredo and Whitney Webb, "The Johns Hopkins, CDC Plan to Mask Medical Experimentation as 'Racial Justice,'" *Unlimited Hangout*, November 25, 2020, https://unlimitedhangout.com/2020/11/investigative-series/the-johns-hopkins-cdc-plan-to-mask-medical-experimentation-on-minorities-as-racial-justice/.
65. Colman, et al., 19; Isaac Stanley-Becker, "Many Police Officers Spurn Coronavirus Vaccines As Departments Hold Off on Mandates," *The Washington Post*, May 2, 2021, https://www.washingtonpost.com/health/2021/05/02/police-low-vaccination-rates-safety-concerns/.
66. Center for Health Security, Johns Hopkins University, *Interim Framework for COVID-19 Vaccine Allocation and Distribution in the United States*, August 12, 2020, https://www.centerforhealthsecurity.org/our-work/pubs_archive/pubs-pdfs/2020/200819-vaccine-allocation.pdf.
67. U.S. Department of Health and Human Services, Centers for Disease Control and Prevention, *COVID-19 Vaccination Program Interim Operational Guidance—Jurisdiction Operations*, October 29, 2020, https://www.cdc.gov/vaccines/imz-managers/downloads/COVID-19-Vaccination-Program-Interim_Playbook.pdf.
68. Center for Health Security, Johns Hopkins University, "Dark Winter: Bioterrorism Exercise," Final Script, June 22–23, 2001, https://www.centerforhealthsecurity.org/our-work/events-archive/2001_dark-winter/Dark%20Winter%20Script.pdf.
69. Center for Health Security, *Interim Framework*, 2.
70. Center for Health Security, *Interim Framework*, 12.
71. Center for Health Security, *Interim Framework*, 5.
72. Raj Kurupati, et al., "Race-Related Differences in Antibody Responses to the Inactivated Influenza Vaccine Are Linked to Distinct Pre-Vaccination Gene Expression Profiles in Blood," *Oncotarget* 7(39) September 27, 2016: 62,898–62,911, https://www.ncbi.nlm.nih.gov/pmc/articles/PMC5325335/; Robert Nellis, "Mayo Clinic Discovers African-Americans Respond Better to Rubella Vaccine," *Mayo Clinic News Network*, February 26, 2014,

https://newsnetwork.mayoclinic.org/discussion/mayo-clinic-discovers-african-americans-respond-better-to-rubella-vaccine/; Carolyn M. Gallagher and Melody S. Goodman, "Hepatitis B Vaccination of Male Neonates and Autism Diagnosis, NHIS 1997–2002," *Journal of Toxicology and Environmental Health, Part A* 73(24) 2010: 1665–1677.
73. Center for Health Security, *Interim Framework*, 12, 14–15; Center for Health Security, Johns Hopkins University, *The Public's Role in COVID-19 Vaccination: Planning Recommendations Informed by Design Thinking and the Social, Behavioral, and Communication Sciences*, July 19, 2020, https://www.centerforhealthsecurity.org/our-work/pubs_archive/pubs-pdfs/2020/200709-The-Publics-Role-in-COVID-19-Vaccination.pdf.
74. Center for Health Security, *Interim Framework*, 12, 20.
75. Glenn Greenwald, "The ACLU, Prior to COVID-19, Denounced Mandates and Coercive Measures to Fight Pandemics," *Substack*, September 7, 2021, https://greenwald.substack.com/p/the-aclu-prior-to-covid-denounced.
76. For an example of the abolitionist focus on surveillance technologies in the prison industrial complex, see *Twenty-First Century Policing*, by the Action Center on Race and the Economy, https://acrecampaigns.org/wp-content/uploads/2021/03/acre-21stcenturypolicing-r4-web.pdf.
77. P. Khalil Saucier, "Traces of the Slave Patrol: Notes on Breed-Specific Legislation," *Drexel Law Review* 10 (2018): 691.
78. Whitney Webb, "Google and Oracle to Monitor Americans Who Get Warp Speed's COVID-19 Vaccine For Up To Two Years," *The Last American Vagabond*, October 15, 2020, https://www.thelastamericanvagabond.com/google-oracle-monitor-americans-who-get-warp-speeds-covid-19-vaccine-for-two-years/.
79. *Jones v. Alfred H. Mayer Co.* 392 U.S. 409 (1968) at 439; William M. Carter, Jr., "Race, Rights, and the Thirteenth Amendment: Defining the Badges and Incidents of Slavery," *UC Davis Law Review* 40(4) April 2007: 1311–1379.
80. *Civil Rights Cases* 109 U.S. 3 (1883).

81. Michael Yudell, et al., "Taking Race Out of Human Genetics," *Science* 351(6273) February 5, 2016: 564.
82. Dorothy Roberts, "Debating the Cause of Health Disparities: Implications for Bioethics and Racial Equality," *Cambridge Quarterly of Healthcare Ethics* 21 (2012): 332–341.
83. Roberts, "Debating the Cause," 338.
84. Farber, *Serious Adverse Events*, 255–256. See Peter Breggin, *Medication Madness: The Role of Psychiatric Drugs in Cases of Violence, Suicide, and Crime* (New York: St. Martin's Griffin, 2008).
85. https://www.webmd.com/hypertension-high-blood-pressure/features/why-7-deadly-diseases-strike-blacks-most; https://www.healthline.com/health-news/why-so-many-people-with-diabetes-stop-taking-metformin.
86. See the classic by William Dufty, *Sugar Blues* (New York: Time Warner, 1975).
87. From Volume 1 of J. H. Bernardin de Saint Pierre's *Voyage to Isle de France, Isle de Bourbon, The Cape of Good Hope…With New Observations on Nature and Mankind by an Officer of the King* (1773), cited in Sidney W. Mintz, *Sweetness and Power: The Place of Sugar in Modern History* (New York: Viking Penguin, 1985).
88. https://www.youtube.com/watch?v=IPogn0cQG38.
89. See Tryon P. Woods, *Blackhood Against the Police Power: Punishment and Disavowal in the "Post-Racial" Era* (East Lansing: Michigan State, 2019).

8

Conclusion: The Abolition Question for Medical Science

The Pandemic Year has sharpened the abolition question into a holistic approach to the police power. We knew before that work kills, while worklessness has its own lethal methodology.[1] We have seen the new ways that "science" as a value and a discourse is used to sanction scientific corruption, profiteering, and widespread harm. We have also seen how the state-corporate nexus maneuvers public health paranoia into greater degrees of social control. High-level government, corporate, and academic leaders, including representatives from WHO and CDC, conducted a global pandemic simulation exercise called Event 201 *prior to* the appearance of COVID-19 in China, in October 2019.[2] The resemblance between Event 201's simulated outcome and the current trajectory of the COVID-19 pandemic is not an uncanny coincidence—it is called planning. In other words, in the face of an eventual pandemic, Event 201 did not focus on rebuilding public health institutions, amending the social costs of corporate practices that leave global society vulnerable to costly epidemic outbreaks, or even how to maintain safe workplaces during pandemic conditions. Instead, it called for vaccination, maintaining travel and trade, corporate partnerships that can temporarily fill in for the state, managing the media message, and the shoring up of "critical nodes of the banking system and global and national economies that are too essential to fail."[3] In planning terms, then, we are mostly on the neoliberal course laid out by Event 201: no public health preparedness to speak of, a massive corporate bailout ("too big to fail" all over again), an emphasis on vaccination, and a reliance on private sector responses to need. For instance, the Gates Foundation, through its Vaccine Alliance (Gavi) and its Coalition for Epidemic Preparedness Innovations (CEPI) worked with the pharmaceutical corporations to fund the biotech research for a COVID-19 vaccine, while Governor Cuomo of New York has invited Gates to reimagine NY education in light of the pandemic.[4]

Accordingly, we are learning more about how nimble the world's largest political economic institutions have become in the digital age. The International Monetary Fund (IMF) is now announcing a "new Bretton Woods moment" as central banks move toward digital currency that allows for total surveillance, real-time adjustments to planning, and control over worldwide transactions.[5] Bretton Woods refers to the post-WWII economic planning meeting in New Hampshire that adopted a new monetary system with the U.S. dollar as the global currency and the IMF as the key international regulator. Since people are already conditioned to online and digital everything, these massive top-down systemic changes are happening backwards: getting everyone to buy into a solution by getting everyone online and digitized now as a necessary step for public health, before they can see where it is all going to end up. All that appears new, however, is based in everything old, such as debt, in which the average person is now further entrapped and desperate for cash flow. Pandemic Year lockdowns also conveniently impacted many of the mass-based mobilizations afoot around the world, from anti-extradition in Hong Kong, to yellow vest populism in France, to farmers in India, to pollution in Wuhan, to police violence, social spending cuts, and xenophobia in South Africa, Brazil, and the U.S.[6] These movements are discrete manifestations of people's common objections to the police power; pandemic public health protocols make managing this dissent far easier than it was before COVID-19.

8 Conclusion: The Abolition Question for Medical Science

These larger realities are difficult to synthesize into one's localized experience living through a pandemic. I have sought to situate an awareness of the multiple levels of our social existence, both the micro and the macro, in terms of policing. The greatest pedagogical utility of the police is their ubiquity in modern culture. The police, or representations of the police, are everywhere; it does not take much effort to discover what they are about, should one desire to see clearly. At the same time, this ubiquity can also be a sleight of hand, if you will, enabling the true nature of police to remain hidden in plain sight. I aimed for a more accurate portrait of what policing is and how it works by turning our attention away from law enforcement and toward the sociohistorical processes by which social control is sought and contested. Policing is better conceived of socially as the police power organized to reproduce an antiblack world. The police power is central, while the police are peripheral.

My conception of the police power as the essential organizing methodology for antiblackness conjoins police and prison abolition with a historical understanding of medical science's emergence as a key institution for reproducing racism. Analysis of the police power reminds us that each discrete institution is set up the way it is to advance the antiblack terms of society. Things are working as designed when black people are disproportionately represented in disease morbidity and incarceration statistics. If criminal justice is working as intended, then so too is medical science. Each facet of the police power equally comprises the whole. The state does not enact antiblack violence in one arena and not in another; it merely uses different methods and discourses to realize the same ends. While the institutions of medical science appear to differ and even conflict with those of criminal law at the level of discourse—health and wellness versus punishment and control—they are in fact aligned with each other in demanding black bodily disempowerment in all arenas as dictated by the structure of antiblackness. Given the litany of injury experienced by black people at the hands of the Western world's medical science, it is a testament to the ubiquitous and disarming reach of antiblackness that black people in particular still look to Western medicine and state-defined public health. This needs to change in the same manner that people need to stop looking to the criminal justice system for "justice" and "security." This history and present reality of medical racism are very much informing some black people's feelings on the current COVID-19 injections.[7] The current pandemic is merely the latest example of the imperative for *all* people to understand state power and its historical practices through the lens of black experience.

COVID-19 is like the police: its ubiquity is both the perfect case study and a test of our analytic powers. In order to explicate COVID-19 in terms of the pandemic police power, I explored three of the generative factors behind the current moment. First, I examined how the edifice of criminal justice was built through liberal reform. The purpose of this review was to prepare us to cut through the sectarianism of the pandemic police power. Electoral politics, political party affiliation, liberal or conservative or progressive or mainstream—these signs are all distractions from the kind of analysis abolition requires. Historical review of both criminal justice and medical science demonstrates that the structure of policing is built with contributions from all points on the ideological spectrum. The reason for this is that the entire spectrum implicitly takes black fungibility as its point of reference. Slaveholding culture—whether in its prime or in its post-civil rights reformed condition—is parasitic on black life, and the history of liberal reform that created the horror of mass incarceration alerts us to the present antiblack leadership of medical science paving the way into a new kind of horror. For this reason, both criminal justice and medical science are able to tout their respective policy failures as self-justifying. Throughout the mass incarceration build-up, criminal justice officials and lawmakers would argue that the crime problem was getting worse, despite soaring prison populations. They successfully used their policy failures to win additional funding and an extension of their policing powers. Today, public health officials inflate COVID-19 death rates in order to justify an extension of emergency declarations constraining social and economic activity. They claim that the virus remains a serious threat, inadvertently acknowledging the failure of the panoply of public health protocols ostensibly used to suppress it, and yet this failure is seen as further justification for more ineffectual restrictions and vaccination—which has its own self-justifying tautology of ineffectiveness.

Second, I addressed how the current challenge to law-and-order discourse has been advanced without uncoupling the race-crime nexus

8 Conclusion: The Abolition Question for Medical Science

and its key articulating figure, the construct of black pathos. This is the failure of abolitionist work thus far: every time the question of abolishing police and prisons is raised *without* contesting the racialized fear of violence, antiblackness corrupts the abolitionist energy into something that works *against* black liberation. Police and prison abolition will only come as a function of overhauling the antiblack structure of humanity. The lesson here for the pandemic police power is that COVID-19 policies are advanced in the interest of the common good, which has historically been defined *against* black life. COVID-19 and its proposed solutions are consistent with the history of medical science that relies upon estranging people from healthy practices, including disease treatment. Black activists rightfully condemn the racial inequities in health care, but in so doing, they do the state's work by pushing for greater integration into its clientele structure. Inequities in health are a design feature of this capitalist democracy, not a sign of flaws in its systems. Gaining access to the toxic mess that is the medical industrial complex is precisely what Malcolm X, James Baldwin, Martin Luther King, Jr., and others likened to integrating into a burning house.

Third, I examined how private capital has quietly shaped the direction of change. Corporate philanthropy has been the shadow partner to the state's counter-insurgency against black liberation since the era of lynching. Foundation involvement in social policy underscores the earlier finding that buttressing state power is not an ideological project: liberal, conservative, progressive, and libertarian ideologies converge on the shared investment in the system of capitalist democracy. Toward this end, private capital is endlessly adaptive to the discourse of anti-racism, as the corporate university makes abundantly clear. Regarding COVID-19 and the pandemic police power, the point here is not to reveal the extent to which private capital has replaced state functions throughout society, from education to health care to information technology—this has long been the case; nor to reiterate that the profit motive supersedes all other considerations across society, surely a mundane point for most people by now. Rather, the crux of the matter is how the corporate-state nexus has already succeeded in implementing a social control apparatus that the public relates to as "convenience," "progress," "security," "care," "innovation," and "independence," when in fact what is taking place is surveillance and disempowerment. Many people who are aware of the mass intrusion of surveillance capitalism brush it off—as in, *well, it doesn't really matter because I'm not doing anything wrong*. This is a luxury that black people have never had, and a fallacy to which non-blacks continue to cling to at their peril. The ubiquity of antiblack violence means that the connection between surveillance and punishment is inevitable for blacks and not contingent on behavior or choice. Black activists today are hamstrung both by their reliance on the very technology used to monitor and isolate them, and by the lack of a critical and robust public sphere in which intergenerational accountability and wisdom are shared. The latter has been steadily eviscerated in the post-COINTELPRO era, but manufactured crises such as the pandemic tighten up the remaining fissures in this social control apparatus doggedly exposed by the social movements against policing. A rigorous abolitionist response to COVID-19 would recognize the necessity of critiquing the state power in *all* of its guises, be it in the corporate university's multiculturalism or in the apparent charitableness of the philanthropic foundation or in the so-called innovations in "personalized learning" of education technology at all levels.

The pandemic is advanced as liberal policymaking, in contradistinction with conversative science denial. It is advanced as good for all, rather than only good for the special interests of the corporate-state nexus, and when the entire premise of the "common good" is parasitic on black life. It is advanced through the sublimation of violence that routinely characterizes the medical industrial complex. And it is advanced by capital as the driving political force. There was a public health crisis long before COVID-19, but the technology and finance industries, not to mention the racist spectrum of the medical science industry and the social control needs of state power, are united in their interest in a vaccine response to health needs. The AIDS debacle reminds us that public health leaders like Fauci have a long track record of fueling public health paranoia, suppressing scientific inquiry, and developing pharmacological therapies that do not work. It is not arbitrary that the Gates Foundation is deeply involved with biotechnology (vaccines) as public health, educational technology for schools and higher education, and surveillance technology for employers and law enforcement. For the billions of dollars spent on

8 Conclusion: The Abolition Question for Medical Science

education technology products and vaccine production, billions of cases of premature death and illness could be averted worldwide if the money was spent on clean drinking water, safe housing, sustainable infrastructure, fruits and vegetables, and actual books. Basic healing principles need as much attention as possible.

In the same way that black leaders in the post-Emancipation period failed to adequately recognize the role of law in pathologizing race, and thus did not contest the connections between convict lease, sharecropping, mob violence, and segregation, today's resistance largely fails to recognize how medical science's pathologizing of the human body and health subverts black freedom. Self-determination and the pathologized body are a contradiction: you cannot liberate yourself when you have submitted control over your body's health to "experts" that view it as a problem to be fixed with external interventions that only they have access to. At root, this was the politic of health sovereignty driving the anti-lynching campaigns, before they were hijacked by private philanthropy; it also informed the push to regain control over reproduction from the state's eugenics practices. Also, just like the liberal reforms that anticipated the challenge of civil rights and built a carceral state foundation that it would leverage to great effect in quelling black liberation, so too the pandemic is the fruit of decades of preparation and will reap further dispossession on scales previously unimaginable. The black movement, and abolitionists of all stripes, should well recognize the harm of the "false positive."

The case against vaccine mandates is strong:

1. Faulty testing grossly overestimates the state of COVID-19 disease and mortality, making it appear far more dangerous than it is in reality.
2. Infection mitigation protocols cause more harm than good. They discount how viruses, bacteria, and germs circulate and co-produce with humans; and they ignore immunological insights about the importance of healthy conditions and systems, above all else. In so doing, the pandemic police power distracts and divests from the holistic production of actual healthy communities.

3. Effective and cost-efficient treatment options exist that preempt the necessity for emergency use authorization for, or compulsory uptake of, experimental biotechnology. These treatment options are far less restrictive and invasive than requiring people to get a COVID-19 injection, meaning that a vaccine mandate should not meet constitutional standards.
4. Only one of the COVID-19 shots (Pfizer) has received full FDA approval. While the existence of one such shot ostensibly undermines the justification for emergency use authorization for the other shots, they all remain on the market under EUA status. EUA requires that taking the shot is voluntary and that accurate risks are disclosed to the public. Neither of these things is happening now: students and workers are being illegally forced to take the shot in order to continue in school or keep their jobs, and the risk for serious adverse effects from the mRNA injections is being suppressed. The thousands of deaths and serious adverse events from the mRNA injections are an utterly avoidable tragedy for a virus that has a survival rate of 99.95 percent.
5. Vaccine development since the mid-twentieth century has advanced according to the eugenicist tendencies of modern science and to the priorities of the medical industrial complex, which taken together, subordinates scientific inquiry and public health needs to racial dominance, profit, and social control. Vaccination is not simply a neutral tool that can be wielded for good or for ill; it is symptomatic of a conception of biological beings that is intrinsically racialized and Westernized—meaning, it rests upon anti-democratic structures geared toward popular disempowerment.
6. Vaccine law has always relied upon an anti-scientific premise that insulates these racial and class hierarchies from critique and challenge. The reason for this is that law follows the police power, which goes a long way to explaining the paucity of legal challenges thus far to the current COVID-19 response. It also means that efforts to remedy the illegalities of the public health protocols ultimately amount to appeals to a superseding law that has already been superseded by the culture of politics. Redressing legal problems, therefore, cannot simply rely upon the law—because at root, they are cultural problems, not legal

ones. A legal response to compulsory vaccination, for instance, must proceed with a clear and sober understanding of law's limits. It must, in other words, advance a political and cultural response, one that intervenes in the culture of politics, specifically, that takes medical disempowerment as unthought, natural responses to health and illness as illegitimate, and capital's interests as primary in the public health establishment.
7. To put it differently, vaccine mandates must be rejected because their purpose is primarily social control, not disease control. We are already seeing the creation of two classes of people: the vaccinated and the unvaccinated, with full social access restored to the former, while the latter remain excluded or marked out as different, risky, undesirable, and subject to serious economic coercion. All the while, actual public health needs remain wanting.
8. The position against vaccine mandates cannot be dismissed as "anti-vax" or based on conspiracy theories. This schema is convoluted politically in the least because "conspiracy theory" was originally a label created by the Right to discount systems analysis from the Left that saw a fascistic and totalitarian dimension to Right-wing control over the state-corporate nexus. Things have not become inverted so much as the so-called Left has lost its structural critique as it has acquired a greater share of power. The number one failing across the literature on the so-called anti-vax movement is that it does not account for the state's track record in systematically creating harms for which it remains largely unaccountable. People who disparage "anti-vaxxers" basically trust the state and take its policies, its narratives, and its science at face value. For this reason alone, the discourse of "anti-vaxxers" should rightfully be understood as a state narrative. The fact that most of the discourse is contributed by non-state actors, such as journalists, university-based researchers, doctors, and everyday folk across society, is an example of how state power is most effective when people internalize it as their own story. The position against vaccine mandates is a critique of state science and its usurpation and corruption of science's democratic tenets.

In short, vaccine law, from *Jacobson* on down, needs complete revision, and lawyers working for the people should inundate the courts with challenges to every facet of the pandemic police power, from vaccine mandates to takings without compensation. But to make the changes they produce lasting, these legal efforts need to follow a change in consciousness. People need to realize that their health is in their hands; when we cede this power to the medical and public health institutions, our communities end up suffering for it. COVID-19 shows that our society is not well: its susceptibility to dominance and disempowerment is as consequential as its degraded conditions for public well-being, all of which are far more consequential than this season's latest batch of circulating viruses.

During the 1971 Attica prison uprising, prisoners took control of the prison and issued a series of political demands as the Attica Liberation Faction. The Attica manifesto asserted that the prison made no pretense to rehabilitation and was nothing but a "fascist concentration camp." As the Attica prisoners put it, "the programs which we are submitted to, under the façade of rehabilitation, is relative to the ancient stupidity of pouring water on a drowning man." The medical science model of health care amounts to 'pouring water on a drowning man': why rely on immune-suppressing drugs and vaccines to deal with a health situation caused by a compromised immune system due to toxified social environments? Vaccinations in particular represent the convergence of interests of finance, technology, the medical industrial complex, and racial hierarchy. It is illogical to expect public health practices to do anything but further the essential parasitic relationship of civil society to black health needs.

I came up working in HIV/AIDS prevention education in New York City in the mid-1990s. The programs I worked with employed a peer education harm reduction framework to prevent HIV community transmission among youth, parents in recovery from drug addictions, sex workers, and the incarcerated. Peer education is premised on the recognition that people learn best from those who are like them in some way. Harm reduction is based on the principle of meeting people where they are at, rather than requiring them to change (as in, stop using drugs or having sex) in order to receive care, and then supporting them

8 Conclusion: The Abolition Question for Medical Science

in reducing their exposure to certain harms that mitigate against the changes they desire for their lives. In short, peer education and harm reduction are both intended to empower people to take control over the circumstances of their lives. Looking back on that time, however, I now see that my work in public health was situated squarely within multiple industrial complexes that undermined the intentions behind this work. I was teaching some of the etiological and immunological fallacies on which AIDS care is based. This faulty foundation, in turn, informed the funding structure of state agencies and private philanthropies that paid my salary and shaped the performance metrics by which meager resources were passed on to the peer educators. Empowerment within a structure of disempowerment. The point is not that change processes can and should be pure from corrupting influences, but that self-determination requires persistent vigilance against such forces of erosion.

An example of this need for vigilance comes to us from the early stages of the Pandemic Year, when one nursing home managed to buck the tragic trend of COVID-19 infections and deaths among the elderly in congregate care settings. Reverend Derrick DeWitt, director of the Maryland Baptist Aged Home, preemptively locked down his facility well before the state issued quarantine orders.[8] He explained that the black community is used to not counting on the state for assistance, so he is in the practice of making his own risk and wellness determinations. As a result of his leadership, his black elderly community did not have a single infection (at the time of the report in mid-2020). This self-determination sensibility is what can cut through the police power in medical science as much as in criminal justice. More than anything, the Pandemic Year underscores the imperative to extend the abolitionist approach to medical science that has garnered substantial support in recent years with respect to law and order. It is time to stop dissenting from the state's criminal justice narrative, while carrying out the state's narrative on public health as if it were our own, because it is not.

Notes

1. Data from the Great Depression parallels trends during severe economic recession: increases in life expectancy due to a decline in accidents are off-set by increased suicides, with the pandemic lockdowns exacerbating these trends—see https://www.sciencedaily.com/releases/2011/03/110324202055.htm.
2. https://www.centerforhealthsecurity.org/event201/. Event 201 is not the first such simulation to immediately anticipate an epidemic. See Whitney Webb, "All Roads Lead to Dark Winter," *Unlimited Hangout*, April 1, 2020, https://unlimitedhangout.com/2020/04/investigative-series/all-roads-lead-to-dark-winter/.
3. https://www.centerforhealthsecurity.org/event201/recommendations.html.
4. Andrew Dunn, "A Coalition Backed by Bill Gates is Funding Biotechs That Are Scrambling to Develop Vaccines for the Deadly Wuhan Coronavirus," *Business Insider*, January 23, 2020, https://www.businessinsider.com/vaccines-for-wuhan-china-cornonavirus-moderna-inovio-cepi-2020-1?op=1; Peter Greene, "Why Bill Gates is Not the Man to Reimagine New York Education," *Forbes*, May 8, 2020, https://www.forbes.com/sites/petergreene/2020/05/08/why-bill-gates-is-not-the-man-to-reimagine-new-york-education/#7b13905779cc.
5. See https://www.imf.org/en/News/Articles/2020/10/15/sp101520-a-new-bretton-woods-moment; https://www.bis.org/publ/othp33.htm.
6. https://www.amnesty.org/en/latest/news/2019/09/hong-kong-protests-explained/; https://www.cnn.com/2020/09/12/europe/yellow-vest-france-protests-intl/index.html; https://www.cnn.com/2021/02/10/asia/india-farmers-protest-explainer-intl-hnk-scli/index.html; https://edition.cnn.com/2019/07/10/asia/china-wuhan-pollution-problems-intl-hnk/index.html; https://www.theguardian.com/world/gallery/2019/may/31/protesters-take-to-brazils-streets-in-pictures; https://www.theguardian.com/world/2019/sep/05/thousands-protest-in-south-africa-over-rising-violence-against-women.

8 Conclusion: The Abolition Question for Medical Science   265

7. *See* Saundra Young, *Black Vaccine Hesitancy Rooted in Mistrust, Doubts*, WebMD (Feb. 2, 2021), https://www.webmd.com/vaccines/covid-19-vaccine/news/20210202/black-vaccine-hesitancy-rooted-in-mistrust-doubts.
8. https://www.pbssocal.org/programs/pbs-newshour/defying-the-odds-1594335644/.

Index

0–9

13th Amendment 16
14th Amendment 16, 35, 36
18th century 18, 47, 48, 171, 243
19th century 13, 14, 34, 46–48, 70, 132, 171, 172, 174, 175
20th century 13, 46, 51, 129, 133, 135, 164, 171, 173, 175, 176, 183, 187, 189, 220, 233, 239
4th Amendment 35–37
8th Amendment 53, 131

A

Abolition 5, 7–14, 18, 20, 21
Abolitionism 6–10, 12, 14, 17
Abu Ghraib 53
Academy 65, 67, 68
Access 6
ACT UP 224
Acute flacid paralysis 184
ADA 197
Adams, Jerome 122
Adjuvant 142
Adverse effect 146
Adverse event (AE) 142–144
Africa 11, 12, 188, 189, 191, 196
African rebels 29, 30, 37
Agamben, Giorgio 19
AIDS 112, 222–235, 243, 245
Alternative medicine 235, 243
Amazon 94, 96
American Civil Liberties Union (ACLU) 240
American Foundation for AIDS Research (amfAR) 229
American Revolution 29, 30
Americas 11, 12
Anaphylaxis 144
Anderson, Carol 45, 74

The Antelope 33, 34
Anthrax 201
Antibiotics 172, 173
Antiblack 4, 5, 14, 17
Antiblackness 4, 13, 14, 17
Antiblack structure 17
Antiblack violence 1, 4
Antibodies 116, 139, 230
Antibody dependent enhancement (ADE) 179, 180
Anti-inflammatory 142
Anti-Vaccination League of America 166
Anti-vaxxers 123, 138
Apple 94
Arbery, Ahmaud 29
Artificial intelligence (AI) 94, 100
Ashe, Arthur 228
Asymptomatic transmission 116–118
The Atlantic 115
Attica 262
Autism 128, 129
Autoimmune disease 119, 128, 142
Autoimmune dysfunction 128, 142, 179, 189
AZT 223, 225, 226

B

Bacon, Charles S. 187
Bacterial disease 172
Bad faith 4, 20
Badges and incidents of slavery 241
Baker, Ella 110, 146
Baldwin, James 218, 246
Balko, Radley 15
Band density 231
Bankruptcy 89

Bayer AG 188
Bayh-Dole Act 198
Bechamp, Antoine 132, 158
Bell, Derrick 2
Benjamin, Franklin 19
Benjamin, Walter 19
Bennett, Lerone, Jr. 70, 85
Biden, Joe 48
Biological race 242
Biometric 100
BioNTech 141
Biotechnology 130, 132, 139, 140
Bi-partisan 46, 48, 56, 57, 60
Black Codes 50
Black community 70
Black criminal stereotype 55
Blackhood Against the Police Power 27
Black liberation struggle 2
Black life matters 218
Black Lives Matter 81
Black news media 227
Black Panther Party 217, 228
Black Power 63, 67, 71
Black sacrifice 4
Blackstone Group 91
Blood clotting 192
Bloods 44
Bloomberg, Michael 96
Boggs, Grace Lee 71, 85
Boosters 137
Breakthrough infections 144
Bretton Woods 254
British abolition 30
British Eugenics Society 191
Brown v. Board of Education 3, 16
Browne, Simone 100, 105, 108
Brown v. Maryland 34, 40
Brown, Michael 45

Brown, Tony 228
Buck v. Bell 186
Burning house 218, 219
Burwell v. Hobby Lobby 35
Bush, George W. 131
Butler v. Wolf 196

C

Caldwell, Earl 228
Camacho, Jorge 68, 84
Cancer 111, 128, 135, 141
Capitalism 7, 134
Caribbean slavery 29
Carnegie 62, 67
Caseload 199, 232
Castile, Philando 64
CDC 112–114, 118, 122, 130, 142, 143, 145
Center for Constitutional Rights (CCR) 240
Center on Health Security (CHS) 237–239
Chemerinsky, Erwin 167–170, 186, 204
Children's Health Defense 193
Chimera 129, 130
Chronic fatigue syndrome 128
CIA 44
Citizen's United v. Federal Election Commission 35
Civil rights 44, 46, 51, 52, 62–65
Civil rights cases 29, 241
Civil War 43, 48, 49
Clean drinking water 173
Cleveland Clinic 126
Clinical trials 191, 192
Clinton, Hillary 48

Coalition for Epidemic Preparedness Innovations (CEPI) 254
Cocaine 44
COINTELPRO 44
Common belief 181, 185, 186, 194–196
Comorbidities 123, 136, 137, 141, 238, 239
Compelling state interest 171
Compulsory vaccination 164–167, 170, 171, 174, 175, 178, 181
Congo 129
Congress 120, 132
Constitutional right 171, 181
Contraceptive 188
Contraceptive vaccine 188–190
Contract law 32, 35
Convict lease 50
Copernican Revolution 185
Coronavirus 119, 122, 130, 137, 142
Coronavirus Aid Relief and Economic Security Act (CARES) 199
Corporate university 69, 71
Counter-revolutionary 30, 37
COVID-19 109–124, 126, 128, 130, 132, 135–146
COVID-19 Policing Project 19
COVID-19 Tracking Project 115
COVID-19 vaccines 123, 130, 138, 139
Crichton, Michael 169, 204
Crime 28
Criminal justice system 43, 44, 48, 49, 59, 67
Criminology 7
Crips 44
Crisis 4

Critical race theory 2
Cross-immunity 116
Crow, Jim 46
Cruel and unusual punishment 53
Cycle threshold 113, 114
Cytokine storm 142

D

Danger 36
Dangerous classes 15, 17, 18
Daniels, et al. v. City of New York, et al. 36
Data & Society 224
Davis, Angela 51
Davis, Jordan 29
Dayan, Colin 53, 78
DDT 183, 184
Debt 90–92
Debtor prison 8
Debt-servicing 90
Declaration of rights of man 30
Deep web 93
Defunding police 46
Deindustrialization 45, 90
Dell 97
Department of Defense 96
Depo-Provera 188, 189
Desselle, Angelia 145
Detroit 70
DeWitt, Derrick 263
Dialectic 125
Diarrhea 173
Digital currency 254
Disneyland 167
Dissent 2, 6, 20
DNA 111, 129, 140
Doe #1 v. Rumsfeld 201
Domain Awareness 96

Douglass, Frederick 49–51
Douglass, Patrice D. 19
Drug addiction 44
Drug crime 176
Drug dealers 44
DuBois, W.E.B. 49, 50, 76
Due process 27
Duesberg, Peter 229

E

Ebola 129
Education 88, 94, 95, 97, 98, 101
Education reform 3
Education technology 98
Eisenhower, Dwight D. 8
Elite university 64, 72
Emancipation 12, 13, 46, 49, 50
Emergency use authorization (EUA) 138
Encephalomyelitis 127, 128
EngenderHealth 188, 190
Equilibrium 124, 125, 128, 136
Equity 27
Essence 4
Eugenics 164, 187–189, 191–193
Eurocentric 8
Europe 8, 10, 12, 13
Eurosurveillance 115
Event 201 190, 253, 254
Ezike, Ngozi 199

F

False positive 58, 114, 116
Family planning 189
Fanon, Frantz 57, 71
Farber, Celia 112, 146–148, 223, 247

Farley, Anthony P. 16, 17, 24
Farrow, Kenyon 224
Fauci, Anthony 119, 229
Fauci, AS. 21
FBI 44
FDA 119, 138, 142, 143, 146
Federal Reserve 88, 89
Fed spending 89, 90
Ferguson, Karen 63, 82
Ferguson, MO 45
Ferguson, Plessy v. 16
Fierce, Milfred 50, 76
Finance 90–93
Financial crisis 90
Flagellin 142
Fletcher v. Peck 31
Flexner Report 133–135
Floyd, et al. v. City of New York, et al. 35
Foot-and-mouth disease 178
Ford Foundation 61, 63, 67
Foreclosure crisis 91, 92
Foster children 222
Foucault, Michel 7, 19
Franklin, Benjamin 37
Fraud 197, 200, 201
Frontline COVID-19 Critical Care Alliance (FLCCC) 121, 136, 150
Ft. Detrick 130
Fungibility 3
Future takings 197

G

Gain-of-function 130, 132
Galton Institute 191
Gang truce 45
Gang violence 44

Gates Foundation 97
Gates 97
Gavi 254
Genetics 191
Geography 19
Germ-free 124
Gilmore, Ruth Wilson 44, 56
Glass-Steagall 197
GlaxoSmithKline 126
Global South 120, 121
Goodwin, Michele 167–170, 186, 204, 210
Google 94–97
Great Barrington Declaration 194
Great Demonstration 175
Great Depression 90, 91
Great Migration 46, 51
Gregory, Dick 228
Guantanamo 53
Guillain-Barre Syndrome (GBS) 184
Guinier, Lani 186, 210
Gupta, Sunetra 194, 195
Gynecology 4

H

Hall, Stuart 15
Harm reduction 262, 263
Harvard 67, 68
Haseltine, William 140, 160
Hayes, Isaac 228
Healthcare workers 170
Health disparities 93, 237, 241
Hedge fund 92
Henderson, Doug 228
Hewlett 97
Hezekiah Wood v. John Davis 32
Hinton, Elizabeth 66–69, 71
HIPAA 197

Hippocrates 114
HIV 112, 120, 127–129
Holland, Mary 192
Holmes, Oliver Wendell 186, 206
Homophobia 234
Horne, Gerald 70, 85
Hospitalization 119, 140, 143
Housing 88, 90, 92, 93
Houston, Charles Hamilton 3
Human genome project 241
Humanity, concept of; structure of 4
Human subjects 140
Hydroxychloroquine (HCQ) 119–121, 136
Hygiene 171, 172

I

Iatrogenic death 135
ICE 188
Immunity 126, 139, 140
Immunology 168, 235
Incarceration rate 43
Inclusion 17
India 184, 189, 190
Industrialization 171
Infection 111, 112, 116–119, 125, 126, 137, 139, 140, 142, 144
Infection mortality rate (IMR) 118, 119
Infectious disease 171, 173–176, 190
Influenza 111, 118, 122, 125, 130, 136, 137, 139
Infrastructure 173, 190
Innate immunity 179
Insurance industry 90
Integration 224

International Monetary Fund (IMF) 254
Ivermectin 119–121, 136

J

Jackson, George 70, 85
Jacobson, Henning 177, 178
Jacobson v. Massachusetts 165, 178
James, C.L.R. 17, 25, 71, 85
Jewish Holocaust 164
Johns Hopkins University 237
Johnson, Charles S. 187
Jones v. Alfred H. Mayer Co. 241
Jurisprudence of racial profiling 35
Justice Collaboratory 67, 68
Justice contradiction 28

K

Kelly, Ray 96
Kennedy, Robert F. 62
King, Martin Luther Jr. 218
Koch, Charles 60
Koch's postulates 229
Kory, Pierre 120, 121
Kuhn, Thomas 226, 230, 248, 249

L

Ladapo, Joseph 194, 244
Lavender, Bobby 44, 73
Law and order 45, 58–60, 64
Law enforcement 29
Lead poisoning 222
Legaretta et al. v. Macias, et al. 202
Lehman Brothers 89
Leicester 175, 176, 179
Levich, Jacob 190, 211

Liberal reform 47, 52, 60
Lifestyle 234
Lipid nanoparticles 141
Lockdowns 117, 118, 123
Los Angeles 44, 45
Lynching 46, 50, 62

M

Madrid v. Gomez 53, 78
Malcolm X 219
Mamdani, Mahmood 189, 211
Manufacturing political economy 45
Marion Sims, J. 4
Marshall, John 31
Marshall, Thurgood 3, 30, 35
Martin, Trayvon 29
Masks 117, 121, 122
Mass incarceration 48, 49, 52, 56, 57, 68, 69
MATH+ protocols 136
Mayhew v. Hickox 196
Mbeki, Thabo 233
McBride, Renisha 29
McCreary, Bill 228
McFadden, Martin 36
McQuade, Brendan 18, 21, 25
Measles 167, 173, 176, 179, 182, 183
Medical education 133–135
Medical experimentation 220, 221, 239
Medical industrial complex 21, 110, 115, 120, 121, 124, 132, 134
Medical malpractice 121
Medical policing 18, 21
Medical schools 134, 135
Medical science 5, 6, 10, 18–21
Medicare 199

Medicine 165, 166, 169, 173, 175, 182
Memorial Sloan-Kettering 220
Mercenaries 8
Merck 121, 136
MERS 144
Microbes 124, 125
Microbiome 124
Microsoft 94–96
Middle Passage 91
Military industrial complex 8
Mississippi appendectomy 187
Missouri v. Celia 49, 76
Mnuchin, Steve 90
Mob rule 51
Modern 132–135
Modern vaccine regime 163
Monkeys 127, 129
Montagnier, Luc 129
Morgan, John Pierpont 166
Mortality 111, 118, 119, 136, 138, 139
Mortgage crisis 92
Movement for Black Lives 63
mRNA 140, 141, 143, 145, 146
Mullis, Kary 111
Myalgic encephalomyelitis (ME) 128, 229, 230
Myrdal, Gunnar 62, 81

N

NAACP Legal Defense Fund 3
National Childhood Vaccine Injury Act (NCVIA) 198, 202
National Institutes of Allergy and Infectious Diseases (NIAID) 119, 130, 132

National Institutes of Health (NIH) 141
Naturally acquired immunity 126
Naturopathy 134, 135
Nazi 220
Naziism 164
Negro Project 187
Neocleous, Mark 18, 21
Neoliberalism 8
New York Panther 21 71
New York v. Miln 33
Nicaraguan contras 44
Nightingale, Florence 132
Nobel 111, 120, 129
Non-violent offender 56–58, 60
Norplant 188
North American colonists 30
Null, Gary 228
Nuremberg Code 201, 221
Nuremburg 220
Nutrition 172, 173, 175, 179, 182, 189, 190
NYPD 36

O

Obama, Barack 46
Omnibus Crime Control and Safe Streets Act 199
Operation Warp Speed 191
Oracle 96
Oral polio vaccine 184
Overpopulation 189, 190
Oxford-AstraZeneca 96, 191–193

P

Pandemic 1, 2, 4–6, 14, 18–21, 109–111, 115, 116, 118, 119, 121–123, 130, 132, 135, 138
Pandemic Police Power 5, 6, 10, 14, 21
Pandemic shutdown 91, 95
Paradigm 110
Paralysis 128
Parasitic 125
Parenti, Christian 15
Pasteur, Louis 132
Pathogenic priming 142, 144
Pathogens 112, 124, 130
Peer education 262, 263
Pelican Bay state prison 53
Pennesi, Luanne 227
Personalized learning 97
Pertussis 173, 192
Pfizer 138
Pharmaceutical companies 223–225
Pharmacological therapies 226, 235, 242
Philanthropy 61–64
Planned Parenthood 187, 190
Police 5, 7, 9, 13–15, 17–20
Police power 5, 14, 16–19, 21
Policing 27–29, 35, 37
Polio 127–129, 183, 184
Political economy 4, 15, 16
Polyethylene glycol (PEG) 141, 142
Polymerase Chain Reaction (PCR) 111–118, 122, 140
Population 116–118, 122, 137, 141, 145
Population council 189
Possessive individualism 11
Poverty 172, 173, 186, 187, 189, 190, 194

Powell, Adam Clayton Jr. 187
Power 9, 12–14, 16, 18, 19, 21
Prevention 111, 140
Prison abolition 5, 7, 13
Prisoners 221
Prison industrial complex 7–9, 14
Private capital 47, 60–62, 71
Private equity 91
Probable cause 37
Progress 3
Property crime 44
Property law 32
Property rights 11
Pseudo-science 94, 100
Public health 1, 2, 4–6, 10, 14, 18–21
Public health failure 182
Public health model 123, 132, 138
Public health policing 109, 110
Public Readiness and Emergency Preparedness Act (PREP) 200, 202
Public school 95, 97, 98
Puerperal fever 172
Punishment 28

R

Race-crime connection 47
Race-specific medicine 242
Racialism 12
Racialization of violence 55
Racial justice 3
Racial sacrifice 239
Racism 129, 134
Radical 110, 123
Ravitch, Diane 97
Raw material 99
Reasonable suspicion 36, 37

Reconstruction 48, 50
Redfield, Robert 199
Rent-backed securities 91–93
Restorative justice 17
Retrovirus 229
Revolutionary 20
Rikers Island 61
RNA 112, 113, 120, 129, 130
Roberts, Dorothy 65–67, 74, 83
Rockefeller, John D. Sr. 127, 128
Rule of law 51, 65
Russia 173

S

Sanger, Margaret 187
Sanitation 171–173, 175, 179, 189
Santa Clara County v. Southern Pacific Railroad 35, 40
SARS 119, 130, 144, 145
Saucier, P. Khalil 240, 251
Scarlet fever 172, 175
School-to-prison pipeline 98
Scientific consensus 169
Security 36
Self-determination 5, 6, 9, 14, 222, 223, 244, 245
Serious adverse event 177, 239, 260
Seroconversion 227
Sex 232, 233
Sharecropping 50
Simmonds, Kristi 145
SIV 127, 129
Skelton, Shawn 145
Slaughterhouse Cases 35, 40
Slaveholding culture 256
Slave patrols 16
Slavery 4, 5, 7, 10–14, 16, 17, 28–35, 37, 91, 92, 99

Slave trade 30, 34
Smallpox 165, 171, 174, 175, 177, 178, 185, 186
Social control 165, 169
Social health 218
Social services 52
Social structures 12
Solitary confinement 54
Somerset v. Stewart 29
Sontag, Susan 195, 214
Soros, George 64
South Africa 191
Southern Regional Council (SRC) 62
Sovereignty 219, 234
Spike protein 140–142
Spontaneous abortion 144, 145
Squire, Clark 71
Sterilization 186–190
Sterilization League for Human Betterment 188, 190
Sterling, Alton 64
Strict scrutiny 181, 183, 196
Subprime mortgage industry 92
Sugar 183
Sugrue, Thomas 70
Surplus value 3
Surrogate human being 4
Surveillance capitalism 94, 99, 100
Swine flu 182

T

Tatum, Bill 228
Taylor, Keeanga-Yamahtta 61, 81
T-cell 232
Technology 88, 93–95, 97, 98, 100, 101
Terrell, Mary Church 50

Terry v. Ohio 35
Threat 29, 30, 36
Torture 53
Transverse myelitis 128
Treasury Note 89
Treatment 111, 112, 118–122, 131, 134, 136, 138, 139, 144
Treatment Action Group 224
Tri-State Healing Center 226, 235
Trump, Donald 21
Trumpism 88, 90
Tubal ligation 190
Ture, Kwame 70, 85
Tyranny of the majority 185, 186, 195

U

Urbanization 171
U.S. Agency for International Development (USAID) 188, 189

V

Vaccination 6, 20
Vaccine 113, 117, 123–130, 132, 134, 135, 137–146
Vaccine Adverse Event Reporting System (VAERS) 142–145
Vaccine efficacy 163, 168, 176, 180
Vaccine mandates 165, 181
Vaccitech 96
Vasectomy 190
Violent Crime Control and Law Enforcement Act 198
Violent offender 56–58
Viral disease 172
Viral epidemics 164

Viral infection 111, 119, 125, 140
Virginia 32
Virome 124, 125, 127
Vitale, Alex S. 15–17
Vitamin A 182

W

Walker, Darren 61
Wallace, Walter Jr. 217
Wall Street 88–91
War on poverty 52
Washington, Booker T. 50
Watts 70
Webb, Gary 44, 72
Wellcome, Burroughs 223, 225
Wellcome, Henry 191, 193
Wellcome Trust 191
Wells, Ida B. 46, 50, 70, 75, 85
Western culture 10
White-collar crime 28, 202
White rage 45–47
Williams, Kristian 15
Wilson, Darren 45
Working conditions 171, 172

Workman v. Mingo County Board of Education 171
World Health Organization (WHO) 114, 115, 118, 119, 122, 127, 136, 137
Wuhan 118, 130
Wynter, Sylvia 99, 107, 219, 246

X

Xenotransplantation 123, 129, 130
Xenotropic murine retrovirus (XMRV) 128

Y

Yale 67, 68
Yellen, Janet 88
Young, Rickia 217

Z

Zoonotic disease 123
Zuboff, Shoshana 94, 105, 108
Zucht v. King 171

Printed by Printforce, the Netherlands